Anonymous

The Present Position of European Politics

Or, Europe in 1887

Anonymous

The Present Position of European Politics
Or, Europe in 1887

ISBN/EAN: 9783337070311

Printed in Europe, USA, Canada, Australia, Japan

Cover: Foto ©Suzi / pixelio.de

More available books at **www.hansebooks.com**

THE PRESENT POSITION

OF

EUROPEAN POLITICS

OR

EUROPE IN 1887

BY

THE AUTHOR OF "GREATER BRITAIN"

LONDON: CHAPMAN AND HALL
LIMITED
1887

PREFACE.

To these six essays, which have appeared in THE FORTNIGHTLY REVIEW, and which are here republished in book form, I have added a concluding chapter dealing with the objections taken by writers in the Press to some of my statements and inferences. I owe my critics the frank acknowledgment that they have dealt more than kindly with my work, and I feel greatly indebted to them for their courteous treatment. To those who have found my conclusions too dogmatic, I would put forward the excuse that in trying to come to a practical solution of practical problems, something like dogmatism can hardly be avoided. I have honestly written to the best of my ability that which I believed would serve the highest interests of my country; have sought to avoid all that might embitter international hatreds, and from first to last have thought solely of how I might best help England and Englishmen to accomplish their work in all parts of the world.

THE AUTHOR OF "GREATER BRITAIN."

CONTENTS.

THE

PRESENT POSITION OF EUROPEAN POLITICS.

I.

GERMANY.

THE present position of the European world is one in which sheer force holds a larger place than it has held in modern times since the fall of Napoleon. The complications which have arisen out of the kidnapping of the Prince of Bulgaria and the mission of General Kaulbars, are only the most recent and obvious signs of the reign of force in European affairs, and the "colonising" mania which has lately possessed several of the Great Powers is merely another indication of the same phenomenon. A few years ago there was perhaps the will to take and hold by force, but the intention was as completely wrapped up and concealed as now it is naked and undisguised; and as regards the extra-European affairs of the European Powers, the desire to grab the lands of the weaker races is also less enveloped now than it was earlier in the century in such specious forms of words as "the blessings of civilisation." It must

B

be understood, then, that in the course of the present work I shall not write so much of what I wish, or of what I may consider to be right or wrong, as of facts and tendencies —facts and tendencies which are not the less deplored because it would be wearisome to state in every line one writes that one deplores them.

The predominance of Germany in Europe may be said to date really from 1866, and nominally from 1870. The present reign of force in Europe dates from the period of the Treaty of Berlin, or 1878. Although the annexation of Alsace-Lorraine by Germany in 1871 was perfectly defen-sible, looking to the circumstances of the war, and necessary according to the opinion of the Prussian staff, not the less it must be considered to have been the real cause of that predominance of force-considerations which has been noted since 1878. The desire of France to profit by the first general war to recover her lost provinces, and the necessity as stated by Count Moltke for Germany to stand in arms for fifty years to defend the provinces which it had taken so short a time to win, were the leading factors in creating that race in armaments which has successively drawn all the European Powers into a rivalry in numbers of men, numbers of ships, and figures of military expenditure. The Treaty of Berlin in itself was, like all treaties at the end of a great war, in form an act of restitution as well as of peace. But the signature of the treaty was accompanied by a number of conversations among powerful people; by secret agreements, some of which have since been published, and some not; by the virtual annexation by one Great Power of a Turkish island which had not been conquered; by the virtual annexation by another Great Power of two Turkish provinces which had not been conquered; by a hint given to a third Great Power (France), that she should occupy another province of that empire; by hints given to a fourth Great Power (Italy), that she should occupy either an island (British hint) or Tunis (German hint); and that which ought to have been the basis of a long-standing if not of a permanent peaceful settlement in Europe, became the opening of a period of despair to the disciples of Richard Cobden. There was nothing very new in these proceedings; what was new was that they were so little veiled or disguised. In 1866—for the policy of *pourboire* was already known— Italy asked at Paris whether she was to join Austria or Prussia in the war, as both of them had made to her the same promise, that Venice was to be the price of her alliance. Italy received, curiously enough, an answer from the Emperor that as he intended to take the Rhine when the combatants were exhausted, what mattered most to him was that the war should last upon pretty equal terms, and that Italy was to take the Prussian, which he, like the great majority of observers, believed to be the weaker side. In 1870, also, Italy was in some doubt as to her course, which also had its price, and Austria acted, or rather abstained from acting, with much deliberate violation of her word; yet not even in 1866 or 1870 was there that public avowal of rapacity which in 1878 assembled Europe made eagerly, although in the name of peace.

It is useless to comment at any length upon the most

recent development of the reign of force in Europe, because it is fresh in the reader's mind.   The abduction of the
Prince of Bulgaria, whether by the actual contrivance of
Russian agents or only with a Russia ready to profit by
the action of the Russian party, an autocracy helping to
use the methods of the dynamo-revolutionists, reminds us of
mediæval Italy rather than of what were until recently the
methods of modern Europe.   Russia indeed has never shown
much respect for her stipulations, but the repeated violations
of her engagements—her defence for which we shall be able
to consider when we come to the present position of Russia
—violations of engagements in Central Asia and elsewhere,
which themselves pale before her recent acts at Batoum,
are, Central Asia, Batoum, and all of them, a trifle when
compared with the audacity of her action against Prince
Alexander and with the incidents of the Kaulbars mission.
Napoleon the Great in his most ill-tempered moments appears
to be the model that the Tsar has in view.   The principles
which he professes at home are those of the Holy Alliance ;
the principles which his friends profess in Bulgaria appear
to be, when necessary, those of the dynamite section ; and
the latest of his actions reminds us of those which were
ignored by the earlier but have been fully related by the
Republican biographers of Napoleon.

   Turning to very different portions of the world which I
couple with Bulgaria as instancing the reign of force in
European affairs, namely, the distant spots where the Great
Powers of Europe have been undisguisedly laying their
hands upon the countries of various independent peoples, we

shall see how those Powers, if any there were, who honestly
did not desire to increase their territory and who did not
believe that increase of territory was increase of strength,
have been forced into following the example of others from
the fact that violent hands were being laid upon all portions
of the globe. In the case of France it was certain, and
in the case of other Powers possible, that differential
duties would be placed upon the goods of the Powers
which refused to annex, and that the trade of the latter
with all those parts of the world would thus be brought
to a close. It is bad enough, by the way, to be robbed by
those who rob, but it is harder still to be robbed of trade by
ourselves. Perhaps it is poetic justice that has made us
suffer heavily through the putting on by Austria of differential duties in Bosnia, the occupation of which we ourselves proposed through our plenipotentiaries, while forgetting to make stipulations for our trade.

The Powers themselves were aware of what was likely
to be the result to Europe of the annexation of Alsace-
Lorraine, and both Austria and Russia sounded Great
Britain upon the subject. Austria, indeed, had reasons of
her own of a very special kind for so doing. When we
come to deal with the weak points of alliances in considering
the military position of Germany in the centre of Europe,
I may have to return to this matter. It is not only
true that Austria had pledged herself to France to join
her in the war, as is seen by the despatch which the
Duc de Gramont afterwards published, but also, what is
less known, that the Archduke Albert had actually made

at Paris with the Emperor Napoleon the arrangements
for the campaign, and that General Lebrun had completed
those arrangements at Vienna, passing indeed by way of
Berlin in order to throw dust in the eyes of Germany.
It is the fact that Austria and Russia both, but indepen-
dently, proposed to us, at London through Baron Brunow,
and at Vienna through Count Beust and the English
Ambassador, to stop the outbreak of war between France and
Germany by guaranteeing to both parties their territory.
The proposal was that Europe should say, "Fight as much
as you please, gentlemen, but you must understand that the
danger to European peace in the future, if one of you takes
away territory from the other, will be so great that we cannot allow that particular result of war to take place in this
case." The negotiations did not indeed break down upon
the merits of the proposal, but upon the mooting more or
less indirectly by Russia at the same time of the question
of the Black Sea clause of the Treaty of 1856, which it
will be remembered she shortly afterwards denounced.
Once for all let me say that in tracing to the annexation of
Alsace-Lorraine in 1871 the evils which have subsequently
occurred in Europe, I am not blaming that annexation,
which was perfectly justified no doubt by the immediate
facts in view, but I am trying to point out that the indirect
and ultimate results have been very different from those
which alone the military advisers of the German Empire had
foreseen.

I now come to calculate, so far as may be, the forces and
the policy of that European Power which is not only the
most central in geographical position, but which is supposed

to be the strongest—the Power which certainly dominates politically the European situation. The first inquiry to be made is, who are the men who guide and direct its policy? and to this question in the case of Germany but one answer is possible, as not only at the present moment, but in my opinion whilst he lives, Prince Bismarck alone counts; and although it may seem a bold statement, looking to popular beliefs in Russia and in France, it is far from unlikely that his sons—that is, his name and his policy—alone will count after he is dead. One doubt which may fairly be held to exist upon this point is raised by considering the future position and the well-known opinions of the Crown Princess. It is no secret that at times the Crown Princess has been unfriendly to Prince Bismarck. They are perhaps two personalities too strong to easily co-exist in the same court; but in spite of perfect willingness to admit this future difficulty in Prince Bismarck's way, I am inclined to believe most confidently that when the Crown Princess of Germany becomes the German Empress, complete accord will reign between Prince Bismarck and herself.

Prince Bismarck's policy we shall have to consider in detail later on, but, roughly speaking, it may be stated to be a policy of maintaining that unity of Germany which is his work. For it, he is prepared when necessary, however autocratic may be his language, to seek sufficient popularity among the people, even by favouring schemes of colonisation, of which he never hesitates in private to express his disapproval, and semi-socialistic schemes which he imperfectly understands. The idea that the Crown Prince has a different policy from his father, and that this other policy will obtain after the old Emperor's death, will suffice no doubt to send up stocks in one country and to send them down in another upon the news of the Emperor's death, and to form the foundation of endless columns of big type leaded leaders, but it has no foundation in fact. The Crown Prince, it must be admitted, intellectually speaking, is, largely by his own will, the Crown Princess; but that most able lady, when she shares the German throne, must inevitably have for her policy the Bismarck policy, the strength and glory of the German Empire.

The Princess Royal is an interesting figure upon the European stage, and of her, in her political capacity, it is necessary to speak. She belongs to a family in which there are many able members. Her mother is, considering the pressure of detail on her daily life, one of the most able persons, king or queen, that have ever sat upon a throne. But the Princess Royal is in some respects the ablest member of the family, and in all respects the ablest member of the family except her mother. And the Princess Royal has that which her mother's perpetual hard labour upon limited and special work has necessarily kept from her—much deep reading and great knowledge of literary and general affairs, which have made her as strong a Liberal in many matters as the Queen is a powerful Conservative. The Crown Princess is not popular in Germany. The reasons of that unpopularity are upon the surface. She has been the patron of reputedly free-thinking clergymen, and popular gossip has accused her of being a complete free-thinker. This makes her unpopular in some quarters. She has often

turned German prejudices into ridicule, and this makes her
unpopular in others. She is very clever, a quality which in
courts makes princes unpopular with fools. She is somewhat
learned, which everywhere makes people unpopular with the
ignorant. Her Royal Highness once asked a certain
Prussian general, before his friends, who was consul at
Rome in a particular year? Naturally that distinguished
officer has from that day been more Bismarckian than the
North German Gazette, or the *Post* itself. The Crown
Princess at one time used to excite hostility in Germany
by proclaiming admiration for France, but that practice is
a matter of the past. She still on occasion ruffles the
feelings of the Court, as, for example, in her sympathy
with the English admiration for the Prince of Bulgaria,
who is a member of a family by no means popular
at the German Court. But there can be no doubt, whatever may be the dreams which have been cherished by
some in France, that when she comes to reign in Germany
she will come to the throne as a good German and reign
as such. Political influence with her eldest son it is said
the Crown Princess has not, but his reign is probably a
long way off, although there are unpleasant stories abroad
about the health of the Crown Prince. The son is Bismarckian, and his wife is orthodox, and probably the difficulties which there may have been, were difficulties upon
questions which affect these matters, and if so they are
obviously difficulties which are likely to be softened or
removed by time.

Those who best know the Crown Prince himself say that

he is conscious of the limitations of his abilities, limitations which are not so much of the mind as of habit. It would be a mistake to exaggerate the difficulties which have existed between Prince Bismarck and himself. At times, as for example at the moment of the issue of a certain imperial rescript, against which the Crown Prince strongly protested, the differences have been sharp, but on the whole the Crown Prince has been content to defend his wife, and it is supposed that, like a good husband, he is pleased to be held by his more energetic consort in silken bonds. The most recent difficulties that have existed at the German Court have been those which have concerned the choice of persons. For example, Count Eulenberg, for many years Hof-Marschall to the Crown Prince, was appointed chiefly because he was a strong Conservative and a strong Bismarckian, holding opinions which are much opposed on most points to those of the Crown Princess, and, in a less degree, therefore opposed also to those held by the Crown Prince. Naturally the result for many years was a good deal of friction, caused by the frequent conferences between Count Eulenberg and the Chancellor. There were matters which arose in connection with the proposal to appoint Count Eulenberg to a post elsewhere which it is unnecessary to relate, but which at one time led to an open breach between Prince Bismarck and the Crown Princess. These difficulties, though still great, are not so considerable as they at one time were, and they may be safely counted upon to disappear.

Prince Bismarck's reputation is so considerable that it is unnecessary to say very much about him. To ascribe to him the astuteness of a Machiavelli, or even of a Talleyrand, is to give him credit for, or perhaps the discredit of a quality which he does not possess. His strength is the strength of a man who knows what he wants, and who, having in years past played very boldly for high stakes, has happened to win, and having won is strong enough to hold his own. In 1866 Prince Bismarck risked everything, even the loss of his head, but he justified the proud words which he flung at the head of the Prussian Parliament, when for the sake of the army he broke the law, and told the members that within a year an indemnity would be voted. Since that victory he has been supreme in Europe, and in a position to have little occasion for the use of diplomatic artifice. It is now, and perhaps in the last years of his life, that, through the growth of the military power of Russia and of France, and through the recent revelations of Austrian military weakness, Prince Bismarck will be called upon to make more serious diplomatic efforts than he has ever yet had occasion to put forth. Those who look upon him as a type-man of the race must regret the neuralgia and the indigestion, because above all he is a strong man, and an almost ideal representative of Prussian power. The story of the interview at five o'clock in the morning in which the completion of the evacuation arrangements of the Treaty of Frankfort was brought about after much deliberation over a jug which contained champagne, porter, and various forms of ardent spirits, blended by the red-hot poker of the German Chancellor, and swallowed with a wry face by the Frenchman for his country's sake, is less familiar than the story of the Ferrières interview, as recounted by M. Jules Favre, and is perhaps not one of dignity, but it is one of those which complete the figure of the man; and I repeat that the neuralgia and the other ailments of Prince Bismarck detract somewhat from that triumph of Prussia which he personifies. A seeming paradox which possibly some day may come to look less like a paradox than it does at present, would consist in the confident assertion that Prince Bismarck after all is much such a man as his own son, who is well known in this country, Count Herbert Bismarck— that is, less an old-fashioned statesman than a strong and very decided person knowing exactly what he means to do and exactly how he means to do it. Prince Bismarck is not mortal, in the sense that his policy and even the impress of his peculiar personality will continue to direct Prussia after he in the flesh is no longer in this world. What is now said of the probable consequence of the death of the German Emperor is not after all unlike what used to be said of the probable consequence in Russia of the death of the second Alexander, in the days when Aksakoff directed the political footsteps of the present Tsar, and made him fine those who spoke German at his card-table—a fine which his august father had frequently to pay. It was generally expected that there would be war with Germany the day that he ascended the throne, but it will be noticed that affairs have gone on since he came to the throne much as they went on before; and so it will be in Germany.

Given the Bismarckian policy, which is clear, the means to the end shift and change day by day. The first point to be considered is that of the relations of Germany to France. Germany permanently alienated all France in 1871, and prevented the growth in France of a peace party, by taking Alsace against the will of the population, and giving a great shock to what those who do not like France call vanity, but what I would call more politely patriotic feeling. The European problem then and henceforward became a military one, which forces politicians of the present day who desire to serve their country truly, and to be anything more than vestrymen, to spend their time in studying works of military strategy, as though they were so many sucking Jominis or Napoleons.

Germany occupies a vulnerable military position in the centre of Europe, with no natural frontier. Her territory is situate between that of three great military Powers, of which only Austria is certainly inferior to her in military strength. She has bound herself in a defensive league to the weakest of the three, chiefly because she cannot bind to her permanently either of the others. France, indeed, was willing for some years to take her policy submissively from Berlin, a fact which was either not known in France, or more probably known, but quietly and patriotically ignored as a horrible necessity; but France, so long as Alsace and half Lorraine are German, cannot be bound to Germany in such a way as not to turn upon her as soon as she is sufficiently strong. Russia, so far as alliances go, is not to be relied upon, because, shifty as may be alliances which rest upon the will of parliamentary majorities, they are stable by the side of those which depend upon the caprice of autocratic rulers. Germany is therefore bound to Austria. Tied thus to the weakest of the three, she is exposed to the

attacks of the more powerful two, with these further considerations, that the military weakness of Austria has lately
become apparent; and that although Italy is also a comparatively weak Power, it is impossible to say for certain that the
assistance of Austria might not be partially or even altogether neutralised by possible though improbable Italian
hostility.   Austria is mistress of the Trentino.   Italy, which
covets many things, especially covets the Trentino, and there
is in this consideration an evident possibility of the neutralisation of the Austrian forces at any given moment.   The
lesser Powers may be left out of account, so small are the
numbers of their forces in comparison with those of the
great.   England in a long war would count for much, but
for little if anything in a short one.   Not that any patriotic
Englishman need feel that the blackness of the European
sky at the present moment extends to Britain in an equal
degree to that in which it darkens the Continent of Europe.
Though might is right, Great Britain, too, in her way, is
mighty, and it is my belief that England's real power is as
great as, or even greater in proportion than, when she first
went into the war against Napoleon Bonaparte, and as great
in proportion as at the time of Waterloo.   But, as I shall
have presently to show, England is, though not weak, unready.
The lesser Powers, in a military sense, I repeat, must be
neglected.   Some of them would throw in their lot with
one or other group of great allies; but it may be safely said
that even at the moment when he was sending the Crown
Prince to Spain, to induce Spain to join the "League of
Peace," which the Spaniards very prudently refused to do,

Prince Bismarck did not attach much real importance to their services. The armies of the Great Powers are now so large that they can afford to detach sufficient territorial troops to watch the forces of the smaller Powers, if need be, without feeling the drain upon their field armies.

We will consider presently the relative military strength of Germany and of France in detail, but obviously the main object of Prince Bismarck must be to prevent a Russo-French alliance by all possible means. Even with a purely defensive attitude on the part of Germany, Russia would hold a German field army of 200,000 men upon the Vistula, and vast garrisons in the German eastern fortresses. Hence Prince Bismarck must be willing to help Russia in the further East, and to help her in the Balkans up to the point where Austria begins to kick. There has been a great deal of nonsense written upon the subject of the Austro-German alliance. The alliance, as agreed upon at Vienna in October, 1879, by a treaty which was ratified at Berlin on October 18th, 1879, was a defensive alliance, directed against Russia and against France, and this is the alliance which substantially stands, for it has survived the three Emperors' league. There is this weak point in the alliance, that it may not be very binding under a great strain; and those who make alliances with Austria cannot but remember that the Austrian alliance with France in 1870 lured Napoleon III. to his destruction. Still the Austro-German alliance has for some years past kept Europe quiet, and it would even now suffice to keep

Europe quiet in the future but for the fact that it is impossible to count upon the policy of Russia, which is simply the personal policy from day to day of a very imperfectly informed person who insists upon having his own way.

The Austro-German alliance, of course, is limited to certain events. It does not refer to all Europe generally, and fresh alliances with a different grouping of the Powers have from time to time been proposed. In October last two great refusals of alliances took place. France, I am told, declined a formal alliance with Russia, and Austria declined an alliance with Great Britain, although in both cases we ought to use the phrase "declined with thanks." France was anxious not to take any step which could precipitate a war, and Austria thought that she should accomplish the end which both her statesmen and Lord Salisbury had in view, namely, the prevention of a war with Russia, better by remaining free. The *Standard* the other day congratulated its readers upon the fact that, however much mischief Lord Randolph Churchill might work in home affairs, he was not allowed to interfere in the field of foreign politics; and this seems certainly to have been the case, for it is not to be supposed that he has suddenly changed those opinions upon the slight value of the integrity and independence of the Ottoman Empire to this country, which for so many years he consistently maintained. The reasons for the French refusal of a formal alliance with Russia are more obvious than those for Austria's refusal of an alliance with Great Britain. The former alliance was a war alliance, the latter alliance was an alliance for peace. All alliances are called alliances for peace;

but the Russo-French alliance might practically have led to war, and the Austro-British alliance would, in my belief, practically have secured peace, as Russia knows that whatever her earlier victories over Austria, England would fight on until she conquered. The view of M. de Freycinet in refusing a formal alliance with Russia was probably that, if war should break out between Austria and Russia, Russia would beat Austria easily, and that Germany would not move if the causes of war were carefully managed; that if Germany did move, Russia could resist invasion even by the com-bined forces of Austria and Germany; and that Germany would be weakened by such a struggle. But the dominant motive in M. de Freycinet's mind no doubt was that a war, even a successful war, would upset the Republic. This I shall attempt to explain at length when I come to write specially upon France.

In the difficult position in which Germany finds herself placed, Prince Bismarck would be more than human if he were to regard with unmixed horror the prospect of a pro-tracted struggle upon equal terms between two of his great neighbours. If Austria and Russia were of something like equal strength, or if England and Turkey were likely to fight upon the Austrian side, still more if the small Slav principalities were to fight for Austria, there would be a long war, which would drain both countries, and leave Germany proportionately stronger. But England has a large peace party—most Liberals would oppose the war, and the Irish party would oppose it. It is far from certain that Lord Randolph Churchill would support it. England,

C

moreover, could not attack Russia by land, nor lend effective
land assistance to Austria in the earlier portion of the war.
It would take England a month to place a single army corps
in Turkey.   It would take her much longer to place there
the two army corps, fully equipped with guns, without
which she would hardly enter upon a Continental struggle.
England, indeed, could strike at Russia, and, in the course
of a very long war, although unable to reach Russia
through the Black Sea, or the Baltic, or the White Sea,
might bleed Russia to death by attacking her at her
extremities, and by repeating at Vladivostock and on the
Amoor the policy of the Crimea.   But European statesmen
look nowadays to rapid mobilisation and to the first four
weeks of a war.   England is innocent of all knowledge of
the rapid mobilisation of large forces, and would not count
for a feather's weight in the first months of a Continental
conflict.   In the meantime the Austrian army would probably
be overwhelmed.   It may be safely said that although France
was much mentioned in the Parliamentary debates upon
the increase of the German army, that which was in the
Chancellor's mind, when he proposed it, was the report of
the German staff upon the military weakness of the Austrian
Empire as compared with Russia.   If Germany were willing
to stand by and let Austria be beaten, Russia could probably
find causes for a virtual attack upon Austria which would
be outside the scope of the defensive alliance between
Austria and Germany.   It is in part the danger of the
Russians attacking Turkey by Erzeroum, but in part, also,
the promise of the exclusion of Austria from Bosnia and the

Herzegovina after the " coming war," that has sometimes made the Sultan subservient to the wishes of the Russian Ambassador; but the obstacle to any rash action on the part of Russia is that, autocrat though he be, the Emperor of Russia cannot go to war unless he is fully supported by Moscow or national opinion, and that Moscow opinion is excited about Bulgaria, and furious at the ingratitude—as it is in Russia held to be—of the Bulgarians and Southern Slavs, while it is indifferent for the moment to the grievances of the Armenians. Looking to the dislike of Russia which exists in Germany, and which unites even Prince Bismarck and the Crown Princess, and to the dislike of Germany which exists in Russia, it is at least possible that Germany would back Austria in any war with Russia into which Austria could be driven. It is less certain that Austria would back Germany in any war into which she might be driven. I have resolved not to write more of history than I can help on this occasion, but history is history after all, and I cannot forget that if dislike of Russia brings together even Prince Bismarck and the Crown Princess of Germany, knowledge of the hollowness of alliances unites two still more bitter enemies in the persons of the Empress Eugénie and M. Ollivier, who must well remember not only the settling of the plan of the campaign with Austria, not only the promises of alliances recorded in the despatches published by M. de Gramont, but the autograph letters from the Emperor of Austria and the King of Italy which are, I believe, still in the Empress's hands.

I have asked those who best know Prince Bismarck's views

c 2

to tell me what they thought, not about the general principle
of his policy, for that is obvious, but about its details.   They
reply, "We shall not allow Austria to do anything calculated
to precipitate a war between her and Russia." The view put
forward, that the treaty of alliance between Austria and
Germany provides only for defence against a joint attack
by two Powers, is not true.   This would have been a leonine
contract to the benefit of Germany alone, for Germany is
more exposed to such danger than is Austria.   But it is true
that it does not bind Germany to espouse every quarrel of
Austria's.   Prince Bismarck will not threaten nor help to
threaten Russia, and he will advise Russia that, if she wishes
to advance, she must offer Austria her price, a price which,
it may be added, Austria is at this moment most unwilling to
receive.   The Magyars, who govern the ruling half of the
Dual Empire, are unwilling to add to the number of the Slav
subjects of the Emperor.

Not only as against Russia, but generally, Prince Bismarck
will not fall into the errors of the first Napoleon.   He will not
bluster; he will not dictate nor help to dictate to people;
and he will not embark in a reckless policy of adventure.
Personal likes and dislikes he shows very strongly, especially
the latter, and he is not at all above that ill temper with
individuals which was one of the weaknesses of the first
Napoleon; but the Corsican's greater weaknesses of swagger
and theatrical declamation are altogether avoided by Prince
Bismarck, who, during the many years that he has been the
arbiter of Europe, has used his power at all events with
discretion.   When the first Napoleon controlled the policy of

Germany, he was never tired of letting the world know it, and at Waterloo he paid for his revelations. When Prince Bismarck for years controlled the foreign policy of France he kept the secret to himself. Moreover, in a military sense it is necessary for Germany to keep quiet. France is isolated unless she will accept a Russian alliance for purely Russian objects, but, if Germany found herself at war, of course at any moment she might have France upon her back.

One of the great difficulties of the existing situation from the German point of view—that of avoiding a defeat for Austria and of keeping Austria in her place as an effective member of the group of Continental Powers—is that Russia is fully persuaded, and probably justly persuaded, that she can beat the Austrian armies in the field, and even beat Austria if allied to Britain before any help could reach her, and that she has the power to prevent that help in Europe being serious by making an effective diversion towards India. Russia is very timid about facing a European agreement, and the pressure put on by Prince Bismarck and the friendship between Italy and England have been very precious to the cause of peace. Austria therefore possibly after all was right in declining, at Prince Bismarck's suggestion, a more formal alliance with Great Britain, inasmuch as while Russia does not greatly fear, in a short war, Austria and England, she does very greatly fear an even less militant demonstration by the four Powers.

It is on the simplicity of Prince Bismarck's policy that all who consider it carefully, have to insist. It is a plain and straightforward policy of the defence of the German

Empire.   People ask, is Prince Bismarck willing to see Russia incorporate the Slav States? will he allow her to establish herself at Constantinople, or does he mean Austria to prevent Russian extension? or is he willing that Russia should go to Constantinople on condition that *pari passu* Austria should obtain Servia and part of Macedonia and Salonica? The answer is that in the present state of Europe a prudent politician is unable to look very far ahead.   Where all is somewhat evil, one may be allowed to use the old phrase, "Sufficient unto the day is the evil thereof," as singularly applicable to the state of Europe.   At the present moment Russia is friendly with Turkey; therefore there is no immediate question of Russia going to Constantinople. Russia has been frightened by the secret lectures of Prince Bismarck, and by the public declarations of the Italian Ministry, and does not intend even to occupy Bulgaria. Two or three months ago the danger of immediate war was greater than it is at present.   Why face the difficulties, when they are of an intangible kind, until they meet us?   Lord Beaconsfield once observed in conversation, "We make our lives miserable by the anticipation of evils which never happen;" and so it is with statesmen who are less gifted with solid strength than is Prince Bismarck. The answer to all the questions is that he will allow Russia to move if he cannot well help it, but that he would much sooner that she did not, and that he will do everything he can quietly to prevent her moving.   If at any time she should insist upon doing so, he will have to consider whether he cannot best avert the destruction of the Austrian Empire as a Great Power by forcing upon Austria a compensation at which she grumbles. National vanity is often more important than national strength, and even though it may be the case that it would be a positive source of weakness and danger to Austria to extend her boundaries, yet it may be necessary that she should do so, in order to keep up the national pride of the people, humbled as it would be by a great increase of Russian territory and an apparent increase of Russian power. In the meantime there is something laughable, although inevitable, in the way in which Austria waits on England and England upon Austria, or, as someone has wittily observed, in which Austria declares that she would be delighted to take the first step, as Lord Salisbury proposes, if Lord Salisbury will begin by taking the second.

In considering from the point of view of Germany the policy of her neighbours, we must bear firmly in our mind that the policy of Count Kálnoky has never varied for one moment since the first day when he came into power, and that while his public words are known to everyone in Europe who is concerned in foreign affairs, his private words are to the effect that Austria not only has no desire to extend or add to the rights which she acquired under the Treaty of Berlin, but that the Emperor personally as well as the Government are of opinion that any such extension would be actually prejudicial to the Austrian Empire. If there is anything in words at all, this not only is an emphatic but sounds like a binding declaration.

The relations of Germany to Turkey are rather indirect, through the bearing of the relations of Turkey to Austria upon Germany, than direct from court to court; still, from time to time Prince Bismarck has carefully considered the condition of the Turkish Empire.   During the last few years Turkey has three times sent special missions to Berlin, and to the Turkish ambassadors Prince Bismarck's language has always been the same.   The Sultan's view of Germany is that he ought to seek for the help of German officers and of German financial guides, on the ground that all the other Great Powers want their pound of flesh from Turkey. France, which first took Algeria and then Tunis, and now desires to take Morocco from the Mahommedan world; Italy, which from time to time casts glances upon Tripoli and upon Albania; England, which took Cyprus and does not leave Egypt; Austria, which took Bosnia and the Herzegovina; and Russia, of which nothing need here be said, are, if friends of the Turkish Empire, hardly disinterested friends.   Germany, on the other hand, in the Sultan's view, from the very fact that she is not specially interested in the Mahommedan territories on the Mediterranean, will give him good advice, and may give him useful help.   Prince Bismarck, in reply, is polite enough.   He warns the Turks that while they may expect good advice from him, and any help which is not costly, he does not particularly value their alliance, because he knows that the Sultan has promised the favours of his alliance to every one of the Great Powers in succession. Prince Bismarck has lent the Sultan financiers; he has lent him officers to improve the Turkish army, although not to serve with it in the field; but he has told the Sultan that he must not dream of regaining any hold on Tunis or any practical power in Egypt; he has warned the Turks that under no circumstances will Germany fire a shot for them, and has declared that Turkey must do the best she can with what is left to her, without attempting a grand policy.

Prince Bismarck's advice at Constantinople for many years past has been friendly to this country, and England ought to view with pleasure the permanent character of German influence at Constantinople, which is always the second influence there, though Russia, France, or England each from time to time exerts the first. When the Sultan's fancy exalts the value of Russia's friendship to the skies, and when he snubs England, as he did once about Mr. Goschen, and lately about Sir William White—an almost incredible folly as regards the former, and a weak act of subservience to Russia's influence as regards the latter of these able and excellent ambassadors—he still keeps an eye on Germany. When, on the other hand, he is on the best of terms with England and is embracing Sir Drummond Wolff, and when Russia is a demon in Moslem eyes, Germany is still consulted. German influence at Constantinople, in a word, is friendly to England, and it is the only influence there that never wanes. The one point which has brought Prince Bismarck into conflict with England as regards the Turkish Empire has been his extreme dislike of what he considers our senti-mental policy of forcing internal reform. The lectures he has addressed to successive English Governments upon this subject have never been published, and never will be; but Prince Bismarck is not in the habit of making a secret of his opinions, and it is well known with what contemptuous

frankness he continually speaks of the pressure exerted upon
Turkey by Sir Henry Layard, by Mr. Goschen, and in a
lesser degree ever since their time by all English Ministers
at home, Ambassadors at Constantinople, and Consuls in the
Turkish Empire, to secure at all hazards internal reform.
Prince Bismarck supports England in keeping the road to
India clear, in keeping order in Egypt, in maintaining the
status quo in the Mediterranean, but he despises England
when by haranguing the Sultan at every turn she sacrifices
her interests at Constantinople to what he thinks the dream
of improving the domestic condition of the Macedonians or
of the Armenians. Prince Bismarck in speaking in public of
course would defend himself from the charge of the possession
of a hard heart by saying that he thinks that pressure at Constantinople does harm, in causing the Turks to resist the
removal of bad functionaries, and in inducing them to delay
reforms which, if left to themselves, they would probably introduce; but while mentioning this defence I do not wish to be
supposed to share the view, for I am too deeply impressed by
all that reaches me from Constantinople that the one necessity
of the Sultan is that of many people, namely funds, and that
every other object is sacrificed to the desire to get money.
Prince Bismarck has a certain admiration for the Turks as
a military people, and considerable sympathy with their view
that reforms must wait when there is not money enough to
pay the troops. As to that shortness of money, an anecdote
is better than pages of statistics, and I will take leave to print
two lines from the last letter I received from one of my ablest
correspondents in Constantinople, who says, " The Turks

must be hard up, for they cannot afford now to buy even necessaries, such as new rifles."* When political economists used to write of "necessaries," they meant food-stuffs, but no doubt in modern Europe torpedoes, new shells, and repeating guns are the necessaries of life.

Prince Bismarck views with a smile the supposed recent increase of French influence at Constantinople. The giving of the Grand Cross of the Legion of Honour to the Grand Vizier and the Marshal of the Palace, and the promotion in the order of other leading Turkish officials, were less a reward for services accomplished than a demonstration. The demonstration was a cheap one, and a very pretty reply to the equally cheap demonstration made by Turkey when the Sultan shortly before embraced a French admiral and ceased to mention Tunis. Prince Bismarck has not always been above suggesting the expediency of the occupation of various portions of the Turkish Empire to his friends among the Powers, but he has always abstained from grabbing for himself, and this is in his favour at Constantinople. The labours of the Berlin Congress, or its festivities, so confused the minds of the plenipotentiaries that they have never been clear who offered what to whom; but it at least seems plain, unless we are to believe that the diplomatists of the Europe of the day exceed Talleyrand himself in their powers of imagination, that a great deal of offering of other people's property, took place, and that some of those offers were suggested by Prince Bismarck. In one case, at least, the same

---

* The contract has, however, been signed since these words were penned. The German contractor seems unlikely to get his money.

thing was offered to two parties, which is an ingenious method of inducing complications which may lead to war.

It is not known what view Prince Bismarck took of the league for the maintenance of the *status quo* in the Mediterranean which was proposed by Lord Beaconsfield in February, 1878. The Foreign Affairs Committee of the then Cabinet, consisting of Lord Beaconsfield, Lord Cairns, and Lord Salisbury, proposed at the instance of Lord Beaconsfield the creation of a Mediterranean League. It was intended that France, Italy, and Greece should be consulted, and then, if they were found to be agreed, that Austria should be asked to join. Italy, however, declined, and the matter went no farther. But the condition of the Mediterranean underwent immediately afterwards an essential change, and a fresh grouping of the Mediterranean Powers became inevitable. Prince Bismarck most steadily resisted the temptation to fall into any anti-French alliance with regard to Tunis. France was, no doubt, furious, after her occupation of Tunis, at the suspicion that England, Italy, and Turkey tried to set Germany at her, but it was mere suspicion, which was not justified, and Prince Bismarck, as indeed is usual with him in great affairs, never held in secret any different language from that of which he made use in public. At a later period, when Prince Bismarck believed in the imminence of a league between the Balkan States, he warned, I believe, Bulgaria, Servia, Montenegro, and Greece that if they entered into such a league he could not answer for the movements of Austria and of Russia, and that they could not be allowed to take steps which would produce a general European conflagration. Nothing, in short, could have been more straightforward and more uniform than the Turkish policy of Germany.

No doubt Prince Bismarck may view without dissatisfaction the jealousies between France and the United Kingdom arising out of Mediterranean questions, but he has never shown his satisfaction, and he has often done much to diminish friction. We shall have to consider the Egyptian difficulties between England and France when I write of France, and it is sufficient at this moment to say that they are not thought worthy of any great attention at Berlin, inasmuch as it is regarded as certain that they will not lead to war. A supposed circumstance which has perhaps caused more hostility in France towards England than even the Egyptian question, connects itself with Germany in a curious way. It is a ludicrous fact, but still it is a fact, that of the several matters which have estranged France from England, of which the Egyptian question is not even the principal one, perhaps the chief is a belief in France that the Queen is anti-French in feeling and especially anti-French-Republican, and that her Majesty's feeling upon this point has dominated the foreign policy of this country. It is not necessary in writing in England to discuss seriously this French popular belief; but although dislike to France, if true, would be supposed to take the form of affection for, or at least sympathy for, Germany, there is no corresponding feeling of close ties on the part of the Court and Government of Berlin, because at Berlin the truth of the case is more exactly appreciated. In fact, some unpopularity at the German Court is attached to certain

ceremonial acts of the English Government for which her
Majesty most improperly has, in German opinion, been held
responsible; as for example, the sending of Garter missions
to small German courts.   Moreover, their Royal Highnesses
the Duke of Cambridge and (in a less degree) the Prince of
Wales are looked upon as friends of the Hanoverian par-
ticularists, and are said to be not too popular in certain circles
at Berlin.   Nothing is too trivial or, it may be added, too
absurd to be taken into account in dealing with either national
or personal likes and dislikes.   It would be impossible to
discover a more ideally perfect ambassador than is Lord
Lyons, but the Republic is not popular in Paris "smart"
society, and while Lord Lyons himself does not "go out," the
Embassy is, like all embassies, in touch with smart society,
which is in opposition, and not with the society, if society it
may be called, of Government.   Just as in Spain, when
Castelar came into power, the English Legation did "not
know" Castelar, so in Paris, though Lord Lyons does his
best by frequent hospitality to meet the difficulty, the British
Embassy does not know the houses of the governing people.
This is true, no doubt, of all the embassies, but as the English are in Paris most in view, and as the English have a
reputation for being disagreeable, well established, though it
is to be hoped not well founded, the estrangement which is
the consequence fixes itself upon the Government of England.

The relations between France and Russia are of the highest
interest to Prince Bismarck.   As I have already stated, M.
de Freycinet told his friends that he would not be a party to
the formal alliance with Russia which he left them to sup-

pose she had solicited. In this he followed the policy of his great rival. M. Gambetta declared times without number to his intimates that Russia was always pulling him by the coat, but he would not stop to listen. There is this difference, however, between De Freycinet and Gambetta, that the latter was deeply prejudiced against Russia, and the former is not prejudiced. Gambetta would have joined an alliance against Russia, even though, as he said, it should be "an alliance at Berlin," although no doubt he had his own hopes as to that restoration of territory which a possible war—in which France should save Germany—might bring about. M. Gambetta had been brought up in the old Polish Republican traditions, which were popular at one time among the French Republicans. His opinions had grown up with him in opposition, and the Poles were always popular with French oppositions. M. de Freycinet's public life has been spent in government, and he knows how necessary it is to France to make use of the dim figure of the Russian power, even if she does not actually ally herself with Russia. I mention merely to reject it the supposition that M. de Freycinet while at the Quai d'Orsay deceived his friends in order to mislead the world, and that an actual alliance between France and Russia has been lately signed. Prince Bismarck knows well enough that there is no alliance between these Powers, but still it suits France to show Russia in the background, as it suits Russia to show France, and while German writers point out that Russia would, if she could, only make use of France for her own ends, still the mere existence of two such military powers upon the two flanks of Germany cannot for one moment be out of the mind of the German staff.

Rumours of wars are bad enough, but it is not easy to see whence at this moment actual war is likely to come. France does not intend that war shall grow out of the Egyptian question. France is not going to attack Germany in a single-handed struggle. Germany is not going to attack France. Russia is the one power which is a comet of eccentric orbit rather than a planet in the European system. The power of Russia is wielded by a single man, or shall I say by two—the Emperor, and the Moscow newspaper emperor, Katkoff. Single-handed war between the United Kingdom and Russia is unlikely, at present and were it to break out the other Powers would be unlikely to be afterwards drawn in. This country has allowed Russia to violate her engagement of 1878 as to Batoum, and she probably would allow Russia to set at naught the Anglo-Turkish Convention, and to violate her other engagement of 1878, if it can be held to be still binding. There are in Europe no secret engagements which are likely to endanger European peace. This country is not under any, as is known, and the engagements that Russia is under towards us are pacific in their nature, though probably worth but little.

I have said that war is not likely to arise even out of that which is in itself improbable, a direct disregard by Russia of the conditions of the Anglo-Turkish Convention. The *Standard* may denounce Lord Randolph Churchill's interference in foreign affairs, but Lord Randolph Churchill's power in the country is not merely dependent upon his personal ability and vigour, remarkable as these are. It is still more largely due to the fact that he more or less faithfully interprets, and almost invariably attempts to interpret, the prevailing opinion of the country. If Lord Randolph Churchill declares now, as he used to declare far and wide, that this country ought not to fight for the integrity and independence of the Ottoman Empire, it is because he believes, and perhaps rightly believes, that the country would not fight for it. There remains Bulgaria.

I have already pointed out that while we may make confident prediction as to the course of action of other Powers by calculating their necessities, and by taking into account their prejudices and their feelings, and arrive at so accurate a result that if we are far wrong the error is due to our own stupidity, as regards Russia it is impossible to predict what she will or will not do, because the destinies of Russia are practically in the hands of a single man whose temper is that which the temper of autocrats usually is, overweighted as they are with responsibility. Although feeling in Great Britain is all one way, still it has frequently and ably been pointed out of late that there is a good deal to be said upon the other or Russian side about Bulgaria. It is true that Bulgaria is politically the child of Russia, that Russian sacrifices during the last war with Turkey created Bulgaria, and that assembled Europe at the Berlin Congress agreed to allow her much power there. On the other hand, Bulgaria now for practical purposes virtually includes Eastern Roumelia, in which it was the intention of the Congress that the Sultan's power should prevail, the result being that

D

Turkey was given control of the militia, while the Balkans were to be held by her troops. But Russia answers that it is rather late to have regard to these provisions now, inasmuch as they all went by the board so long ago as 1879. On the other hand, Russia would not have lost her hold upon Bulgaria had she not abused the situation by first drilling the newly-freed Bulgarians on autocratic lines, and then, when she came to dislike the German prince, by applying to the revolutionary party. On the whole it seems probable, in the opinion of those who know the Russian Emperor best, that Russia will not take any step in Bulgaria that is likely to force Austria into war. Should, however, war at any time prove the issue from the Bulgarian question, a good deal will turn upon the attitude of Italy. Russia is as unpopular in Italy as in Great Britain, and perhaps there is in Italy rather less dislike to the idea of actual fighting over the Bulgarian question than there is with us. Italian opinion has been utterly disgusted by the Bulgarian proceedings of Russia, and Italy is prepared for an alliance with England and Austria against Russia, though "not gratis." Italy would expect English moral assistance in the Harrar, and she would ask from Austria the Trentino, which Austria would of course refuse, but would refuse in such a way as to enable the grant of a strip of territory in the form of an improved frontier line to be given if it could not be avoided.

I have said already that it is necessary for the politician in these days to consider power of armament, and it is impossible to adequately deal with the European position of Ger-

many without taking an exact survey both of her absolute and
of her relative military strength. Both Germany and France
intend to keep out of war, but war between them will some
day come, and it would come the sooner if there were an
obvious disproportion of power between them. France
has done a fabulous amount of military work since 1870.
She has built miles upon miles of fortresses behind which
the least instructed of her men could fight. She believes
that she has a force of 3,408,000 instructed, and 701,000
untaught men, or 4,109,000 in all. As I shall show when
I go on to consider the military force of France in detail,
partly in the present and partly in the next chapter in this
volume, these figures are subject to great deductions in
the opinion of competent foreign critics, but, to summarise
what I shall have to say, it is probable that France possesses
an army of 2,500,000 men, with artillery and cavalry proper
for an army of 2,000,000, able at once to stand in line upon
the frontier, and to carry on simple, though not complicated,
movements in the field. The Germans could only put upon
the ground a force inferior in numbers, if we count the
whole of the reserves upon both sides, but the Germans
have more thoroughly trained men, and they have or had,
until lately, more confidence. In the case of a complete
mobilisation the German forces would be more easily handled,
because the regiments would consist less largely than the
French of men not permanently with the flag, but it is
doubtful, even in the opinion of the German staff, whether
Germany could make any but a merely defensive war against
France, except by a policy which I shall presently describe.

The recent speeches to the German Parliament upon the proposed increase of the army should go for nothing. In every country the people explain the speeches of Ministers by the home or parliamentary necessities of their position, but they seldom accept that simple explanation of what is said in other capitals by the Ministers of other countries. If the German staff thought it necessary that a particular increase in the army should take place, the War Minister and the head of the staff would be likely to use in Parliament the alarmist language by which it was most likely that that increase would be carried. Still, a careful examination of the subject has led foreign officers, looking to the present condition of the French army and also to that of those of Austria and Russia, to agree in the necessity for the increase. As has already been pointed out the most immediate cause for an increase in the German army was the discovery by the German staff of the military weakness of Austria, a factor to which I shall have to recur in the chapters upon Russia and upon Austria. While the Austrian army is much weaker than was supposed a year ago, while the Russian army has been enormously increased of late in numbers, and while the French military system has been maturing itself by lapse of time, the army of Germany, though splendid, has comparatively speaking been standing still.

Germany in a military sense has been living a little upon the prestige of her mobilisations in 1866 and 1870. In 1867, when the figure of 1,300,000 men for the Confederation was given, M. Thiers replied that the numbers were illusory; that if they were true, France must despair, but that luckily the accounts of the German army were all fables, and that the men could not be found. In 1870 they were found. Nearly a million of men were present in ten days, and the forces of the Confederation very soon reached the figure of the books. There can be no doubt that in 1874, and again in 1875, when Russia prevented a war between Germany and France, and England took credit for having done so, Germany could have crushed her rival. It is much more doubtful now. It is little known what efforts were suddenly made in 1874-5 with a view to war, but the time went past. Since that date the Germans have been able to keep the number of men present with the flag exactly equal on the average to the number of men nominally present. Every man who is sent away for any reason is immediately replaced, and the figures which were true in 1870 are equally true with regard to a far larger force in the present day. On the other hand, it is impossible to be certain what deduction upon this point has to be made in the case of France and Russia. The corruption which still exists in Russia, and the wastefulness which prevails in French finance, lead to a considerable shrinkage in the number of men present. It is difficult to find in France the real number of "days of men present" with the flag, but the point is one which is worth care, inasmuch as it affects the national confidence, which is a serious matter in the case of France, and the solidity of the army under mobilisation.

A perusal of the German military budget and a comparison of it with the French are flattering to Germany in one respect and to France in another. France is entitled to credit for the sacrifices which she has made to her ideal of national honour, and for the comparative cheerfulness with which the tremendous charges of her budget have been borne. In the case of Germany, on the other hand, we find machine-like precision; also strict and rigid justice in paying to the last farthing, for example out of the military extraordinary budget—that is, out of the French funds obtained from the indemnity—the pensions of the French Legion of Honour and the French military medal to old French soldiers inhabiting Alsace and Lorraine. We find also that the German staff have made over £20,000 by writing a big book, which is more than most writers can say, and have speculated prudently with the indemnity funds, and greatly increased their sum by fortunate operations on the Stock Exchange. The reason for the difference lies partly no doubt in national character, partly in the fact that in Germany the men who are at the head of the army have spent their lives on the general staff. In France there is a perpetual change of ministers, and there is too much jealousy of individuals to allow much hope that any one man will be suffered to very long control the destinies of the French army. Germany has an enormous advantage in the fact that the German Parliament allows (it could hardly, if it would, prevent) permanence in military arrangements, and that the German Emperor retains in military power a group of men who form a training school of war, and who are at least as remarkable in their offices as upon the field of battle. At the same time, it is difficult to share the pessimism from a French point of view of the generality of French military writers. Their object is sometimes that which we have just been considering in the case of the German staff, namely, to obtain votes from an unwilling opposition.

French military critics write that Germany really has, not 427,000 but 454,000 or 468,000 men actually with the flag, and that these are real figures, for if a man dies or falls ill another man is put in his place, which is not the case in France; that France only instructs 117,000 a year, while Germany instructs 151,000; that the Germans have 680,000 more instructed men than has France, and that the German cavalry exceeds the French by 6,000 sabres. Taking the French nominal figures at 523,000 men, they deduct officers and military police and thirteen per cent. as absent, and reduce their numbers to 414,000 with the flag, of whom they say 71,000 are abroad, chiefly in Algeria, Tunis, and Tonquin, while Germany has all hers at home, and they finally bring out as the result that France has only 343,000 men available in time of peace, to set against the far larger number named above for Germany. The errors committed by many of these pessimistic French military writers are obvious even to the uninstructed eye. They omit officers and military police upon the French side, and count the former, and sometimes the latter, upon the German, and so forth, but it must be conceded to them that, although Algeria has now ceased to be a source of military weakness to France, Tunis and Tonquin, to say nothing of Madagascar, will long continue to make a drain upon her strength in Europe.

After the greatest care in the application of figures, it seems necessary to conclude that, making every allowance for the ill effects of a foolish policy of so-called "colonial" annexation, and admitting that France in the event of a complete mobilisation would have a larger number of half-trained men in her companies and a smaller proportion of fully-trained men than Germany, and would there-fore be less able to undertake difficult operations in the field at the beginning of a war, nevertheless France could put a larger force of infantry in the field than Germany, and possesses cavalry and artillery enough for an army of two millions of men. If we pass from quantity to quality it is more difficult to speak. Most troops will fight well behind walls, and the French frontier is now one great earthwork. Some of those who are disposed to lay down general rules as to the aptitudes of foreign nations, declare that the French never fight well except when they are in good spirits, and that it is absolutely necessary for France that the first battles, however trivial, should prove a success; but Montmirail in old days and Faidherbe's campaigns of December and January, 1870-1, show that Frenchmen can sometimes splendidly fight a losing battle even with untrained troops.

The two great rivals of the Continent are now each too strong for the other. France, even with a Russian alliance, could not easily pass Metz and Strasburg, or cross the Rhine, could not pass through Switzerland, and could not safely pass through Belgium. Germany, on the other hand, except through Belgium, cannot now get into France at all. As late as 1879 France was open to the Germans up to the gates of Paris, and they could have occupied Champagne, fortified its cities against the French, and waited quietly, had they chosen to adopt that plan of campaign. Now Nancy alone is open,

and a short distance behind the nominal frontier there is a
real military frontier, which is inexpugnable. The new
French frontier has been made as strong by art as it is weak
by nature and by the intention of the German staff who chose
it. The French army has been increased till it is superior in
numbers to that of Germany, and rapidity of possible mobilisation is now the same upon both sides. The powers of
railway concentration are equal. The French fortresses,
like the Russian fortresses upon the east, are now superior to
the German. For sixty miles in a stretch along the frontier
every single spot is under defensive fire by heavy guns. Of
a military frontier towards Germany of 270 kilomètres, 200
are under fire, and the two gaps which are left have been left
on purpose, and in German military opinion are impassable.
The French fortresses in the next war, it is safe to say, will
be defended, if they are attacked, as Bitche and Belfort were
in 1870, and not surrendered in the manner in which the
others, from Metz and Strasburg down to Toul and Longwy,
were handed over to the enemy. It was the civil population
which demoralised the troops and forced the surrender of the
fortresses in 1870. In the next war the fortresses will be
detached forts, and there will be no civil population to be
taken into account. There will probably, also, be the employment of the repeating rifle to be faced, and the repeating
rifle is more important in the defence of earthworks than in
the attack. At the worst, the French would lose Nancy in
a direct attack, and the real problem—and it is one of singular importance to us in England—is whether the Germans
will stand on the defensive upon the French as they will

upon the Russian frontier, or whether they will pass through Belgium.

It is a singular fact that the most important point to the future of Britain for the next few years, namely, whether Belgian neutrality will be violated by Germany in the " coming " war, and what England will do if it is violated, had not till lately been discussed in England. One thing may safely be asserted, namely, that if Belgium would make proper preparations for her own defence her neutrality would not be violated; but these preparations have not been made.* While an attack on Germany by France through Belgium is, in a military sense, improbable, an attack on France by Germany through Belgium is highly probable if the Belgians continue to keep so small an army as they do, and to contemplate its withdrawal under the guns of Antwerp. For Belgium to fortify Antwerp on an enormous scale, and to practically fortify nothing else, and to contemplate withdrawal there with the King and Parliament and half her forces, is, if we leave foreign help out of account, much as though England should fortify a portion of the county of Sutherland as the best means for her defence. Antwerp is near the northern extremity of the kingdom, and at the point most absolutely removed from all possibility of attack. Antwerp might be held by any number of troops— by the whole Belgian and the whole British army, for example —without the holding of it being very dangerous to an army of a million of men advancing upon Paris from Coblentz

---

* A great discussion took place on this subject in Belgium shortly after the appearance of this article, and ultimately a Government Bill for the fortification of the towns upon the Meuse was introduced.

through the province of Namur.* I am aware that the Intelligence Branch of the War Office defend in their latest volumes,
which are published for the benefit of the world, the selection
of Antwerp as against Brussels; but Brussels itself lies towards
the extremity of the kingdom, and if Belgian neutrality is to
be safeguarded, it must be safeguarded at Liége* or upon the
Upper Meuse. England, unless she turns over a new leaf in
military matters and adopts a system more in accordance with
modern ideas than her present old-fashioned military organisation, could only place a single army corps at Antwerp in the
time that it would take Germany to place nearly two millions
and France to place two and a half millions of men in the field.
Antwerp cannot be taken, and the defence of Antwerp is
not worth thinking of. It is only necessary to consider an
army which can fight in the open field or advance upon the
communications of the army of the Power which has violated
the neutrality of Belgium. Great Britain, no doubt, could
rapidly place a large number of infantry and some cavalry
in Belgium, not properly organised for war, but in a position
to make a demonstration in what would be a friendly country,
where there would not be much difficulty about supplies;
but no such force could advance, without high risk of
destruction, upon the line of the Meuse, and the war might be
decided before two English army corps and a third corps
composed of half of the Belgian army could appear in the
neighbourhood of Liége or of the Upper Meuse. The
temptation to the German staff is strong, and will remain
so until the French frontier south of Maubeuge has been

* It has since been decided to fortify Namur and Liége.

made as strong as the frontier towards Germany, which will take millions of money and many years. It must be remembered that the French frontier towards Germany is short, while the French frontier towards Belgium is long, for France and Belgium have a common frontier of over 380 miles. Of course I may be told that the plan for the defence of Belgium is the best that can be adopted; that the razing of the fortresses on the Meuse was wise, because they could not have been held by Belgium against either Germany or France; that Belgium is guaranteed by all the Great Powers, which may be expected to come to her assistance; that Antwerp would be the point at which their troops would land; that when a large force had been collected there the offensive could be taken towards the south; and that Germany is too strict an observer of international engagements to make it likely that she should violate the neutrality of Belgium, which even by my own admission it would be to the military advantage of France if possible to respect. Is it quite certain that in a duel between Germany and France any of the Powers would think of coming to the assistance of Belgium? Would not they excuse themselves upon the ground that the treaty is not in the most modern form, and that although in 1839 the country was declared by the Powers to be neutral, when it was practically desired to protect that neutrality in 1870, special and temporary treaties were wanted for that purpose?* In the event of a fresh war similar treaties would at once be entered into if it was not intended to risk the violation; but if it were, delays would

* A misunderstanding of this passage in the French translation caused hostile criticism in France and Belgium, but it contains no inaccuracy.

take place in the consultations of the Powers during which the neutrality itself would be at an end.

The official English book upon the armed strength of Belgium gives as a reason for expecting the presence of a British army at Antwerp after the violation of Belgium's neutrality that England is "supposed to" have an interest in preventing the annexation of Antwerp by a Great Power. This is hardly a sufficiently wide view of the problem. If the defence of Belgium by Great Britain is only to be justified on the ground that it might be dangerous for England if either France or Germany were ultimately to hold Antwerp, it must be admitted that there would not be much more danger in their holding Antwerp than in France holding Cherbourg, and that the increase of danger would probably not be worth the risk of taking part in a great Continental war. That England is bound by treaty to defend Belgium, and must maintain her treaty obligations, would have been a stronger argument for the compilers of the military handbook to have made use of, but in itself would hardly be a sufficient argument to induce the British Parliament to contemplate an isolated intervention. The public law of Europe is an important matter, but people would be inclined to answer that we ought not to stand forward by ourselves to be its guardians. Moreover, suppose the case of a sudden revelation at the beginning of a war of a kind of virtual acquiescence by the Belgian Government in the occupation of a portion of their territory, which is not absolutely inconceivable. In that case it is certain that English opinion would not allow interference, unless all the

Powers were willing to interfere together, which under the circumstances of the case would not be probable, and certainly could not be arranged in time.   The subject is a very serious one, because there can be no doubt that if certain statesmen who might be named were in actual and not merely nominal power at the time, England would be committed to war in defence of Belgian neutrality the moment it was threatened, whereas with other statesmen, such as, for example, it may be safely prophesied, Lord Randolph Churchill or Mr. Chamberlain, England would think twice as to the drift of public opinion before the fatal plunge was made.   Now such a matter ought not to rest upon the chance of any particular individual holding power in this country, but some decision in advance ought to be taken upon the question if our foreign policy is not to be subject to perpetual shifts and doubts.   Mistakes—and in such matters grave mistakes—loss of national dignity, destruction of belief in public faith, and risk of war, can only be avoided by firm adherence to ground taken up beforehand.   The course followed in 1870 by Mr. Gladstone for the defence of Belgian neutrality was approved by public opinion at the time, but it is far from certain, considering the change in the electorate that has since occurred, and the redistribution of political power, and looking to the growth of democracy in both the great parties in the State, that electoral and Parliamentary opinion now would be in accord with the opinion manifested then.

Belgium is, whether justly or unjustly, not only considered less of a British interest now that the memories of

Waterloo have become more dim, as well as the memories of the treaty of 1839, but Belgium, justly or unjustly, is not quite so popular in this country at the present moment as she was a few years ago. The Congo business, and the rumoured secret negotiations of the King of the Belgians with France and Germany successively about the eventual sale of his indefinite African territories, have robbed Belgium of some English sympathy. One point, however, there can be no doubt about, namely, that if we must fight for Belgium against Germany it will be well to lessen the chance of having to do so by inducing Belgium to keep up a proper army to defend her dangerous position, and to arrange a plan for defence which shall admit of the rapid concentration of a sufficient force within striking distance of the Meuse. When once Belgian neutrality is violated by either party, whatever promises are made, her independence will be gone.

I have ventured to forecast the probability in a military sense of German violation of the Belgian frontier as compared with the improbability of French violation. Belgium covers the longest and most vulnerable stretch of the French north-east frontier. It covers more than half the line which France would have to defend, and protects the half which nature has done nothing to guard for France. On the other hand, the shortest, best, and safest line from Central Prussia to Paris goes through Belgium, down the Oise to Creil. The road and railway from Berlin through Maubeuge to Paris are at once the best line of attack and the safest line for retreat in the event of German defeat. But whichever party triumphed, Belgium would have to pay the cost, and either the whole or the greater portion of her territory would pass to one or other of the belligerents, or partition would be her lot.   If the Belgians could be counted upon not to fall back at once upon Antwerp, but to fight sufficiently to force the hand of a possibly unwilling Government in England, Germany would not make their country a battle-field.   But the Belgians do not seem inclined to increase their army.

Surely this consideration ought to show the prudent among French politicians the folly of angering England against France by silly annexations, as in the New Hebrides, or by impossible demands; for to defend Belgium against Germany would be represented to the British electors, by those who objected to the war, as saving France from Germany, which would add to the unpopularity of the war itself if France were unpopular at the time in England.   It is not that there is any desire in Germany to annex.   The considerations which we have been discussing are military considerations, not political.

It is true in one sense, as has been assumed in recent discussions in Belgium with regard to the Bill for establishing a wider military service there, that the greatest danger to Belgium comes, not from Germany, but from France.   True in a sense, because there is little danger of the incorporation of the whole or greater part of Belgium in the German Empire, and the greatest possible danger of the incorporation of the whole or part in France.   If once France should be attacked through Belgium, then, no doubt, in the event of ultimate French success, Belgium, or part of Belgium, would go to France.

There remains the possibility that the next war between Germany and France may be a waiting war in which Germany and France may substantially both stand upon the defensive. The armies of Denmark, of Sweden and Norway, and of Spain are not large enough to cause anxiety to the greater Powers, as the frontiers of France and Germany would be defended against the attacks of the smaller Powers by territorial troops and fortresses. But suppose a waiting policy were adopted by the great belligerents towards each other, they having drifted into war without either of them desiring to attack : which could the better bear the strain ? Had it not been for the French follies of Tonquin, and even, as I think, of Tunis, although Tunis is less distinctly folly than Tonquin, and for reckless expenditure upon all sides by France, there would have been no doubt that at present and for many years to come France would have been the better able to wait. It would be impossible for either to wait long in a complete mobilisation. The next war will in all Continental countries suspend trade except in a few branches, and it becomes more important than ever to the Continental Powers that it should be short. England alone of the Great Powers could maintain a long war, which is lucky for us when we remember how entirely unfit we are to play a part in a short one. Russia, curiously enough, in spite of what is said of her finances, comes next to England in ability to " last," for her army, enormous as it is, forms a smaller proportion of her working population than is the case in Germany, France, Austria and Italy ; and her population are used to hardship, and are moved by a patriotism which is simply marvellous.

E

For any one of the four Powers, a long war is a terrible calamity to contemplate. The dangers of war to Austria are well known in Austria, and they are both military and political. France, which could, were she prudent, best stand the strain, has allowed her finances to become deplorable, partly by spending too much money, and partly by wasting it in costly so-called "colonial" adventures. She would have it in her power to bring her finances into order and to greatly diminish the weakness of her army in trained troops were she boldly to abandon positions which would be lost to her in the event of any future war between England and France. On the other hand, France is now, for the first time since 1870, fully aware of her strength upon her frontiers towards Germany, and, while unwilling to fight, full of spirit as regards a necessary war. Gambetta once said that his Cherbourg speech, which caused a stir in Europe, was the first glass of wine given to the convalescent. After Gambetta's death the convalescent had a relapse, and it is General Boulanger who has first made him hold up his head for good. The gratitude for his cure, due to Providence or to the strength of the patient's constitution, is, as often happens, bestowed by the patient upon the doctor.

In surveying once more the entire field, a fact that must strike the observer is that while the uncertainty of Russia's policy presents the principal danger to peace, there is one obvious consideration which makes against an attack by Russia upon Austria. In simple language it may be expressed by the phrase, "It is heads I win, and tails you lose," for Austria against Russia, for however completely

beaten the Austrian forces might be, Germany could not,
without an intolerable loss of prestige in Europe, allow Austria
to be seriously dismembered. It is the knowledge possessed
in Russia of this fact which, more than the speeches of
Austrian and English and Italian ministers, has caused Prince
Bismarck's advice to be up to the present time followed in
the main at St. Petersburg. Lord Salisbury's language,
therefore, which seemed imprudent to many, both of his
English and of his foreign critics, was a fairly safe example
of the use of what is known to us as Jingo language when its
use is wise. The new generation of Tory-Democratic statesmen are believed to advocate as popular a combination
of Beaconsfieldian language with Cobdenic secret action;
"talk Jingo, but act Manchester" is supposed to be their
watchword. But Lord Salisbury is still supreme in the
conduct of foreign affairs for the Tory party, although
that supremacy may not long continue, and Lord Salisbury
is not so imprudent a politician nowadays as he was some
years ago. I have spoken throughout this chapter as though
Lord Salisbury and not Lord Iddesleigh was our foreign
minister; but I believe that I violate no confidence when
I say that Lord Iddesleigh does not profess to carry out
in the Foreign Office a policy of his own, and that upon
all matters of importance he acts under the direction of Lord
Salisbury.* If I am to give an average outside opinion, free
from party bias, upon foreign questions, I ought to congratulate the country upon the fact that in the hands, under the
Liberals of Lord Rosebery or under the Conservatives of

* First published before Lord Iddesleigh's lamented death.

Lord Salisbury, the foreign affairs of the country are in highly skilled, competent, and wise control.

It now only remains to be discussed whether there are any special considerations affecting England, besides those which have been mentioned, which should be here named. Some few years back it was supposed that Prince Bismarck had taken such a dislike to the English Liberal party as to make the holding of office by that party a matter of danger to the country. It should be remembered that the London press is mainly hostile to the Liberal party, and that when the Liberals are " in " many quotations appear from German newspapers not friendly to this country, which are made to express a hostility seemingly confined to the Liberal party, when as a fact it applies to England under any rule. The *Cologne Gazette* in October last, with the Conservatives in power, was sneering as bitterly at England as it ever did in Mr. Gladstone's days, and declaring that before the Treaty of Berlin and up to the present time England had been of no account in Europe. If we look to the opinions of the German Chancellor and not to the expressions of the German press, it is unnecessary to state that Prince Bismarck has never had any quarrel with the Liberal party as such, nor any love for the Conservative. The new men, the men of the future, as regards foreign affairs, on the Liberal side—or shall I say Liberal sides?—Lord Rosebery on the one hand and Lord Hartington and Mr. Chamberlain on the other, are as acceptable to Prince Bismarck as is Lord Salisbury.

Prince Bismarck differs in one point from those about him :

he does not rate too low the military capacity of England. The German staff, knowing the weakness of our force, the slowness of our mobilisation, the fewness of our guns, the general imperfection of our equipment for rapidly entering upon war, distinctly underrate the power of this country. Prince Bismarck is aware that, although we may have rejected until lately the repeating gun—the introduction of which by all the Great Powers has been slow, for the American cavalry was partly armed with it more than twenty years ago, and it has been occasionally used in war both by the Turks and the Chinese—and although we may not be manufacturing the new shells, or taking any very active steps to fit ourselves for immediate war, we have such wealth, such energy, and such manufacturing power that, whatever may be the ultimate danger to our position in the world, we could crush in a lengthy war the greatest of the European Powers, except Germany, which is absolutely invulnerable by us.

One point about which Prince Bismarck has in recent years come into collision with this country is due to his changed colonial policy. It is a well-known fact that Prince Bismarck for many years was in the habit of expressing his profound disapproval of German colonisation, but of late he has found it necessary to gratify the public taste for "running into something cheap." With singular prudence he has avoided the mistakes of France, and while the countries that he has acquired may not be of any immediate use, at all events their acquisition has been far from costly. They all are countries which have been refused by us, although probably, in the face of the imposition of differential duties against

British goods by certain Powers, the refusal will be seen to
have been founded upon old-fashioned grounds unfortunately
inapplicable to the circumstances of the day.   The non-Dutch
half of New Guinea we might have had at any time for the
hoisting of a flag (Holland has hardly so good a tenure for its
part) ; but half of the half has been allowed to go to Germany.
The Cameroons were offered to England by their chiefs, and
the offer had not been finally accepted at the moment at which
the German annexation took place.   The shadowy French
and German country reachable by the Congo might have
been English had not Lord Carnarvon refused to ratify the
annexation of December, 1874 ; and Zanzibar's rights over
the mainland might have been acquired by England without
difficulty, inasmuch as the Sultan had for many years, in one
form or another, pressed for our protection.   If these countries were not to remain unoccupied, and were not to be
occupied by ourselves, it is not a bad thing for us that they
should be occupied by Germany.   A German annexation or
a German protectorate must for England be preferable to a
French, so long as Germany does not, like France, place
differential duties upon foreign goods. The countries in which
the German flag has recently been hoisted are at present in
truth only nominally German.   The view of the Chancellor's
opponents in favour of German colonies as necessary for the
development of German trade, has been modified by him into
a system of paper annexations in districts where German
trading houses were already flourishing, at Angra Pequeña,
in Central Africa, on the Zanzibar coast, in Northern New
Guinea, and in some Pacific islands.   We might have antici-

pated Germany by having recourse to the same system of paper annexations, against which Germany might have protested, but would not have fought. Still, it is impossible to view with much regret, except in cases which interfere with Australian interests, the nominal annexation by Germany of these territories. In the case of the Cameroons, the main ground upon which it was proposed that this country should accept the cession was that otherwise the territory would be taken by the French, whose commercial policy would destroy our trade ; but as German and not French annexation has taken place, the English trade there will probably be safe enough. The point upon which alone any serious danger was likely to arise, namely, the advocacy by Germany of land claims in the Pacific islands, which, though preferred by German subjects, are often of an utterly indefensible kind, has been tided over by Commissions, and time, precious in such cases, has been gained. On the whole, therefore, with the reservation of Australian interests, far more threatened by France, with its commercial and its convict policy, than by Germany, little harm to English interests has been done by Germany since she became the foremost of Continental Powers, and few occasions of serious difficulty between the countries are likely to arise.

II.

FRANCE.

———

WE have seen in the previous chapter how Germany and
Austria are bound over to keep the peace, and will do
nothing warlike unprovoked; how England is past her
fighting days, unless moved by a very powerfully irritating
cause ; how Russian policy alone is not to be foreseen, and
how the erratic impulses of the Tsar may affect the future
of Europe. We have now to consider the same phenomena
from the French point of view, and it will also be my duty
to try to make plain in what way the personality of the
leading Frenchmen may influence the policy of their country.
Thoroughly as force now reigns in Europe, at least three of
the Great Powers, the first three of the four which have just
been named, whatever be the amounts they spend upon their
armies and navies, are now as peaceable in general intention as the United States. Italy obviously will never begin a war, and the only Powers that are thought likely to
provoke one are France and Russia. What of France ?
It being admitted that the French peasant or the ordinary

French elector is generally of a peace-loving and thrifty disposition, is there in France any man who is likely to play upon national vanity in such a manner as to hurry on a war? A distinction must here be drawn between words and acts. A large proportion of the governing men of France come from its southern provinces, and the Gascon and Provençal are proverbial for the use of language which in England is called Jingo, in Northern France Chauvinistic, but in Southern France is regarded as the ordinary speech of the people. The French Patriotic League not only talks big, but writes big, and publishes statements from which it might be gathered, were they to be taken literally, that Europe is upon the brink of a general war. It will already have been seen, from the necessary anticipations of the previous chapter, that I do not share the view that it is probable that France will voluntarily enter upon war. On the contrary, I go so far as to think that, if Russia were to begin war with England, or with Austria, or with England and Austria combined, France would, if possible, look on, content to reap profit from it at a later moment, if she could do so.

The late Cabinet showed by the official declaration of its chief that it was anti-Chauvinist, although it contained one member supposed to be of a Chauvinist turn. The declaration made by ministers on taking office said nothing of foreign policy, except in vague and general terms, and only named the army incidentally. Nevertheless the French and German newspapers are full of rumours of impending war. It is said that M. de Courcel, the ex-ambassador at

Berlin, gave as his reason for refusing the Foreign Office, that he "would not be the Duc de Gramont of the Republic." Yet the whole of the persons who count in France, have counted latterly, or are likely to count, are, with one possible exception, admittedly peaceable.   The President, who bears a much closer resemblance than does Mr. Bright to the ideal member of the Society of Friends ; M. de Freycinet, a model of cautious statesmanship ; M. Spuller, German not only by race, but by turn of mind ; M. Clémenceau, enlightened, friendly to England, and by no means pro-Russian —all these men are most unlikely to countenance a policy of adventure.   M. Ferry, who may come back again some day, burnt his fingers in Tonquin, and is now as cautious as M. de Freycinet himself.   The one exception, of course, is General Boulanger, and it must be admitted not only that he excites in Germany and in Russia fears or hopes as the case may be, but that he arouses very general public attention even in France.   The personality of the man is strong. He has come very suddenly to the front.   Gambetta, indeed, used to speak of him as one of the best four officers in France, but he put him rather below than above at least two of the four.

General Boulanger is still young; he is handsome, and a good speaker.   He owes his advancement to M. Clémenceau, but he has eclipsed his patron, who indeed never was especially popular.   General Boulanger is supposed to have violated the gentlemanly code of honour, but it is universally admitted that what has happened has not done him any harm.   I shall be disbelieved when I state simply that his personal popularity in France is greater than that enjoyed by any man since Napoleon was at the height of his power, with the possible exception of Lafayette at the moment of the Revolution of 1830. General Boulanger excites a good deal of prejudice in society, but society in France counts less than it does in any other country in Europe. He is probably more popular with the Army than was the Prince-President in 1849 and 1850, and the dislike felt for him by a large number of the superior officers was felt also, and even more intensely, for the Prince-President. So popular is he with the private soldiers and, generally speaking, with the majority of the electors, that it may be said that, in comparison with him, no one else in France, with the doubtful exception of old M. de Lesseps, is popular at all. The politicians are afraid of him, and yet, somehow or other, he is never mentioned without a smile. In spite of his extraordinary popularity no one takes him quite seriously, and the newspapers are able to ignore his real standing with their readers and to go on writing of him as a ring-master, which character they pretend he resembles. It must be admitted that the circus element is not wanting in General Boulanger's composition. He is not only a much advertised man; he has done a good deal to advertise himself. At the same time he is an able War Minister, and the constant kindness which he has shown to the private soldier is probably an honest kindness, with a calculation of the good results of which towards himself he cannot with any fairness be charged. Although General Boulanger's popularity in France is far greater than that enjoyed by Gambetta in his lifetime, he has

never attained in European estimation the same position, nor
does he deserve it.   But in Germany there is an uneasy
feeling with regard to General Boulanger's popularity, and
by some Germans and by the German newspapers he is
thought to be a War Minister who means war.   There never
was a greater mistake made than to think that General
Boulanger is warlike.   He seems to me to have done his
duty as War Minister with no special view of undertaking
an aggressive war, but, on the contrary, to have shown, in
constantly limiting the expeditions intended to conquer so-
called " colonies," a prudence which is laudable from every
point of view.   I cannot agree with those who think that
the strong personality of General Boulanger in any way
affects the situation of France in Europe and her probable
future.   A very considerable time ago I asked a friend of
mine who was going to Paris to find out for me whether
General Boulanger, who was beginning to excite attention,
was a man, a soldier, a mountebank, or an ass.   The report
was of no great practical value because it was to the effect
that the " Bonaparte without a victory " was at once all
four.   But although probably, for the reasons which I have
given, an excellent War Minister, General Boulanger has
shown by his last considerable speeches that his English blood
is strong in him and that he is not a man, as the French say,
" to break windows."

I gave in my first chapter my reasons for thinking that
while France is not likely to move first in a warlike sense,
she is, for defensive purposes, very strong.   There are many
drawbacks to her position.   The instability of her Govern-

ments, although it perhaps has some slight influence in preventing a cessation of financial waste, does not check her
military preparations. The durability of the Republic itself
is often called in doubt. The Republic may be looked upon
as being more safe against internal revolution than would be
any other form of government that could be set up, and as
being, indeed, quite certain to endure as long as peace itself
endures. A foreign observer of France must come now
to believe that what are known as the old parties which
compose "the Right" are very weak. M. Raoul Duval's
attempt to form a new Conservative party which should
thoroughly support the Republic proved a failure, because
it did not suit the personal declarations of the leaders of the
so-called Conservative party; but nevertheless he expressed
the view of almost all the reasonable men in the Conservative
ranks. There are many of those who are ridiculously labelled
"Orleanists" by the "Republicans," who say that, if they
wanted a constitutional king at all, they would as willingly
take M. Poubelle as the Comte de Paris. " M. Poubelle and
his wife are popular," they declare; "he is better-looking
than the Comte de Paris, and she is nicer-looking than the
Comtesse, and more French; they already live in the
Pavillon de Flore, the temporary *préfecture de la Seine*, that
is in the Tuileries, so that they would not have to move." But
then these gentlemen, as may be gathered from their irony,
though classed as Monarchists, really prefer the Republic.

The division of the Monarchists into clerical Bonapartists, democratic and anti-clerical Bonapartists, Legi-
timists and Constitutional Monarchists, some clerical and

some non-clerical, would have fatally weakened the Monarchic party if it had not in any case been so weak as hardly to be worth taking into account. Those who for one reason or other, whether they represent what is called Orleanism or what is called Legitimacy, are in favour of the restoration of the House of France are far stronger than the Bonapartists, but they owe their nominal strength in the Chamber and the number of their supposed supporters among the electorate only to the fact that they poll a large Catholic vote, a large economic vote, and a large discontented vote —votes which are in no sense truly monarchical.

The probability is, that if ever France should want a master, a new man will have a better chance than any member of the families that have reigned in France. As the *Journal des Débats* has lately said, the moderate Conservatives with the Comte de Paris at their head, if he pleases to be there, will separate from the Cassagnacs, who may find a saviour of society in the " dynasty of the Boulangers." If Prince Victor should ever be within a measurable distance of the French throne, it will not be through any help that his party gives him, but because he is a sharp, pushing, good-looking man.

That there should exist persons desirous, as the Comtesse de Paris is said to be, of ascending or of sharing the French throne, is in itself a singular fact. It may be safely asserted that the existence of a king in France would at the present moment, and in any state of French feeling that can be foreseen, only serve to strengthen the revolutionary party. No government in France is likely, for any long time together, to be more conservative than the existing Republic has been during the last fifteen years, and all true French Conservatives admit in private, whatever language they may hold in public, that the best chance for French society, and the best chance for French religion, against anarchy or spoliation, lies in a moderate Republic. The consciousness of this would, if they were free agents, lead them to join and help the moderate Republican party. There is a great deal of ignorance upon this subject amongst ourselves. The natural regret which some feel for the fate of the Empress Eugénie, the ties of others to the excellent members of what is known in England as the Orleans family, even since it has become the House of France, and the somewhat widely-spread feeling of prejudice in favour of a constitutional Monarchy as compared with a Republic, all concur, with irritation at certain recent political action on the part of France, to produce a feeling against the French Republic. That feeling very naturally takes the form of a belief that somehow or other the Republic is to be brought to an end. All governments in Europe, and several in America, are now in this position, that they may at any moment be upset by revolutionary forces, and the French Republic is not beyond the danger. It is conceivable that the Socialists may upset the Third Republic. It is also possible that they may indirectly overturn it by making the Government itself a Socialistic Government, and so producing a violent reaction. But in my opinion France is less exposed to immediate danger from the Socialists than are several of the Monarchies, and I expect to see the Republic, unhurt either by Socialism on the one side, or by Monarchism on the other, last as long as peace is maintained.

Even in 1848 the weak Second Republic proved itself for a time better able to resist violence than was the Constitutional Monarchy, although the latter was no doubt weakened by the extreme limitation of the suffrage. No Republic would have fallen so easily as fell the Monarchy of July :—no Monarchy could have survived even for a time the days of June. At the moment of that remarkable insurrection the Socialists were stronger in France and possessed abler leaders than at the present time, and it is an extraordinary testimony to the power even of a weak Republic that it should have crushed them, although indeed it perished later on. The French Third Republic is not likely to die of Socialism, or to die at all except by war.

The English people are—thanks to the English press—so much better informed upon foreign affairs than are the people of other countries, and are in fact so well and frequently addressed upon the subject by thoroughly competent men, that only prejudice can account for the mistaken view which widely prevails in England among the wealthier classes as to the durability of the Republic. The expulsion of the Princes from France was all but unanimously, if not quite unanimously, condemned by the English Press. If it had been simply condemned as unjust, I should have had nothing here to say, because I am here not expressing opinions upon what is just or what is unjust, or giving my personal preferences, but attempting only to state facts. The English newspapers did not content themselves with arguing that the measure was unjust, but almost all of them went on to prove by the most conclusive arguments that it was inexpedient from the point of view of the French Republic. This is an excellent example of the class of delusions of which I speak. It has turned out that the French Republicans knew their own business best, and that the Conservative reaction, which a year ago was shown by the results of elections to have reached a considerable height, has been checked by the expulsion of the Princes. The French electors, as was notably displayed in the recent elections in moderate departments, have welcomed what they regard as a necessary act of national dignity and of commendable vigour.

We saw just now that General Boulanger is not likely to be any especial danger to peace. Is he likely to be a danger to the Republic? I have said that in the event of France desiring a master, she is more likely to look to a new man than to a member of the late royal families; and, when this is said, people begin to ask, with that attraction which is always felt for the element of personality, "Have you such a person in view?" I have in view, not the present War Minister in particular, but the Generalissimo of the French forces in the event of war, whenever that may come. France is unlikely to be badly beaten in the next war, for the reasons which I have given in the article upon Germany. If, however, she is to have any chance of success, her Ministry must trust the best general that they can find, and let him virtually assume a dictatorship during the continuance of the war. A Generalissimo, thus placed with full powers at the

head of an army of some four millions of men, may be successful. If so, all will admit that the Republic will run a
danger through his success. If he is not successful, the
strong probability is that France will not be driven back
far within her frontier, and to some extent will be able to
hold her own, with an ever-increasing amount of suffering
caused by the pressure of taxation, and the withdrawal of
men from agriculture and from trade. If the Generalissimo
has been fairly cautious, is he not likely, even in these circumstances, to be almost as formidable a person to his
colleagues as he would be in the event of a successful war?
In case, however, of a severe defeat of France, the Republic
would certainly be upset in favour either of the House of
France, or of some individual who had been less compromised
in the failure than had others; some general, for example,
who had made a gallant stand. I cannot but think that a
calm observer must fear that war, either successful or unsuc-
cessful, must be fatal to the French Republic. Not necessarily
in name, however; not even probably in name. The next
man who upsets the French Republic will, if he is a prudent
man, retain Republican forms.

Under ordinary circumstances, that is to say, supposing
that there is no war soon, General Boulanger will not rise
higher than he has already risen. With his popularity, with
his face and figure, he would have a good chance of being
elected President if the election of President were by a
national vote; but he has little or none as matters stand,
the election being made, as is well known, by both Houses
sitting together in congress. Like the popularity of the

Prince-President in 1850, General Boulanger's popularity is one which lessens as you go upward in the social scale. Those who wish to know his weaker side will find it described in an article lately written by M. Cherbuliez (under his other name of Valbert) on " M. Cambon." It was the circus-master's side of General Boulanger that came out in Tunis, but during the war of 1870 he showed that he was a brave colonel, and lately, as minister, he has proved that he pos-sesses both sense and prudence, though " he is only the more dangerous when he is prudent " is the observation made to me by Republican politicians. General Boulanger's popu-larity has survived his disavowal of the D'Aumale letters, but his enemies lately thought that they had him on the hip. An attack was made upon General Boulanger, M. Clémenceau and others with regard to the circumstances under which Dr. Cornelius Herz received the cross of a Grand Officer of the Legion of Honour. This foreign gentle-man was stated to be a shareholder in *La Justice* and a subscriber to M. Clémenceau's election fund, as well as the entertainer of General Boulanger. It seems to have been thought by the latter's enemies that he would not survive a financial scandal, but, unfortunately for them, they failed to prove his connection or that of M. Clémenceau with any discreditable financial transactions. No doubt there is a good deal of monetary corruption at Paris, for, with the exception of the short-lived Second Republic, the Restora-tion was the last pure governmental period in France. The Monarchy of July, the Second Empire, and the Third Republic have all been marked by considerable financial

scandals, but M. de Freycinet's enemies admit that his hands
are clean, and General Boulanger's opponents failed to show
that his connection with Dr. Herz, even assuming for the
sake of argument that there was anything wrong about the
schemes of Dr. Herz, was any closer than that of M. de
Freycinet himself, or than that of General Menabrea, the
Italian Ambassador.   The net result of the efforts of General
Boulanger and of his enemies has been that, whilst he is still
a young man, the General's popularity greatly exceeds that
of the next most popular Frenchman, who has been many
more years before the country.

M. de Lesseps cannot well be Generalissimo ; General
Boulanger could and would be Generalissimo if there were
war at any short interval from the present time.   Some
suppose that there may be civil commotion in France, and
that he may be the general who will put it down, and that
in this way, as well as in war, there may be danger to
Republican institutions.   In my opinion that is not so.   If
there should be civil troubles, put down by force, the general
who puts them down will have incurred violent resentment
and will not be popular enough with the whole country to
found for himself a dictatorship, supposing that he wished to
do so.   But with war it is different.   Whilst an unlucky
war might even restore the House of France, and a doubtful
war might produce a dictatorship, a successful war would give
to the Generalissimo who brought to France Alsace or
Belgium, a supreme power veiled under Republican forms.
It is certain that the next French Cæsar will have no arch-
chancellors in breeches and silk stockings about him, and it

is probable that he will be styled President of the Republic. But the virtual autocracy of a strong man is not by any means out of the question.

In spite of General Boulanger's present popularity, it is quite possible that within a few years, as he grows older, he may be forgotten. In France men, even useful men, are thrown aside more easily and more completely than is the case with us in England. In England almost all the men able and willing to give useful service to their country are "in," or "out" and certain to "come in next time;" otherwise they are "in the running," to use our most expressive phrase. In France, not only are the declared partisans of the House of France, or of the Bonapartes, excluded, as well as men, however remarkable, who have failed, as, for example, M. Ollivier, but even men such as M. Léon Say, perhaps the most eminent of French statesmen. In France, M. Léon Say seems to be looked upon as destined never again to hold power, for no sufficient reason that any Englishman can see. The men of small compromises and of expedients hold on the best, or those of extraordinary caution, like that three-times Minister,* "the little White Mouse."

Given not the fact, but a belief on the part of the President and of the more cautious of his advisers, that war would upset the French Republic, we must cease to wonder at the refusal of a formal alliance with Russia, and we must expect that, whatever may be the language used in various countries, peace will last. The understanding between

---

* Written before 25th May, when he was again called upon to form a Ministry.

France and Russia was last autumn strong enough, without any formal alliance, to produce in many respects the consequences of a real alliance. The pressure of the confederates at Constantinople was immensely strong, and one noticeable fact about it was that, to judge by the attitude of the German Ambassador there, Prince Bismarck did not appear to mind it in the least. Twice within the last six months there suddenly arose the story of a Russo-German alliance, which was believed, because not contradicted at Berlin or St. Petersburg, but only at Vienna. Just as there was in the autumn no formal alliance with France, so there was in the spring no formal alliance with Germany on the part of Russia. Prince Bismarck and the Russian Emperor both gain by the assertion being made, but Prince Bismarck must contrive to contradict it at Vienna, for he could not tolerate that disruption of the Austrian Empire which would be caused by the revelation of an alliance which, if complete and formal, would be really directed by Russia against the Austrian policy in the East.

The Russians have set the report going at Constantinople that the English Conservatives now agree with the English Liberals that the possession of Constantinople by Russia would not be a danger to this country. They tell the Turks that England is now altogether indifferent to their fate, and that the only chance for them, if they wish to avoid absorption into Russia, is to be what is called good neighbours; that is, to allow Russia absolutely to direct their policy. With the apparent assent of Germany, the Sultan is rapidly coming to play the part of a Bey of

Tunis to Russia's France. At the same time the private
relations between Paris and Berlin are not of the nature
which might be expected from the recent coquetting
between Paris and St. Petersburg. Whilst the first-class
clerks whom the French Foreign Office sends to Berlin as
Ambassadors now no longer draw the Foreign Minister's
policy from the German Chancellor, yet there has been no
apparent change in the good private relations which exist
between the countries, both at Paris and at Berlin. Count
Münster is not an ambassador in whom Prince Bismarck
confides, and therefore it is the communications at the
Berlin end which count; but M. de Courcel met with no
serious difficulties during his residence in Berlin, and the
same has been the case, I believe, with M. Herbette.
Although people in this country are inclined to flatter
themselves that Germany must be really friendly to Great
Britain at all times, yet even as late as when Lord Salisbury
was Prime Minister in 1885, the relations between France
and Germany were distinctly better than the relations
between Germany and England. Sir E. Malet has been
able to some extent to change this state of things, but it is
a fact that for some years France was taking her policy
from Berlin, whilst England was too proud to do so, and a
good deal of friction was the result. The personal relations
between Prince Bismarck and Lord Ampthill were always
excellent, but Lord Ampthill was not allowed to bend the
knee, and the dislike which his attitude occasioned fell not
upon himself, but upon the country which employed him.
Lord Rosebery was looked upon as being very German, and

his tenure of office coincided with a great increase in the military spirit of France, which led to an attitude of independence on the part of that Power. While no breach in the relations of Paris and Berlin has yet occurred, and while Germany will avoid one as long as possible, the relations with England have become more close.

I see no occasion to modify the estimates of the relative armed strengths of France and Germany, which I ventured to make in drawing some comparison between them in the first chapter. The French army is becoming more democratic, whilst the German army in this respect is not undergoing change. The one-year volunteer system in Germany is so carefully regulated that its effects upon all sides are excellent. In France, abuses have from the first crept in, and the consequence is that the system itself will be destroyed, and service for a uniform period made universal. The failure of the one-year volunteer system in France appears to show that the French, although both a warlike and a scientific nation, are behindhand in the combination of science and war, or the application of scientific principles to war. The small number of German one-year volunteers become in nearly all cases most valuable non-commissioned officers, or officers of reserve. This is not the case with the vastly larger number of one-year volunteers in France, and the impatience of the French character displays itself in the probability that the system will be swept away instead of being modified until it becomes good.

Some doubt has been expressed as to the accuracy of my figures. One writer thinks that a reduction of 40 per cent.

should be made on the 4,000,000 French soldiers; but a reduction of 40 per cent. on the actual figure, which is above 4,000,000, gives that 2,500,000 men of which I wrote as the real force. It is well known that on the twentieth day of war, which is the last day for complete mobilisation, France will have 1,200,000 in the front line, 400,000 in the depots, and all her fortresses full of men, without counting the Algerian and Colonial forces—figures from which the same total of 2,500,000 men is reached.

Much criticism has been aroused in Belgium by what I have said of the military (not the political) prospect of an attack on France by Germany through Belgium. The Belgian writers who treat this subject, such as the editor of the chief organ of opinion at the capital, General Brialmont, and that other distinguished general who, previously to the appearance of my article of January last in the *Fortnightly Review*, had written the series of leading articles in the *Revue de Belgique*, but who, though signature is the rule in that periodical as in the *Fortnightly Review*, preferred like myself to keep his anonymity,—all think the violation of Belgian neutrality almost certain, and differ from my view, where they differ at all, only because they think the danger is from both sides, and not from Germany alone. This difference does not affect, unless to strengthen, the warning which I addressed to England. The enormous accumulation of supplies of every kind in the entrenched camp of Cologne is of itself enough in military eyes to prove the truth of what I said in the last chapter. Belgium is not disinterested, and it might be said that Belgian arguments are the arguments of alarmists. I am content then to rely upon an almost universal consent of military opinion in disinterested countries.   As regards political considerations, I would ask those who believe in the value of the " neutralisation " of Belgium to read the correspondence of 1870, at the time when Austria and Russia declined to support our action in defence of Belgium, until, France being hopelessly beaten, they found that it involved no responsibility.   I would also refer them to the Prussian circular of Dec. 3rd, 1870, in which Prussia declared that the Royal Government would "no longer consider itself bound to any consideration of the neutrality of the Grand Duchy" (of Luxemburg) " in the military operations of the German army," and which contains illustrations of the difficulty Luxemburg and even Belgium would experience in maintaining their neutrality in the event of another great war.

France is forced to trust solely to her army and her navy for her strength, for she cannot rely upon friendships.   The Emperor of Russia detests the French Republic, but is of course very willing to make a certain use of the military power of France for his own ends.   The Sultan merely follows the Russian lead ; but where in Europe can we say that France now has real friends ? As regards governments, nowhere ; for the traditional friendship of Sweden for France is checked by the understanding between France and Russia, Sweden's hereditary foe.   In the event of a general war, Sweden would be compelled to make choice between her old sympathies, and her desire to attack Russia in her own former province of Finland, and would probably be neutral,

as she was under even more powerful temptation during the
Crimean War. Austria follows Germany ; Italy is hopelessly
estranged from France ; Spain is condemned to immobility
by her internal circumstances and her geographical position.
Spain is ruled—although this is one of the facts that are
disguised from us by correspondents who are amenable to
hospitality—by an unpopular, because a foreign, queen.
The Spanish people are divided into Republicans and Indif-
ferents, and the spirit of the country is upon the Republican
side.   France cannot find an ally in Spain, but, on the
other hand, Germany will not be able to make Spain march
so long as France resists the temptations which lead her to
Morocco.

Not only the most interesting to ourselves of questions
which concern the friendships or the enmities of France,
but the most important even from a French point of view,
and the most difficult, is the question of her relations with
England.   So many are the points at which French and
British interests come into contact in various parts of the
world that conflicts between the two countries continually
arise.   Had the Monarchy of July, or the Second Empire,
taken as little trouble to avoid circumstances of irritation
as has been taken of late years by the Third Republic, there
would have been war between the two countries in the
middle of the present century.   That there has not been
war in recent years has been due to the strong peace feeling
in England, and to the inward consciousness on the part of
French Ministers that there is, underlying a good deal of
hostility towards England, also a real peace feeling in France.

Sufficient causes of war have been continually arising, and they have not been dealt with in all cases with discretion. Take, for example, the New Hebrides. The conduct of the French Government in this matter has looked at times as though it were purposely intended to exasperate English feeling.   In the Madagascar case the treatment of British subjects was of such a nature, that had the telegraph line to Tamatave been in existence, so that the facts had been published day by day in the English papers, war would probably have broken out.   But the first of all questions in men's minds when they talk of the relations of England and France is that of Egypt.

I shall write on this question with all the moderation that I can command, because I know that if I say but half as much against the policy of France as has been said against it in leading French newspapers by leading Frenchmen, I shall be thought to be yielding to national prejudice, and not to be writing with the impartiality which ought to be shown by one who professes to write of facts alone. The French will bear from Frenchmen—like M. Weiss for example, " the first pen of France," as M. Gambetta called him when he made him despatch-writer to the Foreign Office—that which they will not bear from Englishmen. The editor of the *Times* cannot with impunity contrast the Germany of the day with the France of the day, somewhat to the disadvantage of the latter, or describe the German officer as walking among his men with the " demeanour of a god." Thus far does M. Weiss go in his last book, and even in his reassuring preface he cannot say more for his own country than that it is "not substantially inferior" to Germany. In this book, by the way, too, M. Weiss admits that which has never before I think been admitted in writing by a leading man in France, that Prince Bismarck had been, whenever he wished it, the real Foreign Minister of the French Republic. If I were to say but one-tenth of what M. Weiss has said, I fear that if ever again I wished to visit Paris, and my identity were to become known, I might find myself conducted back between two constables to Boulogne or Calais.

Let us try to appreciate the French position with regard to Egypt. Russia, France, and Turkey, are now pressing us to say how long we intend to stay there; and we reply as we have replied for years, that we do not intend to stay permanently, but that we do intend to stay until our work is done.* It is useless for us, so far as affecting French opinion goes, to say that France backed out of her share in the protection of the Government of Egypt (after having, by suggesting the dual note, given that protection a militant character), and that she has refused to spend her money in preserving order there. It is open to the French negotiators to reply that they personally regret that their country did not take a more active part, but that the previous abstention cannot be allowed to affect the future. Now, England has by far the greatest interest in the Canal transit, and she has the same interest in the land transit through Egypt, because the land transit, which existed before the Canal, might replace Canal transit at the time of a

---

* Written of course before the negotiation of May.

Chinese war or of an Indian insurrection, if the Canal were blocked, as by accident or pretended accident it might easily be. France, however, is attempting to raise an empire in the further East, she has military necessities arising out of her difficulties with Madagascar and with China, and she is not prepared to allow that the question of Egyptian transit is not also vitally interesting to herself. Looking to the splendid ports possessed by France upon the Mediterranean, and to the difficulty England would have in using the Mediterranean in a time of general war, it might even be argued that in certain eventualities Egypt might be of greater use to France than it ever could be to England. Still, free transit has always been the object which England has had in view in Egypt; and it will be remembered that in the famous conversation between the Emperor Nicholas and Sir Hamilton Seymour, the latter refused Egypt in the words that "English views upon Egypt do not go beyond the point of securing a safe and ready communication between British India and the mother country." In refusing a later. offer of Egypt by Napoleon III., Lord Palmerston said, in words which ought to be remembered to his credit in these days of general spoliation, "How could we combine to become unprovoked aggressors, to imitate, in Africa, the partition of Poland by the conquest of Morocco for France, of Tunis for Sardinia, and of Egypt for England? and how could England and France, who have guaranteed the integrity of the Turkish Empire, turn round and wrest Egypt from the Sultan? . . . . As to the balance of power to be maintained by giving us Egypt, in the first place, we don't want to have Egypt. . . . We want to trade with Egypt and to travel through Egypt, but we do not want the burden of governing Egypt, and its possession would not, as a political, military, and naval question, be considered in this country as a set-off against the possession of Morocco by France."

It will be seen that Lord Palmerston did not set the value of Egypt to this country high. In 1878 Lord Salisbury declared that we did not desire to establish any territorial settlement in Egypt, and similar declarations have repeatedly been made since the destruction of the joint control. The interest of this country in Egypt is the interest of free communication both by the Suez Canal, and, as an alternative, by land across the isthmus, and the interest of British trade. As the means to the end, we think it desirable that Egypt should continue to be indirectly part of the Ottoman Empire, and essential that no other Power should effect a settlement there. We think the honour of this country bound to the present Khedive, but France, which is also bound to him by a solemn declaration of her own suggestion, has, from time to time, proposed his deposition and the substitution for him of Prince Halim. Our interest in Egyptian finance is not a peculiar interest, and might be entirely provided for by general European stipulations.

Under the Goschen control, it will be remembered, England had the higher position, but France was largely represented; under Lord Salisbury's control, the English comptroller had still, at first, the chief place of authority, but there was a closer similarity between the functions of the two men; and under Lord Salisbury's control as modified in November, 1879, the distinction between the two comptrollers ceased, and they became of equal standing.   At Christmas, 1881, England and France declared together to the present Khedive that they considered his maintenance on the throne as alone able to guarantee the present and future good order and general prosperity of Egypt, in which England and France were equally interested, and they stated in menacing terms that the two Governments were closely associated in their resolve to maintain the present ruler by their united efforts against all causes of complication, internal or external, which might threaten him, and which would certainly find England and France united to oppose them.   M. Gambetta, who had suggested this declaration, fell, and was succeeded by M. de Freycinet, who was opposed to armed intervention, and who, after long opposition, agreed too late to a naval demonstration by England and France and armed intervention by the Porte, having first proposed the deposition of the present Khedive, which was refused by England.   M. de Freycinet attached much importance to the employment of Turkish troops not being mentioned, and he finally backed out, or was disavowed by his colleagues, a proceeding which indeed caused the revolutionary movement in Egypt to come to a head.   After this he agreed to a small Anglo-French demonstration, but the French Chamber refused the money.

That which followed is well known, and so is the fact that after the French occupation of Tunis the Sultan's alarm and indignation at the proceedings of France were such that he also followed the example of the Emperor Nicholas and of the Emperor Napoleon III., in offering Egypt to this country, only to be once more refused. The Sultan has, indeed, throughout been of two minds, sometimes inclining to the view that it would be best for him to frankly recognise the fact that he has lost all real hold over both the Egyptian and the Arabian populations and to compound for tribute, and sometimes inclining to the view that it would be possible for him, after the English troops had quitted Egypt, to reassert there some actual authority.

The intention of England when she went to Egypt to put down a military insurrection, was to leave that country as soon as possible. The delay in leaving was caused by Turkey's refusal to allow troops to be raised for the Khedive within the Turkish dominions, and by the difficulty of organising an Egyptian army that could stand alone. The proposal for the absolute annexation of the country which was strongly pressed by some persons in the autumn of 1882, was steadily resisted by Mr. Gladstone, and the policy was laid down of gradually withdrawing the army of occupation to Alexandria, and of reducing it to under 3,000 men, which, although it has been delayed by events in the Soudan, continues to be the policy of the present Government. The decision not to accept Egypt for ourselves had virtually been taken long before this time. The annexation of Egypt, which would have been possible at any time between 1870 and 1875, or 1876, was set aside by the Conservative Government of 1874—80, in the successive steps by which they established the Anglo-French joint control, and recognised the high position of French interests, which they ultimately admitted to equal recognition with our own.

Another difficulty in the way of those who would indefinitely hold Egypt is the self-denying protocol of the Conference of the summer of 1882, while the strongest fact of all is that we have voluntarily but repeatedly informed the Powers that we intend to leave the country when our work is done.   On the other hand, we cannot forget the rejection by an enormous majority of the French Chambers of the Bill making provision for carrying out the agreement to which even M. de Freycinet had come with us for a limited French concurrence in the military steps to be taken against Arabi in Egypt.   It is of course held in England that by abstention from taking her part in the restoration of order in that country, France forfeited her rights.   At the end of 1882 the proposal to give France a certain share in the Egyptian Government, although a comparatively small share, was rejected by France, which took up the position that after our intervention in Egypt the institutions which had been upset revived, and amongst others the Anglo-French control.   The French Government were on strong ground in maintaining that obligations regularly entered into by three States could not properly be abolished or modified without the concurrence of all the contracting parties.   The position of England was that the appointment of the comptrollers was the act of the Khedive, and that there was no engagement that the control should be perpetually maintained. The control was abolished under French protest, and has disappeared for the last four years. In the summer of 1884 it will be remembered France offered to renounce the idea of re-establishing the dual control, undertaking also not to substitute a French for the British occupation, nor to send French troops to Egypt without a previous understanding with England ; in return for which England was to express her willingness that the withdrawal of British troops from Egypt should take place at the beginning of 1888, provided that the Powers should then be of opinion that such withdrawal could take place without risk to peace and order. These arrangements were to be subject to the success of financial proposals to be made by England to the Conference ; but the Conference itself broke down. The financial views of the English and the French were laid upon the Conference table, and subsequent experience has shown that the French were more nearly right than ourselves.

In connection with the Conference of 1884, the English Government announced its intention of proposing a scheme for the neutralisation of Egypt on the basis of the principles applied to Belgium. It is probable that if the English troops ever leave Egypt, that country will, in spite of the objections of the Sultan, be declared an independent and perpetually neutral State, bound to observe neutrality towards all other States, and placed under the guarantee of the contracting parties. The shadow of connection with Turkey and the payment of tribute to Turkey are not inconsistent with neutrality, as is shown by the case of the

Lake district of Savoy, and other cases which might be adduced.

The present position of the question is, that when the French ask us to name a date for leaving Egypt, we reply that it is impossible for a weak native government to rule the country so long as the low-class Europeans who inhabit Alexandria in great numbers, and in lesser degree the other towns, cannot be dealt with by the ordinary law; and as it is known that the French object to modify the Capitulations so long as we remain in Egypt, we in turn charge them with doing nothing to facilitate our leaving it, but on the contrary with making the difficulties which are the cause of our staying there.   As long ago as 1857 this question of Europeans of bad character in Egypt had become urgent, and it is a curious fact, though only historically curious, that the opposition to proper police control over low-class Europeans in Egypt came originally from England. It is to be feared that a subject very important in itself is being used now upon both sides deceptively.

As to the duration of the English occupation, there is this thing to be said, that, so long as the French violently denounce the occupation, it is likely to continue.   Some of the more moderate and more reasonable of the French news-papers have themselves pointed out that England went to Egypt with the consent of Europe to re-establish order ; that she went alone and at some risk and with much cost, and, indeed, they might add that we asked first France and then Italy to go with us, and went alone only after our invitation had been refused by both; refused, in the case of the former, by the Chamber after acceptance by the Government. These moderate journals argue that the English must judge for themselves whether it is yet safe for them to leave the country which they undoubtedly mean some day to leave; that it would be a folly for France to court refusal by asking questions too definite in form, and a still greater folly to fight for such a cause. These journals have pointed out the extraordinary reversal of French policy which is involved in the proposal to use the Turks to morally drive England out of Egypt, France having always been throughout her history the most reluctant of all the Powers to admit the existence of Turkish sovereignty in Egypt. Is France willing, they ask, to restore the supremacy of the Sultan in Tunis or Algeria?

It is indeed true that the French agitation against the English occupation of Egypt, which reached its height in November last, may well be pleasing to Russia, and has awakened illusions for the future, as well as cynical thoughts about the past, in the Sultan's mind. The class of feelings which it has aroused in Turkey finds expression in harmless notes to the British Government, which I take it are hardly read, although they are occasionally replied to. The feeling aroused in Russia by the action of France may possibly bode more danger to European peace, because although there is no alliance between Russia and France, yet if France backs all the proceedings of Russia in Bulgaria, Russia in return will find herself forced to back all the proceedings of France with regard to Egypt, and the result may be some wound to British pride which conceivably may lead to war. Except as regards Russia and Turkey, France of course only increases her isolation by her Egyptian policy. Italy is forced if possible farther away from France, whilst Austria and Germany remain indifferent, or think only of themselves. It would almost seem as though no real calculation of interest presided over the policy of the French Foreign Office. Provided that France can show herself able to make a sufficient noise in the world, it would seem as though French politicians were indifferent to the driving of Italy and England into the arms of Germany and Austria while France secures only the approval of Turkey and the Platonic alliance of Russia. Clearly French politicians do not adopt that elementary maxim of diplomacy which rivals in simplicity the "Never prophesy unless you know" of daily life; namely, "Never make a fuss unless you see your way ahead." Obviously, France, in telling England to leave Egypt, only postpones the date of the evacuation. Lord Randolph Churchill, whose power, so long as he terrifies the Tories by sheer energy, and paralyses the Liberal party by receiving Mr. Chamberlain's support, it is difficult to over-estimate, does not, unless he has strangely and suddenly changed his views, believe in the expediency of a British occupation of Egypt, much less in the necessity. But Lord Randolph Churchill is an Opportunist even more distinctly than a peace-loving Democrat, and he knows that the English will not leave Egypt as long as France bids them do so, so that he will probably not oppose Lord Salisbury's policy. The net result of the French demand is simply to court refusal, and drive England into alliance with Germany, Austria, and Italy.

The real value of a position in Egypt, whilst it is admittedly important as regards an Indian rising or a war with China, is easily exaggerated. In a great war in which France was against us, or in which Italy (though, in the present circumstances of Italian friendship, this may be neglected) was one of a coalition of hostile Powers, the Suez Canal would be useless. It is practically impossible to run past France and Corsica on the one side and Algeria and Tunis on the other, and to command the Mediterranean sufficiently to convoy troops, supplies and goods, while keeping our command in the Channel and patrolling the seas of the whole world. We cannot, in short, safely carry troops through the Mediterranean against either Italy in a combination or France alone, and this whether Russia be or be not at Constantinople, and be or be not at war with us. In a war in which France was against us, it may safely be asserted that France could not communicate with her Eastern possessions at all, and we with ours only by way of the Cape, and that the Suez Canal, as regards belligerents, would virtually be closed. But nations do not fight for points which are vital and neglect all points which are not. Nations generally fight for sentiment; and it is certain that in the present frame of the British mind and state of the British temper we shall not go out of Egypt so long as France orders us to go.

The raising of the Egyptian question has confirmed the prospects of peace, by placing on the one side four Powers and on the other side two units. In the next chapter I may have to consider whether an arrangement between England

and Russia is or is not possible, and whether Europe is likely to arrive at a lasting peace based on the isolation of France. Since the raising of the Egyptian question by France, Germany has ceased to find it necessary to proclaim a constant willingness to help French interests in all parts of the world. The change was not coincident with the return of the Conservatives to power in Great Britain. If it had been, we should have been inclined to ascribe it to the dislike felt by Prince Bismarck for some English Liberal politicians. But while three years ago Prince Bismarck by no means completely endorsed our Egyptian policy, and occasionally joined with France to slight us, as he also did at one time as regards the Congo; and although he backed up French aggression in the case of the New Hebrides, yet the change which took place on his coming to an agreement with us about Zanzibar—an agreement distasteful to France and made without consulting her in advance—was rather coincident with the revival of strong feeling between England and France about the Egyptian question than with the change of government. Even after the present Government came into power we seemed to be floundering between the hostility of France and the hostility of Germany. France was flouting us about the New Hebrides, and Germany was openly ridiculing us through her official press. It pleased Mr. Ashmead Bartlett to ascribe the isolation of England as well as her feebleness to Mr. Gladstone, but it must be admitted by any fair observer that its causes lay deeper than party. We seemed unable to mollify either France or Germany, and yet still to want the one or the other as our friend, and to be without a friend in the whole world.　It looked as though Italy were our only friend when Mr. Gladstone was in power, but as though we had none at all when he was succeeded by Lord Salisbury.　Suddenly all this was changed, and we became firm friends not only once again with Italy but also with Austria, and through Austria with Germany.　This change may partly have been aided by wise policy on Lord Salisbury's part, but the most important factor in producing it was aggression on the part of Russia and aggressive language on the part of France—the action of Russia in Bulgaria, and the language of France upon the question with which we are here concerned.

If England had been inclined to let the Egyptian debt take care of itself; to insist during the occupation on defying the Capitulations, as French generals would have defied them ; to take her own course, which she firmly believes to be the wise and scientific course, as to quarantine; to insist on simple justice as regards the taxation of foreigners, France would have grumbled, but probably would not have fought, and Egypt would have been the better for the action of England and none the worse for the grumbling of France. England did none of these things.　Throughout the occupation she has been courteous and, internationally speaking, law-abiding to the verge of weakness.　On only one occasion has she allowed of the faintest infraction of international agreement, and then under the pressure of necessity, and her action was immediately succeeded by an apology and explanation, and condoned by the general opinion of Europe.

The French, instead of quietly holding the English Liberal

party to its declarations, and, through it, the country, noisily stepped in and greatly increased the difficulties in the way of withdrawal.   The Conservative party in England would have left to the Liberals the unpopularity, whenever they should next come in, of actually quitting Egypt, and so risking a fresh rising, or the trouble of carrying out the arrangements for neutralisation.   But, under the rumour of French menace, the neutralisation scheme of the Liberals, with any personal leaning towards it of Lord Randolph Churchill, temporarily vanished, and both parties (*pace* Mr. Labouchere) were for the illogical but safe *status quo.*   " Il n'y a que le provisoire qui dure," and it looks as though a temporary occupation had been given a longer life by the recent language of France and Turkey, and by the demonstration of the existence of a Franco-Russian understanding at Constantinople.   Powers and parties are human, and self-interest itself is often a less strong human motive than the desire to annoy one's neighbours.   Bentham somewhere proves that there is such a thing as disinterested malevolence, and I fear that if it exists at all it is occasionally to be discovered in nations, at all events as highly developed as in the proverbial dog in the manger.   There are in England a great number of persons who are persuaded that the military occupation of Egypt is a source of strength to England.   But a large majority of these, who are themselves not a majority of the electorate, are persuaded that we are bound by promises voluntarily made to Europe that the occupation is to be temporary, and for practical purposes these count on the side of the persons who are against the occupation. France herself has greatly increased the number of those who will strain a point to avoid giving immediate effect to our promises, and must have increased the number of those who persuade themselves that the remaining in Egypt is a British interest.

If France would help us in Egypt; if she would strengthen the hands of such men as was M. Barrère, as is M. d'Aunay, in resisting the selfish action of individual Frenchmen at Cairo, when they behave in a manner really hostile to the higher interests of the French nation ; if the French Government would give up the Capitulations and replace them by a proper system of police and a just criminal law ; if we were aided and not thwarted—evacuation or neutralisation at an early date might indeed become possible. So different has been French action, that many, after seeing M. Barrère unable to cope with the *Bosphore Egyptien*, and M. d'Aunay in later times forced to support his compatriots, jump very wrongly to the conclusion that M. Barrère, as well as M. d'Aunay— that, in fact, the French Consul-General as such—must be the centre and soul of French resistance to the occupation. Both M. Barrère and M. d'Aunay are very able men, neither of them perhaps too much burdened with pedantic principle, while both of them speak and write English perfectly, and have lived long in England, which is a help towards understanding English ways and modes of thought. M. Barrère indeed is a man who found himself equally at home on the barricades supporting the Commune at the age of twenty and, at the age of thirty, on the European Commission of the Danube, patronising aristocratic Austria herself, a man to whom English is so familiar that a drawing-room at Albert Gate, when he already held the rank of minister, once presented the singular spectacle of a French ambassador and a French minister discussing between themselves in the English tongue, into which, in the course of their conversation, they had unconsciously dropped, the problem how their country might best get the English out of Egypt.   M. d'Aunay inherits from his direct ancestor Lepelletier a habit of courteous give and take, and speaks and writes English, if not with the British vigour of M. Waddington and M. Barrère, at least with great skill. These men understand how to get the English out of Egypt and how to keep them there, and if they have had to keep them there, it is because persons in France, incompetent to judge of policy, have imposed on them, as well as on their masters, a line of action of which they see the folly. Some of the Foreign Ministers of France of recent years have been of the calibre of chairmen of the Metropolitan Board, but M. de Freycinet was a cautious statesman of European fame, and whatever faults he may have had, knew perfectly—as well as M. Barrère, whom he detested, or as M. d'Aunay, whom he trusted—how mistaken the policy was which he was forced to pursue.

The Opportunist politicians, or successors of Gambetta, composed the party which was most active in the anti-English outcry.   Just as, the moment after their leader died, they advocated alliance with that Russia which he abhorred and against which he looked to Germany to protect the world; so, while Gambetta followed the earlier statesmen of France in detesting the presence of the Turk in Africa, and was a representative of the Frenchmen who backed Mehemet Ali, his party, immediately after he was gone, began to prompt the Turk to express to England his desire to return to Cairo. The change in the Egyptian policy of France, when she began to back up the Sultan's supremacy, is perhaps more extraordinary in suddenness and completeness than any modern national change of front except England's when Lord Beaconsfield offered Herat to Persia in 1879.

It is assumed by the English press that the word was passed by the French Government to the French press to attack England about Egypt. The *Temps*, however, which is the organ of the Foreign Office, was very moderate in its language. The most violent papers are not under Government influence. This violence, as I have shown, was calculated to do harm to the interests of France, as M. de Freycinet, who is a wise man, must have been well aware. I believe, therefore, that, so far from being desired, it was inconvenient to the Government of France. The French Government lagged behind public opinion in place of leading it, and the Government position, as expressed to England, was as follows: that France, which made the Canal, and has a large amount of money invested in it, and which is also historically and sentimentally interested in Egypt, does not desire to press England to leave Egypt at once, but merely reminds her of her promise to leave it, and asks, not for a fixed date, but for some sort of approximation to a date at which the English troops will leave. France is willing to engage that French troops shall not go to Egypt, and desires to enter into

an engagement to secure the absolute neutrality of the country, or to carry out the restoration of the "status quo ante Arabi,"
but with some security taken against the Arabis of the future.
The moderation of the French demands is, however, the
result of failure to bring pressure to bear upon England,
except, indeed, at Constantinople, and it is possible that, if
French views had received more support, the language officially employed would have been much more emphatic.

In the meantime France does not help us to withdraw. She
protects seditious newspapers published by French subjects ;
she insists upon maintaining to the letter the Capitulations,
by which the administration of Egypt, not only by England,
but after England is gone, should England incline to go, is
rendered dangerous in the extreme. At the bottom of the
unwise and somewhat illogical action of France there lies, as
there almost always lies at the bottom of unwise acts on the
part either of nations or of individuals, a fit of temper. France
knows that, if England was to go to Egypt at all, France
should have accompanied her. France agreed to go, but the
Chamber rejected the agreement. It was M. de Lesseps who
really prevented France from doing that which she had
promised to do, and, after the collapse of Arabi, leading
French politicians blamed M. de Lesseps for misleading them
as to Arabi's power. And so the French, profoundly dissatis-
fied with the inevitable consequences of their own inaction,
have striven to avenge their mistake by thwarting the English in Egypt ; and every check to the French arms, whether
in Madagascar or Tonquin, has but intensified their malevolence. Mutual sulkiness on the part of France and England

in regard to Egypt is likely to continue. France does not mean to fight for Egypt, and yet is not satisfied to have been ousted from it. And England will stay there, although nearly all Liberals and many Conservatives desire the neutra-lisation of the country, just because England will not leave Egypt under pressure, and there will continue to be pressure enough exerted by France to make it impossible for England to leave. The troops will be brought from Cairo to Alexan-dria, and be reduced to under three thousand men, but com-plete evacuation will not take place.

In the writings of French newspapers upon Egypt there is a great deal of exaggeration. The popular belief in France, which is not shared by the men who control her destinies, is that England is an annexing Power, anxious to lay hands upon all possible portions of the world, and checked only here and there by France and Germany. As a matter of fact, for many years past, with the exception of the movement upon Burmah, which was caused by the action of the French agent there, England has made no annexations except in self-defence against the annexation policy of Germany or France, and has declined to annex the Cameroons, Zanzibar, and Egypt itself, not to speak of other countries, over and over again.*

I have assumed that France, however much she grumbles, does not intend to fight for Egypt. If France intended even to risk war for Egypt without actually provoking it, she would take one step which is always in the minds of French politicians. She would take England out of the most favour-

* The recent annexation of Zululand has been caused solely by the neces-sity of protecting the natives against the Boers.

able and place her in the most unfavourable column of the
French tariff, at the same time allowing free entry into
France for certain classes of yarns which are absolutely
needed in the French cotton-spinning industry.   Everything
else that France absolutely needs and that she at present gets
from us, she could, it is argued, get from Germany and
Belgium, and a very slight rise in the price of certain goods
would only be an inconvenience of the same nature as the
inconvenience which she bears already in the form of duties
for the sake of protection.   Another step that France would
take would be to raise some pretext in Egypt for interference, and French troops would be landed, nominally as
against Egypt, at some point on the Egyptian coast, with a
declaration of perfect friendliness towards England, but with
the intention that they should remain there as long as our
troops remained.   The friendship of Italy and our joint naval
power prevent all chance of a sudden attack by France on
Egypt, and make it impossible for France to hope to hold
Egypt in the event of war.   It is true, however, that we
ourselves in that case should derive little or no benefit from
its possession.   But no strength of our own and no strength
on the part of Italy could prevent a landing of French troops
in Egypt on pretence of some violation of the Capitulations
against a French subject, and it is not very easy to see how
a termination could be put to a virtual joint occupation
except by that neutralisation which France herself demands ;
a neutralisation, the name of which scares people here, though
in my opinion, if properly secured, it would offer nothing but
advantages to this country.

There is another view of the action of France with respect to Egypt, which is, that when M. de Freycinet talked of Egypt it was the Canal that he really had in view, and that, knowing as he did that he would not be able by pressure to get his way in regard to Egypt, he must have meant only to get it with regard to the Canal. The most authoritative statement of the French views upon the subject is M. de Freycinet's own, when he said that England and Italy had put forth one view and that France had put forth another, but that the other Powers insisted that England and France should agree, and that he hoped that it would not be long before that agreement was reached. The only difficulty in settling the question of the Canal is caused by the fact that the Conservative Cabinet somewhat hesitates to settle it for fear of Parliamentary attack.

Everybody seems to mean the same thing with regard to the Canal. There is no real difference of opinion upon the subject itself, but only a divergence of language between the proposals which England and France have made respectively. Proposals to secure by international agreement the freedom of the Suez Canal at all times for all ships, whether of trade or war, have been made by England at least twice. Now France can come to an agreement with England upon this subject whenever she pleases, and if she uses language of insistence it is only for the purpose of breaking through a door which is already open, so as to be able to celebrate a triumph. The other Powers, with the exception of Russia, which will do what is most agreeable to France, in order to keep up the shadow of an alliance, think the English

H

Canal proposals sufficient and satisfactory, and the only difficulty has been a difficulty about words, and the only reason why there has been no agreement has been because there was no real desire for agreement, inasmuch as each Government is afraid of its Parliament. The statement which has been repeatedly telegraphed to various journals that England declined to entertain French proposals for a neutralisation of the Canal which would prevent the passage of the English fleets in time of war, is a mere confusion, for France has never made and never intends to make any such proposition. The Powers agree that the Canal should be made free to all, and should be protected against blockade, but no one of them desires to limit its use by excluding ships of war. The disputes about words have been formidable, no doubt, and have been intensified by the peculiarity of the problem, for there is no diplomatic question in the world similar to that of the Suez Canal. According to a witty remark ascribed to Baron Solvyns, the Belgian minister at this Court, a diplomatic career consists in passing one's life in explaining to others things which you do not understand yourself, and there has been a good deal of that kind of diplomacy employed upon the questions relating to the Suez Canal.

It is rather a startling statement, but one which is perfectly true, that the Canal has been neutralised from the first, and is neutral at this moment. Its neutrality is read into the original firman by a reference to the Act of Concession. The action taken by France during the Franco-German war constituted an admission of this neutrality, and was consistent with something more than that which we have always meant by it, namely, equal freedom for the use of the Canal by all Powers. In the Russo-Turkish war, Russia engaged not to bring the Canal within the sphere of operations. M. de Lesseps at one time made a proposal for the neutralisation of the Canal in terms which were approved by the French Government, but to which the English Government saw objections which they did not explain. After Arabi's insurrection, further plans for dealing with the Canal were discussed between the Governments, but an ambiguity arose from the use of the word neutralisation in two different senses. England at one time rejected a suggestion of neutrality, understanding that neutrality meant the closing of the Canal against all vessels of war at all times, which was never, as a matter of fact, intended by France; but England proposed as her own, in a subsequent communication, a measure precisely similar to that which had been proposed by France in 1877.

The English proposal is that whilst all ships at all times should be allowed to pass through, there should be a limit of time as to ships of war of belligerents remaining in or about the Canal; that no hostilities should take place in the approaches to the Canal; that no fortifications should be erected on or near it; and that the Canal and its neighbourhood should not be made the base of military operations. I repeat that there is no real difference of opinion between England and France, and that an arrangement could be concluded at any moment if there were on both sides a wish to come to terms.

There are a good many differences between England and France besides those which concern Egypt and the Suez Canal. In the New Hebrides there was a violation of an engagement with us, as well as that complete disregard of native rights which has now become usual on the part of European Powers. In Madagascar, where the Government of England have decided not to interfere, there is carried on in the name of France a violation of every principle which keeps civilised mankind together, an outrage which rouses the indignation of English High Churchmen, Congregationalists, and Quakers, who are all strongly represented in the Madagascar missions, and attracts to their views upon the subject the sympathy of members of other religious bodies. Moreover the formation of a French military establishment at Diego Suarez or British Sound, is regarded by English naval men as directed against this country. On the Upper Niger the French are coming into conflict with the interests of the British traders established on that river, as they are also upon the Congo.

The French are annexing other islands in the Pacific besides the New Hebrides group, and are threatening to use them for convict stations, to the intense dissatisfaction of our Australian colonists. In some of these cases France has annexed islands the independence of which she had engaged herself to this country to respect, as for example, Raiatea. On the other hand, in China as in Egypt, and as in Madagascar indeed, but that Madagascar is an evident case of wolf and lamb, the French consider that they have grievances against us. In the case of the Newfoundland fisheries and "French Shore" questions, each country finds grave fault with the other.

It is necessary for us to examine these questions at some little length, because out of almost any one of them war might easily arise. The French nation is not united upon these questions. The most powerful newspapers in France by no means adopt the "Colonial policy." M. Clémenceau, one of the strongest of French politicians, condemns it, as it is condemned also from the other side by the Monarchical Opposition, and by independent financial reformers. With a deficit in every Budget for the last four years, which has risen from two millions sterling, five years ago, to ten millions sterling last year, and about ten millions this, France cannot afford to pour out gold upon Tonquin, and Madagascar, and Senegal, and other pestilential places, which will never bring in a tithe of what they have cost. The "Colonial policy" greatly weakens the military position of France in Europe, and disorganises her finances, while it compromises the efficiency of the only thing which really counts in modern European war, the rapidity of the mobilisation of the reserves. The "Colonial policy" has obviously increased the work to be performed by the French army and navy in time of war, and has given hostages to England, who would be able to cut the communication between France and all these so-called colonies, as soon as war had been declared. France has acted in Tunis in a way that has irritated Italy; she has incurred the lasting resentment of the Australian colonies of Great Britain, which one day will

form the third Power in the world, and she has permanently
alienated that which will probably be one of the strongest
military empires—China.   The Tonquin policy of France
has increased the chance of China joining England whenever France joins Russia, and a Chinese alliance in the
Pacific is certainly not to be despised.

The French Colonial policy has always been a very costly
one.   French subjects in the French dominions outside of
Algeria and France cost France about £1 per head per year.
British subjects in the British dominions outside of the
United Kingdom cost us about 2d. per head per year, excluding indirect naval expenditure upon both sides.   The French
Colonial policy from the time of Colbert to the present
day has been closely connected with the French doctrines
of protection, and the dominant idea in connection with the
extension of French rule is to place differential duties upon
foreign goods.   In some cases, but not in all, a religious
persecution on a small scale also plays its part, and the
French flag, which does not protect Catholic interests at
home, gives them something more than an equal chance
abroad.   I suppose it is useless to speak of the rights of the
native inhabitants of the countries which are annexed by
France.   Looking to our own past, it does not come well
from an Englishman to do so.   But we may hope that
when the historian of the future comes to deal with the times
in which we live he will point out that England in this respect
grew better whilst France grew worse.   It is necessary to
bear in mind, in considering the subject, that the French
colonies are all of what we should call the Crown colony

type, and that none of them resembles Canada or Australia
or the Cape in getting its own way. Where the supposed
commercial interests of France come into conflict with the
interests of the colonists, as seen by the colonists themselves,
colonial interests have to give way, and where the colonists
have desired to buy in the cheapest market, the French have
frequently compelled them to buy, by means of differential
duties, the dearer goods of France.

The present difficulties between France and China, in
which the French suppose, rightly or wrongly, that the
Chinese have us behind them, have grown gradually out of
the difficulty which arose during the Tonquin war. English
sympathies will naturally go with China in her desire herself
to undertake, in concert with the Holy See, the protection of
Catholic interests. We know how in the past these real
interests have been placed in jeopardy by their connection
with the political interests of France. We know that on the
whole the London Missionary Society has succeeded perfectly
of recent years in dealing directly and peacefully with the
Chinese; and we desire to see the causes of future quarrel
lessened, as they would be if Catholic interests in China
received the peaceful protection of the Vatican rather than
the gunboat protection of the French Republic. In the long
run, China, upon this subject, is certain to get her way.
China is now too strong for France to take Pekin without a
struggle which would greatly reduce her continental fighting
power. But France could, single-handed, still take Pekin,
because the Chinese will not yet make an intelligent modern use
of their splendid men, and their officers are still silly beyond

description. War between France and China, if a real war, and not the ambiguous state of things which prevailed on a recent occasion, would be so serious for us, with eighty per cent. of the China trade in our hands, as against the three per cent. which France possesses, that it may be considered that an effective blockade of the Chinese coast could not be enforced by France without the certainty of such irritation arising on our side that we ourselves should be drawn into the vortex. As the French have something to say for themselves upon the Egyptian, so, too, with regard to the Chinese question. It is true that our influence at Pekin is great, and that it is not of a description very friendly to the French. If our influence there is menaced, it is not by the influence of France; and it is not a Frenchman who is likely to obtain the key of the position by becoming the future Tsung Shui Wu Sze, or Inspector-General of Imperial Maritime Customs.

As regards the French position in non-Algerian Africa, it is well known that vast sums of money have been spent in Senegal in the attempt to lay out a railroad towards the Upper Niger, and much also has been expended in trying to found an empire upon the Congo, efforts which Germany has done all in her power to promote, because she agrees with English observers as to the weakening effect upon the French power in Europe of the new French colonial policy. In the case of the Niger, French and British interests at one time came sharply into conflict, but the West African Conference held at Berlin in 1884 laid down the respective spheres of influence and established the principle of commercial freedom for the Niger, so that difficulties are at an end for the present. At the same time if the French choose to go on spending sufficient money, they will ultimately, although at vast cost, reach Timbuctoo both from the side of Senegal and from that of Algeria. The French expenditure in the district is, however, probably connected in some degree with hidden designs against the empire of Morocco, which form a source of possible European complications for the future, inasmuch as Spanish pride would be greatly wounded by the conquest of Morocco by the French, whilst England possesses in Morocco a considerable trade. As regards the Congo, I know that I attempt to swim against the stream of English opinion in regard to the help given by this country to the exclusion of Portugal from what I believe to have been her ancient possessions upon the Congo coast, and I also differ from many in England in thinking that the International Association, which has now become the personal Congo kingdom of the King of the Belgians, has by no means shown by its past that it was any more worthy than Portugal, which was not thought worthy, to receive the control of vast districts in the interior. While by the policy of the West African Conference and by the assistance given by Prince Bismarck both to France and to the King of the Belgians in 1884, France has been admitted to the Congo on one bank, an enormous district in the heart of Africa has been made over to the King of the Belgians, with, however, the happy condition of freedom of trade.

Engagements between two Powers with respect to African annexation, or, indeed, with regard to any of the countries of the world which are what is styled "unoccupied," that is, occupied by the black people to whom they properly belong, are apt to be of very little use. For example, in 1862 there was an agreement between England and France that neither would interfere with the independence of Zanzibar, but Germany has now taken away the greater portion of the Sultan's nominal territory there. And there is always this risk of a third Power stepping in. On the other hand, whatever the French may think, English interests in Africa are secured when freedom of trade has been secured, and the extension of the principle laid down in the conference at Berlin in 1884 would suit England better than increase of territorial responsibilities. These considerations leave out of view questions of right or wrong; but while England has not in these matters always acted upon the principles which at all events a large portion of her public men have professed, in the case of other countries there has never been much desire to take questions of ethics into consideration in dealing with weaker peoples.

In the days of the Holy Alliance, when Christianity was nominally laid down as the guiding principle of the great Continental Powers, it was nevertheless England which had invariably to take the first step in all matters which concerned the suppression of slavery and of the slave-trade, and her suggestions were viewed frequently with as little private favour, whatever may have been the public language held, as is extended now by Prince Bismarck to English views upon the subject of Turkish reform. Just as England led the way with regard to the slave-trade, and was followed

for very shame by the rest of Europe, let us hope that now
that her own desire for annexation has passed away, she will
gradually be able to induce the Continental Powers to show
some small regard for the independence of the dark-skinned
races. The real interest of Europe as such is the same as
the interest of civilisation, that these countries should be
open to healthy trade, not a trade confined to arms and liquor.
But to the Protectionist Powers open trade has hitherto meant
British trade, and it is a remarkable fact that Germany should
have had the prudent courage in 1884 to make a new departure in proclaiming herself the champion in such countries
of free trade. France, however, in her annexations has
always in view the exclusion of British and German trade
by means of differential duties, and this fact heightens the
regret with which her aggressions in Madagascar and other
places are viewed by the English people. So long as the
dark-skinned races are treated as they now are, it must be
sorrowfully admitted that in the foreign affairs of the Powers,
as too often in the business affairs of individuals, that common
Christianity disappears which is practised in some, at least,
of the daily affairs of life by most men in the United
Kingdom and the United States and Russia, and in a less
degree in Germany and the Austrian Empire. No one asks
what is right, what is just towards natives. All look only to
what is selfishly best from the narrowest and most grasping
point of view.

Of Madagascar I need hardly speak, the circumstances are
so well known in England, and there is the less necessity to
dwell on them, because it seems improbable that France will

for the present make a serious attempt to carry into effect the designs which all the writers upon her colonial policy openly proclaim. There is, however, the fact to be borne in mind that the English Government have evidently decided not to resent a French occupation of Madagascar, or even the creation of a Gibraltar at British Sound. But, in the case of some of the French annexations in the Pacific, there is a direct interference not only with the interests but with the treaties of Great Britain, and also with the interests of the Australian colonists. Of such annexations it is necessary to say a word.

The Australian colonists have for years protested against the transportation of French convicts to the penal settlement in New Caledonia. The first great quarrel between Australia and France was caused by a custom of the Governor of New Caledonia, who used to grant free passages to time-expired convicts intending to proceed to the British Australian colonies, a custom which somewhat reminds one of a former practice of the Channel Islands, when they transported their convicts to Southampton. The Australian colonies have followed the lead set by Victoria, a free colony from the first, in resenting bitterly the effects of the transportation system. Victoria it was that stopped the transportation of English convicts, first to Tasmania, afterwards to West Australia, and thus, at last, altogether. In 1882 there were frequent debates in France upon the subject of the transportation of habitual criminals, which had been strongly recommended by M. Gambetta, and the rumour spread that it was to the New Hebrides they were to be sent. Now in 1878 an agreement

had been made between England and France which formed
a distinct pledge on the part of these two Powers not to
annex these islands, and this agreement has latterly been
renewed. Yet in spite of it the French flag has been
hoisted in the New Hebrides, and France appears in the
most distinct manner to have broken her twice-pledged
word.

The view of the Australian colonists is that the French
intend to do to them what in 1872 we prevented the French
from doing to ourselves. After the suppression of the Commune the French Government began to make England a
penal settlement by expelling people from France whom
Germany and Belgium and Switzerland and Italy would
not receive, and who, destitute and without papers, were
sent away from Calais and Dieppe to be landed in English
ports and to become chargeable upon the English poor rates.
The Australians believe that France intends to ship large
numbers of habitual criminals to islands in the neighbourhood of Australia, and then, by keeping a very lax guard
upon them, to allow them to escape and so to avoid the cost
of their detention. To suppose that this is likely to be done
upon a large scale as part of a system is, no doubt, to
exaggerate, but it is certainly the belief in Australia,
where panic upon this subject has of late years been frequent.
In 1852, an Act was passed in Victoria to protect that colony
against even pardoned or time-expired convicts, and although
it was disallowed, the Governor was afraid to make known
the fact of its disallowance. A temporary Act was afterwards
passed, to which another Governor assented, on the ground

that, if he had not done so, the colonists would have taken the law into their own hands. Ultimately, the Home Government gave in, and the colonists were allowed to pass Acts upon this subject which were contrary to every principle of English law, and the Stockade near Melbourne was filled with persons who were, no doubt, many of them, undesirable colonists, but who, according to British principles, were properly free men. When the French first occupied New Caledonia, the Government of New South Wales informed the mother country that they feared the occupation of these islands by a foreign Power would, at no distant date, be a source of much trouble and anxiety, both to the Australian colonies, and to the British Government. This prediction has proved too true, and it is likely perhaps to be even more completely justified in the future. The strength of Australian feeling upon the subject of transportation has never been kept within the limits of law, and for this country to insist upon its strict rights towards Australia in the matter, and still more, for it to maintain the strict rights of France, or of any other foreign Power, against the outburst of Australian feeling, would be simply to produce separation, if not separation coupled with war. To take a somewhat similar case, when the Irishmen who had given evidence against criminals in their own country, and had to be protected by the Government, were shipped quietly to Victoria, the Victorian Government refused to allow them to land there, although they could not even pretend that they were legally justified in their refusal.

It is in the light of what has happened in the case of New

Caledonia that we are compelled to regard French action in the New Hebrides. In the case of the New Hebrides the Australian objectors will have their hands strengthened by the fact that the French occupation of New Caledonia was legitimate according to the accepted view, whereas the occupation of the New Hebrides was, had our Government chosen to resent it, a *casus belli*. The French are behaving in regard to the New Hebrides now as they have behaved, since 1879, in regard to the Society Islands, and our Government have met their action with a protest, but with a protest only, for which the French do not seem very much to care.

The New Hebrides were discovered by Captain Cook. They were partially civilised by English and Scotch missionaries. In 1857 the chiefs of the largest island requested the protection of this country. In 1858 the expediency of the protection was recommended by the officer commanding the naval forces upon the station. In 1858 and 1860 the chiefs again offered the cession of their island, which was formally declined. In 1865 the colony of New South Wales began to interest itself in a movement for excluding from the New Hebrides any other European Power, without annexing the group ourselves. In 1876 it was pointed out that there was a large Presbyterian mission in the group, and that there were sixty Englishmen, three Swedes, and only one Frenchman residing in the islands. It was also in 1876 that the French Government informed us positively "that there did not exist, and never had existed, any intention, on the part of France, to take possession of the New Hebrides." In 1878 the French Government spontaneously proposed a declaration of the intention not to annex the group, and a French statement was replied to by a similar statement on the part of England. In 1878 also the New Zealand Government set up a claim that the islands were actually theirs, and also remonstrated against the joint declaration, but were promptly replied to by the Government at home. The New Zealand Government still, however, held that the New Hebrides were theirs by the charter of 1840, and that the Home Government had acted without consideration in 1878 in agreeing to the joint engagement. In 1879 the French declaration was renewed; as it was again in 1883. The breach by France is not, as in the case of Raiatea, the breach of a somewhat old agreement (the date in that case is 1847), but the breach of a brand new engagement proposed by France herself in 1878, and renewed in 1879 and 1883.

The case of the New Hebrides is almost as interesting to the English religious world as is that of Madagascar, in which, however, there is no breach of treaty. English missionaries have for thirty-eight years been working in the New Hebrides, and a very large proportion of the natives have now become civilised and Christian. There can be no doubt, from the concurrent testimony even of travellers who are favourable to the French, that the population are as opposed to the idea of French annexation as are even the population of Madagascar. There are large holdings of land in the New Hebrides by British subjects. There is a great amount of British money expended in churches, schools, and mission stations. There are over a hundred British subjects

in the group, and fewer French, except the troops who have
lately been sent there to form three military posts. It is a
serious matter to quarrel with France about anything, and
certainly about an island which we do not want ourselves,
and which we have over and over again refused, but it is a
still more serious thing to allow a solemn declaration volun-
teered to this country, and accepted by her, to be contemptuously set aside; and if the Government condone this action
on the part of the French, it must be because an occupation
of Egypt weights us with a heavy burden in our dealings
with France in other portions of the world. Clearly it is
useless for us to enter into engagements with other Powers
in the future, if we allow engagements thus to be set at
naught; and there are circumstances in the case of the New
Hebrides which make the aggression such as even the
greatest of lovers of peace may properly resent.

The case of the Ecréhous rocks, near Jersey, is a curious
one. They have always been looked upon as belonging to
Jersey, and have been occupied every summer, from time im-
memorial, by Jersey fishermen and Jersey seaweed-gatherers;
they have never been claimed by France in the past, whilst
they are actually included in a Jersey parish and have a
few permanent inhabitants who are Jersey men. Crime in
Ecréhous has been punished in the Jersey courts, and no
attempt was ever made until quite lately to raise any question about the matter. In this case no act of aggression
has been committed by France, and no false claim has been
asserted by the Government of France, as such, but the
violence of the French press in its declarations that the

I

Ecréhous have been lately seized by England is founded upon a complete misapprehension of the facts. This question is closely connected with that of the fisheries upon the coasts of the United Kingdom, into the intricacies of which I will not enter here, for it, like the Newfoundland question, would claim an entire and not very interesting article to itself; but I will merely mention them among the causes of dispute between this country and France which may become serious at any moment.

Some French Chauvinists have lately been setting up pretensions more extravagant than even those which have led to the French action in the New Hebrides which I have described. Just as in the case of Italy there is an Italia [Irredenta, of which the boundaries are continually stretching out, so in the case of France there is now a Francia Irredenta, a Gallia·Irredenta, or what shall we style it? French Canada has not yet been asked for, but the Newfoundland grievance is kept alive, and the "French Shore" will continue to be claimed until there comes a day when a proposal will be made to us for the exchange of St. Pierre, Miquelon, and the "French Shore" for the Mauritius. There is no doubt that those Frenchmen who pushed on the Madagascar expedition expect that one day the Mauritius will fall under French rule, and believe that the French-speaking inhabitants of the Mauritius ardently desire the coming of that day; in which belief, according to the information at my disposal, they are entirely wrong.

It is wonderful, looking to the number of the causes of difference between England and France, that the two countries should manage, as the phrase has it, "to get along" at all. That they have done so during the years in which French Chauvinist feeling has, in order to forget Germany, been turned against England, is largely due to the tact and caution of Lord Lyons. May I be allowed, without the ascription of any but patriotic motives for so doing, to deprecate the proposed shelving of our most able and most representative diplomatist, at a critical period, by the application of a hard and fast superannuation rule.* Lord Lyons may be seventy, and he has never been physically a very active man, but intellectually he is in the prime of his vigour, and we shall not know how much we lose in him till he has gone, if, unfortunately, he is made to go. It is difficult to overestimate the effect which Lord Lyons' admirable direction of the British Embassy in Paris has had upon the relations of England and France. They are far from good, it is true, but it is really difficult to say how bad they would have been by this time had it not been for the ability, the unfailing courtesy, the splendid hospitality, and, above all, the patience of Lord Lyons. England is well served in many ways and by many men, but it must be admitted by all who know what Lord Lyons has done for us, that it is not possible to find a man to efficiently replace him. Lord Lyons is a man of a very curious type, not only unenergetic, but, shall I say, even lazy physically, hating to put his head outside his door. He is, officially, the most energetic of men. Always seeing the right people

---

* The danger now appears to be over for the moment, though I fear that Lord Lyons means to leave Paris at the new year.

at the right time; writing as much as all the other ambassadors and ministers of Great Britain put together, in the
enormous private correspondence which he constantly carries
on; writing always with his own hand, never writing an
unnecessary word, for his letters are always clear and
always to the point, Lord Lyons has never practically been
a lazy man, except indeed when pressed by his Government
to say or do something which he thought would irritate the
French without really benefiting British interests. Then
Lord Lyons is a lazy man. The patience of the most energetic
or of the most obstinate of Foreign Ministers would wear itself
out before he induced Lord Lyons to actively press at Paris
a claim or an object of this nature; for Lord Lyons possesses
a staying power and a power of resistance which are the most
British of all his British qualities. I believe that Lord
Lyons has never but once been known both to be really angry
and to show it in the course of his career. This was when it
was stated in Parliament by one of the Irish members that he
himself had been followed by Government spies in Paris,
and when it was not at the same time explained that the
spies—if spies there were—had not been employed by the
Embassy, and had not reported to Lord Lyons. This anger
is characteristic, because Lord Lyons is essentially an English
gentleman, and has managed in the course of a long life
to deal successfully with a great many people who were not
what we call gentlemen, without ever forgetting his own
position for one moment, or letting them forget it either. In
a capital where ministers set spies on one another, and
ambassadors set spies on their own friends, Lord Lyons did

not like to be even for one moment so much as suspected
of having set spies upon those who were at that time the
confessed enemies of his country. He has no illusions
upon the subject of the Governments of France, or indeed
upon any subject of any kind, and some might call him
cynical, but he is as kind as he is courteous; and if fairly
peaceable working relations are to continue to exist at all
between England and France, it is Lord Lyons who must
preserve them, as long as he will consent to do so.

III.

RUSSIA.

———•———

In the two preceding chapters it has been shown how
Germany and Austria from the fear of a Franco-Russian
alliance, how England from preference for peace and want of
sufficient motive, and how France, from the real peacefulness
of the majority of its electors, are unlikely to begin a war.
There remains Russia, the country which, intensely patriotic
but not yet very sure of its position in the world, ridiculed
as barbarous, and therefore very sensitive, and ruled by an
autocrat of uncertain temper, is alone in a position to provoke
a conflict. Will it do so?

There appeared lately in a number of Russian newspapers some remarkable articles on the same question on
which I am writing here—the present position of the
Great Powers. These articles, indeed, teach us nothing
except the arrogance, or the consciousness of strength, of
Russia, which scarcely seems to care what other Powers may
or may not do, and the extraordinary ignorance which
prevails among even the best-informed real Russians in
the empire. I say real Russians, because there are at St.
Petersburg a number of able and highly cultured persons

who are in the Russian service, and have no illusions upon the subject, but are either not of Russian race or are so much in touch with foreigners through constant travel or long residence abroad that they have ceased to share the more dangerous among the illusions of their countrymen Unfortunately, however, it is the Russian Emperor who governs Russia, and not these gentlemen. Some of them, as for example MM. de Giers, Jomini, and Vlangaly, are occasionally consulted by way of form, but their private opinions do not receive official sanction or become that policy of the Russian Empire which in public (and most conversations at St. Petersburg may be looked upon as public) they defend.

To justify what I have said about articles in the Russian journals, let me quote the doctrines of one from the *Novoe Vremya* upon "The Western Powers and Russia." The phrase "the Western Powers." does not apply only to Great Britain and France, the meaning which it used to bear, but it includes five Powers, or what we style the two central and the two western Powers, with the addition of Italy. The writer states that if Prussia has managed to make an apparent German unity towards the exterior, it must be remembered both that German Austria is not yet included within Germany, and that there is no internal unity even among the kingdoms that are included. South and Catholic Germany, he declares, detests Prussian and Protestant Germany more than ever, and the southern states will seize the first opportunity to throw off the hegemony of Prussia, and once more make Austria supreme in the German Empire. Schleswig-Holstein too is a serious weakness to the Empire.

Germany is hated by Austria as well as by France, she suffers internally from Socialism, she has alienated Great Britain by her colonial policy, and she could not even depend on Italian friendship unless she were willing to help Italy to take away from Austria the Tyrol, the Trentino, and Trieste itself, and this she will not do. Germany therefore is absolutely isolated. The Emperor and Prince Bismarck himself will die before German unity has made a step, and the only chance they have of maintaining themselves lies in a Russian alliance. A somewhat flattering picture this, indeed, of what Prince Bismarck has done for Germany! The writer passes on to Austria. Austria desires to regain leadership in Germany, she refuses to become a Slav Power and insists on remaining German, she is waiting only for the death of Prince Bismarck, but is too wretchedly weak to harm Russia. Turning to France, the writer points out that she has quarrelled with England and stands alone, whilst his glance at England, as might be expected, reveals to him the impossibility of her defending either her colonies or her trade, the danger that she incurs from Ireland, and the certainty that she will put up with anything rather than fight. The conclusion of the article, of course, is that Russia alone among the Powers is quiet, strong, and really great, that if she gave to Germany her alliance she could wipe out Austria from the face of Europe, and force France to remain at peace. If, on the other hand, she chooses a French alliance she can destroy Germany, whilst the destinies of England are in her hands, inasmuch as she could easily deliver India from the British yoke. The writer thinks it laughable to suppose that Russia will ask the consent of any Power to settle the Bulgarian question in the sense which she may prefer. It is hardly necessary to indicate the weak points of this article, and I shall have occasion to deal with the strong points, and to reveal the grain of truth that it may contain, in demonstrating the immense power of the Russian Empire. That with which I am here concerned is only to show in what a fools' paradise those Russians live who really direct the external policy of their country—the Emperor himself and the leading journalists, who, however, it must be observed, are themselves powerless, except through the immense influence of one of them, the autocrat of the *Moscow Gazette*.

I am aware that much that I say in the course of this chapter will produce protest, for while I shall offend those who believe in the moderation or truth of Russia, I shall, on the other hand, displease those too patriotic Englishmen, if there be such a thing as an overdose of patriotism, who dislike Russia so much that they cannot recognise either her power or the patriotism of her people. All that I shall try to do in this, as in my other chapters, is to ascertain the facts, and the exact bearing of the facts with which we have to deal. I address myself to those, if there be such in these days, who are free from party prejudice, from prejudice personal or national—to those, in short, who try to see things as they really are.

The fact upon which it is necessary to insist in considering the position of Russia is that she has of all the European Powers by far the largest homogeneous population. There are about as many Great Russians, speaking the same language, without any dialects, as there are real Germans in all Germany. In addition to these there are millions upon millions of closely-connected Russians of other Russian tribes, of which the fourteen millions of Little Russians are the most numerous and the best known, furnishing as they do the picked men of the Russian guards. Some careless observers are apt to make seriously an exactly opposite statement, namely, that there is such a diversity of races under the Russian flag that Russia must be bound but loosely together, and be always on the point of tumbling to pieces. No doubt there are great numbers of picturesque peoples of various races, tongues, customs, and religions who are under the Russian rule. Travellers affect their provinces, and are rather repelled by the uniform black dulness of Russia proper ; but all those peoples bear to the mass of the Russians only about the same numerical and political importance as the sotnias of Persian, Armenian, Georgian, Mingrelian, Circassian, Bashkir, and Uralian Cossacks, who figure in the Emperor's body guard at a great review at St. Petersburg, bear numerical and military importance to the fifty or sixty thousand men of the guards who are upon the field. No doubt the Fins of Great Finland and the Samoyeds of Northern Siberia, and the Sarts of Central Asia and the yellow-faced and slit-eyed Kalmucks of Astrakhan, the Golden-Horde Tartars of Kazan, the Turcomans of the Caspian steppes, the Tchuvassi, Vatiki, Mordwa, and other Asiatic Fins upon the Volga, and countless other tribes and peoples who might be named, differ very greatly the one from the other, and all of them from the

Russians; but on the whole they do not form a weakness to the Russian Empire, and their existence within its confines does not detract from the essential fact that there are some sixty millions of Russians who speak virtually one tongue.

This nation, numerically the superior of any nation except the Chinese, and China is not yet organised for modern war, is also more religious and more patriotic as a body than is any of the other Great Powers of Europe. The accuracy of this remark will be contested, but hardly I think by those who know Russia well. The Russians are as religious at the least as are the people of the English colonies or of the United States, and they are as patriotic as the citizens of the latter country. In the union of patriotism and of religion they present, I know no nation in Europe which can approach them, although they may be rivalled by the people of the United States. We have here in Russia, obviously, from the facts which I take to be admitted by careful observers, a Power which, by the very nature of things and apart from any movement which she may make, is formidable in the highest degree. There are some fossil politicians in England who still think that Russia is weakened by the existence of a Poland. Poland died in 1863, and died for ever. The men who, either in their own persons or in the persons of their ancestors, have illustrated literature by their genius, and countless battle-fields by their splendid courage, may refuse to recognise the extinction of their country; but the Poles, considered as an anti-Russian force, were an aristocracy, in the best as well as in the common sense of the word. The

Polish peasantry, though often led by them against Russia, were never anti-Russian to an unpurchasable degree, and a large portion of the Polish peasantry have now become as attached, through agrarian legislation, to the Russian Empire as the German peasantry of Alsace were to France by the agrarian legislation of the Revolution. At the time of the Crimean War Poland did not rise; but looking to what afterwards happened in 1863, it is impossible to say that it might not have been roused. Poland could now no longer be raised against the Russians; and in spite of the fairly successful attempts which have been made by Austria to conciliate the Galician Poles, there are Slavonic subjects of Austria who could far more easily be raised against the Dual Monarchy than any Polish or other Slavonic subjects of Russia could be raised against the Tsar.

It is difficult for us to realise the attraction of Russia for some of the weaker members of the Slavonic races. Where, as once in Servia and lately in Bulgaria, Russia has had a comparatively free hand, she has often alienated Slavonic feeling; but where Slavs have been the subjects of another Great Power, and especially where they are subjects of Hungary and Austria, Russia is to them a friend on whose power they build their hopes. The Ruthenians of the Dual Monarchy are so many Russians lost within its boundaries. There is no similar German or other colony lost in Russia, for what aliens there are are too few and too much dispersed. Some think that Russia is weakened by the German element in the Baltic provinces. Here, again, those who think so are behind the times. The Baltic provinces were never German, so far as the peasantry are concerned. A German aristocracy, with German traders in the towns, ruled over a peasantry of the Esthonian, Lettish, and Lithuanian races. To this peasantry the Russians, with all their despotic measures against the landowners and against the German tongue, have come as deliverers. Because Russia is very violent in her language and in her acts, we too often fail to see how a peasantry which an aristocratic government or a government of political economists could never win, is won over by her to her rule. The Moscow men failed in Bulgaria, but in Poland they succeeded, and in the Baltic provinces, too, their methods and their policy have not been found wanting, and the problems that have so long perplexed this country in her relations with Ireland would have been solved in a week by Samarin, or Miliutin, or Prince Tcherkassky.

Some are disposed to think that Nihilism constitutes a great danger to the Russian Empire, weakening not only her offensive but even her defensive force. There can be no doubt that in Russia, in spite of the recent so-called cadet and staff conspiracy, the general belief of the best informed is that at this moment Austria and Germany have more to fear from Socialism than Russia has to fear from Nihilistic conspiracies. I shall have to return to the subject generally when I come to my Austrian chapter; but as regards Russia I may say that my latest information leads me to agree with Russian writers upon this point.*

There can be no doubt, I think, in the mind of any reasonable observer as to the real and lasting strength of

* This statement has proved to be erroneous.

Russia; and the question which it is more interesting to consider is in what manner that strength is likely to be used. Russia is, though old in some senses, politically as young a country as the United States, and has not yet by any means passed the growing period. She is strong even while growing fast, but will be still stronger in her prime. In considering her power let me, in the first place, protest against the action of those Englishmen who allow themselves to be scared out of a policy which a short time ago they thought right and wise. The fact that a number of gentlemen have come to realise the strength of Russia has led them to begin to declare that they were quite wrong a few years ago in saying that this country ought to keep Russia out of the Balkan Peninsula and away from Constantinople, and out of Herat and away from the Persian Gulf; and that on the contrary England should embrace Russia with open arms and enter upon an alliance with the Power which a short time ago they thought to be their country's mortal foe.

No doubt it is impossible to maintain the principles of Lord Beaconsfield's speeches of 1878; and it is a waste of time to examine how completely the so-called settlement of that year has broken down. All that has happened was prophesied by clear-sighted observers at the time. Sir Samuel Baker then stated that our policy "might terminate in a friendship between the Russians and the Turks to the detriment of British interests and to the confusion of the assumed protectorate." He was alluding to the Asia Minor Convention and the appointment of military consuls throughout the Turkish Asiatic provinces, and his prophecy has come true to the letter. In 1878 we were told that England had restored to Turkey the greater portion of her provinces, but Eastern Roumelia was counted into what was " restored," and Bosnia and Herzegovina were not counted into what was taken away, so that the inquiry need hardly be pursued. We were told that our action had not only restored her provinces to Turkey, but had insured the reform of their administration. No one I suppose can imagine that much progress has been made in that direction. We were told that Turkey had been given in the Balkans an " impregnable frontier ;" that the power, " military and civil," of the Sultan in Eastern Roumelia was complete, and that it was " absolutely necessary for securing the safety of Constantinople." All these considerations, however, were examined at the time, and the only extraordinary thing is that, even by a portion of the public, and even for a few months, they should have been believed.

The whole fabric of our policy in 1878 having sunk in collapse, we are now told, by some of the same persons who were instrumental in misleading us on that occasion, that Bulgaria is not a British interest, that Constantinople is not a British interest, that the continued existence of the Turkish Empire is not a British interest, and generally, that nothing is a British interest which our own military unreadiness would make it difficult for us to protect by force of arms. Just as a large portion of the public refused to accept the guidance of these gentlemen in 1878, so it is possible that a portion of the public will refuse to accept their guidance now, and will insist on examining the question for themselves. When we all but went to war in 1878 for the Sultan's supremacy in Eastern Roumelia, and were told that we had secured it, we soon found that we had only secured it upon paper, and we were then assured that the idea must be replaced by another. British policy, we were asked to believe, had shifted, because circumstances had shifted, and the spirit of freedom found to exist in the Bulgarian race, and especially in Eastern Roumelia, was to form the new bulwark against Russia—a bulwark better than the Balkan line. But as soon as Austria declined our alliance, and Russia refused to make terms with the Bulgarians, then our instructors began to tell us that even Bulgarian independence was not a British interest, and it seems now to be generally understood that Constantinople itself is not to be defended by this country, unless Hungarian feeling should make Austria fight, and unless a scratch pack of other allies can also be obtained.

Just as in the Belgian question, which I discussed in my first chapter, and to which I shall return in the last, it is desirable that England at all events should know what she means to do and should make up her mind, so too in this question of the Balkans and of Constantinople. Not that the question is likely to be raised at present in an aggravated form. The Sultan, knowing that he is now deserted by the most influential men in both the English parties, and that Austria will not fight for him if she can help it, because she knows that she is not a match for Russia in a military sense,—expecting also, as he does, a rising in Crete, a Greek advance upon Janina, and a rising in Southern Macedonia whenever he is attacked,—is forced to pretend to make terms with Russia, which practically means that his empire is to last his time. This habit of trying to make things last their time is common with the pashas. A Turkish plenipotentiary once said to a representative of one of 'the Great Powers, " Why cannot the Greeks and Bulgarians keep quiet a little? They will get all the territory they want some day." The Sultan is forced to sit still whilst his empire crumbles. He is at this moment only asked to permit what he cannot prevent, the nearer approach of Russian influence ; nothing really under his rule is for the moment to be taken from him ; and he can persuade himself that after all he will be no worse off in any point than he was as early as 1879, when the Eastern Roumelian part of the Treaty of Berlin was seen to be a dead letter. There is nothing new in the friendship of Russia and Turkey. Russian troops held garrison in Constantinople when it was menaced by the Egyptians under Mehemet Ali, and the two countries worked cordially together under the auspices of "Mahmoudoff" in the winter of 1879–80. The Russians have been slow upon their way. Baron Blumberg, as long ago as 1684, called Turkey that " body condemned to death, which must very speedily turn to a corpse ;" but the corpse is not yet laid out. The Russian advance, however, though slow, is sure. From time to time she makes one long step further towards her goal.

At the time of "Peace with Honour," Lord Beaconsfield, speaking of the danger of Russia gaining "such a prize as Constantinople"—such was the language of the instructions which he received, curiously enough from Mr., now Lord, Cross—puzzled the Protocolists by alliteratively styling it

K

"the capture of Constantinople." We shall have presently
to consider the chances and the probable results of a struggle
between Austria and Russia, and also of a struggle between
England and Russia ; but it must, I think, be recognised that
neither France nor Germany shares the view that the " capture of Constantinople " by Russia is any danger to the world,
provided that, in the case of Germany, it can be reconciled
with the continued existence of Austria as a Great Power.
In order to estimate the probabilities of a contest we shall
have briefly to consider the internal condition of Russia,
and to compare it in some degree with that of Austria, which
will be further investigated in the next chapter.

I spoke just now of Russia as being, above all, a patriotic
country. France is a patriotic country. Frenchmen are
patriots, from M. Grévy down to M. Drumont; but probably
neither M. Grévy nor M. Drumont possesses that kind of
patriotic courage which would lead him to get himself
quietly killed for his country's sake if he could well help
it. The Russians have a different sort of patriotism from
the patriotism of other European peoples—there are few
Russians who would hesitate to die if their death could
help their country's cause. Possibly this may be a mark of
barbarism; some pale-faced philosophers, I have no doubt,
may think it so; but it is a factor in the present position of
the European Powers.

Poland and the Baltic provinces and Nihilism may not be
sources of weakness worth counting; Russia's real weakness
is the absence, inevitable under an autocracy such as hers,
of a trained upper and middle class. The sharp contrast

between the simple piety of the Russian peasant, which makes of every meal a celebration of a Sacrament, and his occasional outbursts of drunkenness and violence, is excelled by one still sharper between the piety of the peasants and the profound scepticism of the upper classes. I do not speak of religious scepticism alone, but of that practical scepticism which thinks nothing worth doing well for any cause, and which while in Russia 'consistent with the use of patriotic language, and perhaps with the existence of certain patriotic sentiments, makes of the class which is undermined by it a feeble instrument for the purposes of the Russian Fatherland.

I said in the first chapter that in Russia there are only two men who count—but the second whom I named counts in a double way, both as an individual of ability and as the editor of a newspaper, which, in a sense, may be described as the most powerful in the world, because it is all-powerful or nearly all-powerful in one great empire.

The Russian press is only powerful through Katkoff's power. The official and semi-official papers say only what might be expected of them, and, as a rule, do but mark time. The *Moscow Gazette*, which asserts that there is no free press in the world except the Russian, enjoys a freedom which is, however, personal to itself or to its great editor. In constitutional countries, it declares, the whole press is enslaved by party. The *Moscow Gazette* knows no party, for Russia knows none that is worthy (or unworthy) of the name. It succeeds in doing what it pleases in Russian home affairs; but although in foreign affairs its anti-German sentiments are contradicted by *Le Nord* and do not prevail, at all events it is allowed to utter them.

Katkoff counts as Katkoff, and counts also as the mouth-piece of the Moscow, or national " party," which may better be styled the Moscow Group. This " party " is composed of a knot of men, who may have their differences, but who to the outside world appear to hold opinions which are identical, because they are identical as against the outside world. Aksakoff, Samarin, Miliutin, and Tcherkassky, belong to a past generation, and now represent Moscow in the Elysian fields. Prince Vassiltchikoff, and others who could be named, have continued their traditions, but whether in the Conservative shade of the *Moscow Gazette* or in more Liberal journals, the expression of Moscow or National opinion has always been substantially the same in questions which concern the outer world. We talk of the Moscow party, but one great strength of Russia lies in the fact, which I repeat, that it has no parties. Russians nearly all agree, with the exception of those whose hand is against everything—agree, that is, in a large number of general views which are almost peculiar to Russia. Even the Nihilists and all other Russians are at one upon some points, as, for example, in ridiculing Parliamentary government. The dominant note with all is confidence in the future of Russia, and a pro-tective affection for the Slav races outside the empire, pro-vided they will look up to Russia, take their policy from Russia, and profess the orthodox religion.

The late Emperor was affected and controlled by Moscow opinion, but the present Emperor shares it, which is a very different thing. The present Emperor is as national as was Peter the Great; but, unfortunately, he hardly shows Peter the Great's ability. In a family where all the members have been made by absolute power unlike other men, he resembles rather, in the type of mind, Paul and Nicholas than Alexander the First or Alexander the Second. Both the Alexanders were melancholy Germans as contrasted with the present obstinate and thoroughly Russian Tsar. In spite of the fact that he was trained by men who knew Russia well, I fear that, like the traditional Irishman, he might remark with truth that he himself knows nothing of his own country and still less of any other. Those who surround, and mainly advise him, are strongly Conservative in tone. Pobedonostchieff, Count Tolstoi, and Katkoff are men who are accused by the reformers of being the somewhat pretentious exponents of an ignorant old Tory obscurantism, but to a foreign observer there is not much difference between a Russian Liberal and a Russian Conservative. In the English sense of the word, Liberalism is somewhat out of place in Russia. Parliamentarianism, so dear to us, will probably never be fully adopted there, and it must be admitted that Russian patriotism holds it not so much in aversion as in contempt.

The one great weakness of Russia, the absence of a really trained middle or upper class, is intensified by a kind of proscription, which is a result of autocracy. Half those men of ability that the country does possess are shut out of office because they, not being in the least able to help themselves, used to bow somewhat low before the lady who since the death of Alexander II. has been in foreign countries styled his widow; to whom indeed the Imperial family themselves,

also because they could not help it, used to bow rather low
in the late Emperor's lifetime. This proscription is in itself
a consequence of the obstinacy of the Tsar, who likes to be
served by submissive or by pliant men, but who in spite of
his liking for pliancy does not himself know how to forgive.
M. de Giers, as one of his colleagues once told an Englishman, who knew him well, "stands at 'Attention,' one thumb
on the seam of his trousers and the other at his cap, and
says (the minister was speaking in French), 'Oui, sire;
oui, sire.'"

When we talk of "spread-eagleism" we are generally
thinking of the United States, but the real spread-eagleism
is that, not of the American Republic, but of the Russian
Empire. The Russians habitually talk of the time when they
will be masters of the whole world, and if, instead of writing
of the facts of our time, I were tempted to prophesy con-
cerning the next century I should have to admit that, if we
exclude America and Australia and confine our thoughts
to the Old World alone, it is at least conceivable that their
dreams should one day come true. The only foreigner who is
known to the Russian peasantry is the German, and the name
for German and for foreigner with the peasantry is the same,
and the hatred of the "dumb men," as they call their German
neighbours, is intense. The peasantry know little of the
English, and if you listen to their sentiments you discover
that it is their belief that one day there will be between them
and Germany a war compared with which, their soldiers
say, that of 1870 will be child's play, and that if Germany
wins this will not be the end, but that war after war will

follow until Germany is destroyed. This feeling is to some
extent held in check by the Russian Court, although one day
they may take it up and use it ; but court dislikes are turned
for the present less towards Germany than towards Austria.
We will consider presently the military strength of Russia
as compared with that of her great neighbours. Russia,
in spite of her enormous debt and its tremendous annual
charge, is growing in power, and that power, great in itself,
gains by being surrounded by the terrors that encompass
the unknown. She has by far the largest army in the world,
and, with a complete mobilisation of her forces, has upon
paper a force at once of four and ultimately of six millions
of men. Some are inclined to think that the men will not
be found when wanted, but great progress has been made
by Russia since 1878. Her artillery has as many guns as
that of Germany or of France, her cavalry is perhaps more
numerous than that of France and Germany together, certainly more numerous than that of Germany and Austria
combined. This cavalry force is admittedly the best there is
for that service to which cavalry in modern war is limited, if
it is not to be destroyed on use. With moderate prudence
the resources of Russia cannot but grow and grow, for Russia
from many points of view is a young country, and Siberia,
territorially considered, is almost another United States.

With her magnificent natural position, and with her
unrivalled chain of fortresses upon the German frontier,
Russia can always wear out German patience. It may be true,
as Count Moltke says, that 200,000 men upon the Vistula,
along with the German fortresses, might prevent Russia from

invading Germany; but even in that case there would be 200,000 men withdrawn from the French frontier in face of a French army more numerous than the German, and they would not suffice to prevent Russia from crushing Austria.

It is a curious commentary upon the repeated protestations of affection which have passed between the Emperors of Germany and of Russia during the last few years, that since 1870 Königsberg has been converted into an entrenched camp upon an enormous scale, that the forts of Thorn have been iron-plated and topped with iron turrets, that Dantzic has been greatly strengthened, that Posen has been greatly strengthened, and that Cüstrin is being strengthened now, as is also Glogau. Russia, growing daily in military strength, sets in the scale against the Germans more than Austria can bring to restore their equilibrium. It may be confidently asserted that it is now far too late for Germany to strike her possible enemies one at a time. For Germany to attack either France or Russia now would be madness if not suicide, and Germany will go on with her declarations of friendliness towards Russia although with a perfect willingness to see coalitions formed against the Northern Power. Prince Bismarck has one immense advantage in dealing with the Russians; he is face to face with the worst informed of European Powers. The Russian Emperor has some of the best-trained men in Europe at his back if he would use them, but they are retiring from business or growing old. One of them is not what he was when Minister in China; another is not what he was when he settled certain private difficulties in the Imperial family, which needed more tact and even wisdom for their settlement than do the affairs of nations. In the concerns of the Powers blunders are repaired by the simple process of casting swords into the scale, and the most solid of arguments after all is based upon the adding together the troops and fortresses of allies, and deducting the troops and fortresses of the enemy. This simple plan of dealing with affairs of state is inapplicable to the affairs of courts, but Baron Jomini has an hereditary understanding of the one class of considerations, and an inborn power over the other, which make of this Vaudois-Swiss "bourgeois" of Valangin the best foreign servant that wears the livery of the Slav, whose very tongue he cannot speak. But he is old, and set aside for clerks and sergeants. Prince Lobanoff, who is a really great diplomatist, is allowed no power. Were I to say how great, I should fear to be read by M. Katkoff, or by M. de Giers, and to do the ambassador hurt by causing his patriotism to be suspected. M. Zinovieff, of the Foreign Office, is also a good man and also has no real power.

Prince Bismarck, I repeat, is to be congratulated upon having to hold his own against the worst-informed of Powers. Austria could not exist at all, if she were not well-informed; with her mixed nationalities and with her servants of many tongues, she is well-informed, as if by the law of her being; and Germany is well-informed, because it is her business to be well-informed, and she does all her business well; but Russia and France are by far the worst-informed of all the Powers. The Russian Emperor now reads nothing, whatever he may have read when only

Tsarevitch, and rejecting the advice of the men of ideas, who are suspected of the deadly sin of " Europeanism " or " Westernism," is advised by those who are mere sergeants by obedience and discipline, and by the old Tory bureaucrats and pedants. Russia need only be pointed out as a country in which every .foreign newspaper is tabooed. France, I am sorry to say, though she allows foreign newspapers to enter freely enough in all conscience, is, for practical purposes, almost as ignorant. M. John Lemoinne may know, the *Temps* may know, but France as a country does not know, and the electors and the Assembly are vain enough to suppose that they know better for themselves by natural lights than they could be taught by those who have been trained to teach or govern.

So greatly is the instability of governments in France displeasing to Russia, that there have been dreams of late of bringing about an arrangement for a lasting peace by a revival of the Three Emperors' League and the complete isolation of the French. This is possible rather than probable. In order that Russia should cease to menace Germany and Austria with France, it is necessary that Russia should be completely contented in all parts of the world, and it is difficult to see how Austria can willingly be a party to contenting her. There is no great love lost between the English Conservative Cabinet and the Bulgarian Government. The most prominent member of the English Tory party would count it a cheap way of pacifying Europe, if peace could be aided by the isolation of France, through letting Russia work her will in the neighbourhood of the Balkans.

Lord Randolph Churchill was one of the steadiest foes of Lord Beaconsfield's foreign policy in 1877–8. On the other hand Lord Salisbury is not a man to throw away the possibility of a good alliance, or to leave Austria in the lurch, and he keenly sees the possibility of making an anti-Russian policy in the Balkans popular by using the popularity of the Roumanians and the Bulgarians. Moreover, there is an argument by which an anti-Russian policy in the Balkans can be recommended and which appeals to John Bull with peculiar strength. It is the breeches' pocket argument. Every country annexed or virtually annexed by Russia is closed for ever to our trade by means of heavily protective duties, although, as I have shown in the case of Bosnia, I fear that I must admit that the same is very nearly true of our Austrian allies.

Russia, it may be seen by what has been said, is really working her will on Bulgaria by Prince Bismarck's help. Austria is hardly strong enough to resist. She is terrified at the prospect of a war with only an English alliance. She expects Prince Bismarck to back her policy at St. Petersburg, and he himself is not strong enough to do so. From time to time the Russian Emperor pretends friendship with France, or at all events shows France in the background, in the way in which a fowler "shows a dog" to drive wild fowl here and there. There is not and there will not be a Russo-French alliance till a European war has begun, if even then, but France is necessarily always ready.

The less decided of the opponents in England of Russia's Bulgarian policy (for it has in England not one single friend) extenuate it by a comparison with British action against Arabi in Egypt. Now, granting that Arabi represented Egyptian feeling as much as the Sobranje represents Bulgarian, an assumption which the British Government would deny, and putting out of sight the fact that the organized Government of Egypt was in part destroyed by Arabi, whereas in Bulgaria the Regents have taken charge, by consent of the last Prince, of the organized Government of the country; yet, even so, no fair comparison is possible. An English Kaulbars has yet to be discovered. In going to Egypt England did not act alone. The ultimate action taken was the consequence of the joint note, and the joint note was proposed to the English Cabinet in 1881 by France; France moreover agreed to take part in the expedition, and would have done so had her Chamber been willing to vote the funds. When France refused to go, England applied to Italy, and Italy all but consented. England, in fact, moved with the unofficial approval of most of the Powers, whilst all the Powers, without exception, officially congratulated her on her success in restoring order.

From the moment when Great Britain, through Lord Salisbury, saved the Prince of Bulgaria at the Constantinople Conference it became certain that Russia would dethrone him. He was dethroned accordingly, but merely to dethrone was not sufficient to restore the Russian prestige in Bulgaria, and further steps were necessary. Prince Alexander had done nothing against the Tsar of late, and nothing at all that has been proved, though I am aware of much that has been asserted. He had even been unduly submis-

sive. But he had been independent, and Bulgarian independence, whether in tongue, in religion, or in the sphere of
foreign affairs, is intolerable to Russian patriots. I am one
of those who are unwillingly driven into a position of hostility
to Russia, for I have much sympathy with the aspirations of
the Slav race in general, and even with those of the Russian
people in particular. Strongly anti-Russian as I am, there
are, as has already been seen in this chapter, many points
upon which I have the highest possible opinion of the
Russians ; but I must admit that the outrage to Europe of
the Kaulbars mission, after the circumstances of Prince
Alexander's deposition, is tremendous, and I fear irretrievable.
It is a death-blow to the smaller states, and the proclamation
or consecration of the doctrine that might in the affairs of
nations makes right.

The Russian press is now claiming Bulgaria as virtually
a province of Russia: its concerns are a matter of internal
policy with which the Powers have nothing to do; and
resistance to orders from St. Petersburg is the same thing in
Bulgaria as in Poland. Whether or no the Russian policy
has been wicked, it certainly seems to have been foolish
from the Russian point of view. There can be no doubt
that the Bulgarians are alienated from Russia by that
policy. They adored Russia, or rather the figure of the late
Emperor, before the Russians came. The Governor of
Bulgaria during the Russian advance, the leader of the
Moscow party himself, wrote during the war to one who was
once the friend of himself and Samarin, and of both the
Miliutins and both the Vassiltchikoffs, that the Bulgarians

would not commit what he called the folly of the Poles, but would resemble the Ruthenians of Galicia in welcoming the Slavonic headship of Russia. Now the Russians had this advantage in Bulgaria, that there was practically no religious difficulty. The English Quakers are loved by the Bulgarians for the quiet good that they have done in the burnt villages, and there is much American Protestant influence, besides that of Dr. Washburn's people from Robert College; but, neither the Quakers nor Robert College have tried to proselytise, and all Bulgaria is Orthodox. At the same time it is democratic, and those who welcomed the Russian liberator did so with a strong belief that their local independence would be preserved to them.

The Bulgarians, according to the majority of ethnographic writers, are not of Slavonic race, but I will at once admit that this matters little. They are as completely Slavised as the Slavs of old Prussia have become Germanised. If Prince Bismarck himself, like Justinian and Belisarius, is a Slav by race, he is as German in fact as Justinian and Belisarius were Roman. The Bulgarians undoubtedly came from what is now the heart of Russia, and had their empire upon the Volga, from which they take their name; but although when they came in the fifth century they were not Slavs, by the eighth or ninth century they were almost as completely Slavised as they are now.

On the other hand the Russian Governor of Bulgaria and his young men from Moscow, who came with him, failed to understand that the Bulgarians had not risen against the Turkish rule for the purpose of substituting one sort of pashas for another. The Bulgarians gloried indeed in the marvellous strength of Russian patriotism and the Russian desire for extension and for increase of strength, but they did not want them exerted at their own expense. The Russians, on the other side, feel that Bulgaria is now, from some points of view, so close to Moscow that absolutism in Russia will be at stake if Liberalism is to prevail within Bulgaria.

Russia is a country without a Liberal party. The old-fashioned Tories there are weak, and the empire ought to please Lord Randolph Churchill, for, being without Liberals and almost without old-fashioned Tories, it is a sort of paradise for a Tory-Democrat. The descendants of the Dekabrists are dead; the old Anglo-maniacs and aristocratic Liberals are dead; and all the Russian politicians of the day belong to the Moscow national school, although some of them affect a Tory and some of them a pseudo-Liberal strain. I call it pseudo-Liberal when I remember their policy in the occupied provinces during the Turkish war, when they insisted that all opinion should be Orthodox; and that all opinion should be subject to the Emperor's will. It was always certain that Russia could not easily absorb a Catholic population, and it was always doubtful if she could ever hope to absorb an Orthodox population belonging to the Hellenic branch of the Eastern Church, but the Bulgarians were not supposed to be endowed with so much love of independence and power of resistance that they were likely to stand out against Russia. By doing so they have embarked, however, in a hopeless struggle in which the sympathy that is bestowed upon them is hardly likely to find expression in action.

There are some persons in England, haters of Russia, who believe that the Bulgarians have nothing to do but to hold out some time, and that Russia will fall to pieces of herself or undergo some remarkable change. But even a great disaster in foreign war, which alone would upset the established order there, would not in overturning it make much difference in external questions of this kind. Men point to the assassination of the late Emperor, or the acquittal by a St. Petersburg jury of officials and nobles of the assassins of the Grand Police Master, Count Trepoff, but the stone-throwing spirit, the self-depreciation of the capital, and the occasional outbursts of violent Nihilism are only the natural results of the autocratic system. Like Malet's conspiracy before the campaign of France, they reveal weakness, but their existence is not inconsistent with that of a wide-spread patriotic feeling, or of the power to make patriotic sacrifice.

Cold comfort, I fear, all this for the Bulgarians and for the weaker generally in the Balkan States and in the world outside; and yet the Bulgarians have deserved better things of us. By their wise and prudent policy, and by the self-restraint which has been exercised by the whole people, they have on the one hand held their own, and on the other, made an armed occupation difficult. Their spirit of independence was well known, but the ability which they have displayed in war and in finance was somewhat of a surprise. Russia believed that the withdrawal of the Russian officers would disorganise them, and immediately afterwards they were successful in a very serious war. Through all the provocations of the Kaulbars mission, and in the total absence of a supreme direction of their affairs, although under a monarchic system, perfect order has never ceased to reign, nor the taxes to come in with regularity. Verily, the Bulgarians deserve the thanks of all free men in Europe. It used to be said by Russian officers that the road to Constantinople lay through Vienna, but it now seems as though there were a still greater difficulty in Russia's way in the unconquerable spirit of independence of the Roumanians, the Bulgarians, and the Southern Slavs. Every attempt at coercion only makes them more permanently hostile to autocratic rule, and when the opposite policy is pursued and they are left to themselves, they do not appear to repent at all.

The possession of such remarkable qualities of self-government by these small peoples has led many to try of late to force to the front in practical politics that which has long been one of the favourite dreams of political speculation. It may be considered to be the policy of the more liberal elements in English Conservatism and of the more prudent amongst English Liberals, to set up, if there is a possibility of doing so, some kind of Balkan confederation. If, indeed, a Balkan confederation, even with the support of Austria and of England, would not in a military sense be strong enough to hold its own against Russia, nevertheless, in any time that may be left to us, before Russia once again presses on, it may be possible to bring about, if not confederation, at all events a cordial understanding. Certainly the Greeks, the Roumanians, the Bulgarians, and the Serbs are young peoples, worth helping to defend. One of the difficulties in the way of producing anything like settlement in the Balkan question, or, let us say, in the European

L

branch of the Eastern Question, has been the existence of mutual jealousies or even hatreds. The Greeks dislike the Austrians, partly because the Austrians are supposed to intend some day to go to Salonica, and so to cut Greater Greece in half, partly because the Austrians are the protectors of Servia, and the Servians claim some part of Macedonia and Albania, which the Greeks expect rather to come to their share. On the other hand, although both the Greeks and the Bulgarians have been at various times somewhat pro-Russian and anti-Austrian, there is the most violent hatred between these two races, because Bulgaria was promised in the Treaty of San Stefano many districts which are claimed as Hellenic by Greece; and because, in short, both peoples have a longing for the same parts of Macedonia.

A confederation in the Balkan provinces must mean the confederation of Greece, Bulgaria, Servia, and Roumania, of which Roumania, Greece, and Servia almost equally dislike Bulgaria. Such an arrangement seemed at first sight to resemble a confederation between three not very friendly cats and an altogether hostile dog. The difficulties are still very great, but they are not so great as they were, for the dislikes are now distinctly less accentuated. King Milan has even privately suggested a personal union between Servia and Bulgaria, thus raising questions which I will discuss in the next chapter. Bulgaria, too, has appointed a diplomatic agent at Athens. Unless Hungary, with her anti-Russian policy, should prevent it, Austria would still look with disfavour upon a Balkan confederation of the smaller Powers, and would be inclined to join with Russia to prevent her own permanent exclusion from the Mediterranean coast, to which she does not at present desire to go, but from which she does not wish to be entirely shut off. By our action at Berlin we cut the Southern Slavs in half by planting Austria between Servia and Montenegro, an arrangement which does not seem likely to be permanent. The Austrian difficulty is, perhaps, the greatest difficulty which now remains in the way of confederation, and it is no difficulty in the way of the formation of a Balkan confederacy under Austrian headship.

There is another incident, beside the one just named, which shows that the relations of Greece to Bulgaria are better than they were. An arrangement had been concluded between M. Tricoupis and the Bulgarian Government, before the deposition of Prince Alexander, for the delimitation on a map of the respective spheres of influence of Greece and Bulgaria in Macedonia. This dividing the skin of the beast before he is dead, which is as a rule imprudent, is perhaps necessary in the case of Turkey, to prevent those conflicts of interest, occasionally threatening even armed struggle in the field, which break out from time to time between the Greeks, the Servians, and the Bulgarians. Unredeemed Roumania is chiefly Austrian, and therefore we hear little about the completion of the unity of the Roumanian people, although, curiously enough, the majority of the Roumanian people live outside Roumania, but the other three principal states of the Balkan peninsula are bitterly at enmity among themselves about Macedonia—Servians arrayed against Bulgarians, and Greeks against both. The troubles in Macedonia which were expected by Lord Salisbury in January last came, however, from none of these, but from Russia as he believed. The delimitation of the sphere of influence which had been arranged, of course meant an agreement in advance whether Bulgaria or Greece should conduct insurrection in particular villages whenever Turkey was *in extremis*, and which should annex them whenever Turkey was extinct. There would not be much desire, it appears, on the part of Greece to hurry matters if once she had a clear agreement upon this point. The present Greek Prime Minister, at all events, would be content that Greece should wait for any number of years, provided that this question were not to be settled against her in the interval. Greece asks, of course, for Janina which was promised her by the Powers and which is one of the chief cities of her people. She believes that Albania will gravitate towards her, although she is apprehensive both of Austrian and of Italian ambition in that quarter; but the point to which she attaches the most importance is delimitation in Macedonia, and then she will be content to wait a century if need be, for, as one of her chief statesmen lately said, " A hundred years is nothing in the life of the Greek nation." Apparently the Greek dream of Constantinople is dead; at all events it is no longer put into words.

As Balkan confederation is not likely for many years to come, or is not likely soon enough to be of effective value to stay the approach of Russia to Constantinople, we have to admit that if Russia is to be kept out of the Macedonian plain, Austria, with or without alliances, must bar her advance. Unfortunately Austria is not strong enough. As Austrians and Russians have not been tried the one against the other, it is impossible to accurately gauge quality, but roughly speaking it may be said that putting quality on one side the Russian army ought to be equal to the armies of Germany and Austria combined. The Russian annual contingent of the regular peace army has risen to 227,000 men, which is only slightly under those of Austria and Germany together. The Russian peace army is nominally in the present year 840,000 men, but, really, if we take into account the Cossacks permanently embodied, it amounts to 890,000 men, whilst even the smaller figure exceeds the peace armies of Austria and Germany combined. The total force of trained men which ought to be easily and rapidly mobilised by Russia, considering the figures of her contingents and the character of her military system, is about 4,000,000 as against 2,000,000 for Germany, and 1,250,000 for Austria. More slowly, if she has guns for them—and guns if not in stock could probably be pretty easily obtained—Russia could place six millions of men in the field. The power of Russia to realise in fact the promise of her paper figures has recently been denied, but the necessity of taking into account the Russian military movement which began after the failures of 1878 has not been sufficiently kept in mind.

If we were to credit the figures given by the German Government to the German Parliament in January last, we should believe that these results were secured by Russia at a cost exceeding the annual charge of the united army budgets of Germany and of Austria, for the official German figures give 785,906,259 marks for Russia. But Prince Bismarck deceives the German Parliament by estimating the rouble at three shillings when it is worth less than two. It is the Russian "gold" or "metallic" rouble that is worth a little over three shillings of our money. The "silver" rouble is the paper rouble, now worth but twenty-one pence three farthings. Rau, Marga, and most, if not all, of the authorities, except the Intelligence Department book, have made the same mistake, and reckon the rouble at from 3·75 francs to 3·50 francs. On the other hand, there is a large extraordinary military expenditure in Russia which it is not easy to find in the Russian Budget, as, for example, a large part of the expenditure upon the Transcaspian Railway now being rapidly constructed by General Annenkoff; and calls are made upon both the village communities and the provincial Zemstvoes for matters which in other countries would be at the charge of the State. In any case, however, the figure given by the German Government as 785,906,259 marks, is the figure of the Russian budget which should have been stated at 495,428,078 marks only (at the rate at which the rouble then stood ; now less)—a pretty considerable deception practised towards the German people. Men are cheap in Russia.

By whatever test we take, excepting quality, which has not yet been employed, Russia ought to be from two and a half to three times as strong as Austria. The trained cavalry of Russia is even stronger in proportion than are her numbers generally. It outnumbers the trained cavalry of Germany and of Austria together, and is sometimes even said to be more than three times as numerous as that of the Dual Monarchy, although Austria-Hungary is strong in cavalry, and has almost as large a cavalry force as France.

It may be assumed that Germany will not only give no cause of offence to her tremendous neighbour, but will try to avoid being compromised by Austria or by England. If she had ever to intervene as against Russia she would try to do so when Russia was already weakened by a long struggle. There are no very probable causes of war between Russia and Germany, except indeed the intensely bitter feeling between the two peoples, for Germany has ceased to concern herself with the Russification of the so-called German provinces of Russia, and is herself engaged in the similar policy of Germanising Prussian Poland. Russia is well protected by fortresses against a possible German advance whilst she might be engaged elsewhere, especially by the Polish quadrilateral, in which of Mödlin, Demblin, and Terespol, the last-named is familiar to us now as Brest-Litovsk, but the others are hardly recognisable at all under their new names. Russia has lately taken to the Japanese system of frequently changing the names of cities, just as the Town Council of Paris changes those of streets. Towards Austria Russia has till lately had virtually no fortresses, and the difference is instructive, for Austria is far more likely to be her enemy than Germany. Lutzk, now to be called Michaïlograd, and Dubno, old places of arms, are to be re-fortified, and there is a talk of an entrenched camp, but substantially the Russian frontier towards Austria is an open one, where, instead of fortresses, Russia has troops, especially a numerous cavalry.

And yet it is on this frontier that she expects to have to fight. The meaning of this absence of fortresses upon one frontier and of their presence upon the other is, that in a war with Austria Russia expects to act on the offensive, assisted by a Ruthenian insurrection in Galicia; and so she no more fortifies her frontiers against Austria than she fortifies them against Turkey. On the other hand, it may be noted that she fortifies her frontier towards Germany, so as to be able quietly to attack Austria at her will. Russia proudly refuses to fortify her capital, a fact which would be significant of her consciousness of strength, were it not that Vienna also is virtually an open town, for the fortifications were stopped owing to the objections of the town council in 1867.

The probabilities are that, in the event of a war with Austria, Russia would be able to enter Galicia, along an open frontier of more than 600 miles, and take Przemysl, Lemberg, and Cracow, in spite of the fortifications now being pressed forward with feverish haste.* Looking to the nature of the Polish climate it is to be hoped that it will not be discovered when spring comes that snow-works form the bulk of the new fortifications. The disposition of the Russian railways alone is sufficient to plainly show that she means to take the offensive. She has special reasons for occupying Galicia. She would be glad enough to keep it, because it is at the present time a gathering-place for disaffected Poles. She would easily gain popularity there, by giving to the peasantry the lands of the Polish nobles, and thus could raise the Ruthenians. Galicia forms the road

* Published 1st March.

towards Vienna, where the Eastern Question is to be settled. In the vast plains of Galicia 200,000 Russian cavalry would find a splendid field for war, and there they would be able to carry out against Austria those wonderful manœuvres of the new dragoons with horse artillery, which the foreign officers, in 1886, were not allowed to see. The Russian manœuvres of 1886 were conducted by forces of 40,000 men at Krasnoe Selo (for the edification of the foreign officers), and of 162,000 men, of whom nearly 20,000 were cavalry, with 528 guns, between Wilna and Warsaw. Germany does not put 202,000 men with 650 guns in the field at the annual autumn manœuvres. Austria is miserably equipped with fortresses and is trying in haste to repair her deficiencies in this respect.

Austria in a Galician war with Russia would have no special advantage that I can see, save one, that, namely, of being able to raise a splendid but not very large fighting body of aristocratic Poles from other lands to serve against the hereditary enemy of their race on behalf of the least unpopular of the three partitioning Powers. No doubt Germany, without actually appearing to move, would quietly collect troops on the Polish frontier and watch Russia, but it is doubtful whether she would be able to detain a very large force of Russian troops in Poland proper, except militia and garrison battalions. She could not prevent the loss of Galicia to Austria, though she might interfere to prevent the ultimate destruction of Austria as a Power. A partial dismemberment of Austria, by a Russian annexation of Galicia, Germany might not very much regret, because Austria in Galicia protects the Poles, a course which is a permanent slur upon the action of Germany in this matter. But a further or really considerable dismemberment of Austria Germany could not permit, unless under downright fear of France.

Italy would possibly not have the will, and England and the small Balkan States, (even if not divided amongst themselves or partly neutral), would not have the power, to give rapid and effective assistance to Austria in the field. Italy would be to her a more useful friend than England or the Balkan States. I have already said, in a previous chapter, that Italy would not save Austria gratis; but it is not improbable that she might save or try to save her for a price, and although a curious fact, it is a fact, that Vienna is more likely to be saved from a temporary Russian occupation by Italy than by Germany. Russia is anxious to weaken, and if she cannot really weaken, then to hamper Italy, and is not unacquainted with the origin of the recent attacks upon Massowah, a fact which the French press denies, but of which the Russian newspapers boast. It is certain that Italy regards the Russian policy in the Balkan peninsula as iniquitous, as harmful to European interests generally, and as hurtful to Italian interests in particular, and that Italy would join a group of Powers to oppose it by force. If opposition by force is impossible, owing to the weakness or the fears of Austria, or even to the buying off of Austria by Russia, then Italy would join England in putting on the drag as much as possible. Whatever may be the feeling in Hungary, it must be admitted that Austria will put up with a good deal from Russia rather than fight. She has done so in the past; and to give a single example of humiliation out of many, I need only mention how at various times and on various questions she had to remonstrate with the Bulgarian Government in the days of the "Russian Ministers" in Bulgaria, and received from the latter replies couched in terms of gross and intentional discourtesy.

I have assumed that England would be unable to rapidly assist Austria in the field. In such a war our part, if we were drawn in, would probably be the same as in a single-handed war against the Russians, namely, to defend India in Central Asia, to try to raise China against Russia, and to adopt the policy of exhausting Russia by a very strong attack on Vladivostock; but if Italy were with us, it is probable that we should be tempted by the possession of a formidable allied fleet to attack Russia in the Black Sea—an enterprise in which we should undoubtedly fail. The Russians expect to be attacked in the Black Sea, but a careful examination of the character of that sea, as well as of the Baltic, shows that not by the strength of her fleets, but by the natural strength of her position Russia is in those directions virtually impregnable. There are some who think that the Mahommedan population of the Caucasus might still be made use of against Russia, but this view is as obsolete a superstition as the belief in Poland. The Russian colonists of the Caucasus have now become Cossacks for military purposes, and Russia has no more patriotic people than the Black Sea and the Caucasian Cossacks. Those who think that while India could defend itself upon the Helmund the troops from England, with a Turkish army—if the Turkish alliance were obtained—should be thrown into the Caucasus in order to prevent the despatch of troops by the Caspian towards Herat, are proposing a course which the highest authorities reject.

Colonel Malleson is the chief exponent of the view which I wish to combat. I know not which, indeed, it is that he proposes—a landing at Anapa and march on Stavropol, or a landing at Poti and march on Tiflis. In the latter case we should be destroyed by fever, and in the former crushed by Russian numbers. Colonel Malleson seems to think that the Caucasus has not long been Russian. Stavropol and its district have been Russian since the seventeenth century, and Tiflis since 1801. It is the Circassian highlands which alone held out against the Russians, and into them we cannot penetrate. Or does he wish us to repeat Hobart's 1877 experiment of a Soukhoum Kali landing? This is mere map-maker's warfare. From Soukhoum Kali we could go nowhere, and our spies when sent into the mountain valleys would discover that the Circassians are gone and replaced by Kouban Cossacks. But even during the Crimean War the Caucasus did not rise, though Schamyl was in his home. The Jingo plan appears to be to march on Tiflis in winter, but the Vladikavkas military road, which I know well myself, is perfectly passable in winter for Russian troops, and even the *Géographie Militaire*, which asserts that it is sometimes blocked by ice, admits that the interruption of communications does not average more than seventeen days a year. I cannot agree in the Yate or Malleson proposals, and feel that there is indeed no arguing with gentlemen who believe that we can make use of Persians against Russian troops.*

* I will refer in the last chapter to an answer, "The Fortnightly Reviewer and Russia," which appeared in *Blackwood's Magazine* for April.

Whilst the Austrian military position, in spite of the desire of the Emperor for military reform, is still weak, I cannot find words too strong to praise the political ability with which the Austrian Empire is being kept at peace and kept together. The Austrian Empire is a marvel of equilibrium. The old simile of a house of cards is exactly applicable to its situation, and just as in the exercises of acrobats, when seven or nine men are borne by one upon his shoulders, it is rather skill than strength which sustains them; so if we look to the Austrian constitution, which we shall have to consider in the next chapter, it is a miracle how the fabric stands at all. At the same time it is impossible for Austria, although she can maintain her stability in times of peace, to impose upon either her Russian or her German neighbours as to her strength for war. Prince Bismarck is obliged, with whatever words of public and private praise for the speeches of the Austrian and Hungarian statesmen, to add the French and Russian forces together upon his fingers, and to deduct from them the Austrian and the German, with doubts as to the attitude of Italy, and doubts as to the attitude of England.

If Austria could have presented Prince Bismarck not only with an English alliance, but with an English, Turkish, and Italian alliance, he might possibly have allowed her to provoke a general war; but with the difficulties attendant upon a concession of territory to Italy, except as the last resort, and with Turkey at the feet of Russia, it was difficult for Prince Bismarck to go further than to say to Austria, "Fight by all means, if you feel yourself strong enough to beat Russia single-handed. France and Germany will 'see all fair,' and you can hardly expect anybody effectually to help you." Prince Bismarck deals with foreign affairs on the principles upon which they were dealt with by King Henry VIII. of England, when that king was pitted against the acutest intellects of the Empire and of France. His policy is a plain and simple policy, and not a policy of astuteness and cunning, and almost necessarily at the present time consists in counting heads.

A good deal of indignation has been lately wasted in England upon the Turk. The Turk may be frightened by Russian pressure from the Caucasus, a territory which, instead of being a military weakness to Russia, as the ill-informed suppose, is in fact a splendid base for offensive operations; or the Turk may be bribed by the promise of getting Bosnia back; but in reality his position is a very painful one, for he is weak, and he would be between the hammer and the anvil whichever side he took, and would suffer about equally either way. No one who knows the present state of the Turkish Empire can suppose that Turkey could effectively deal with a Russian attack by Erzeroum and an insurrection in Macedonia, not to speak of a rising in Crete and a permanent revolution in Arabia. The efforts of the last war have left Turkey weak; and although in the course of a few months, if they were given to us, we could collect and ourselves arm and equip a Turkish army which would prove a formidable force, the time would not be given to us, and long before anything could be done Macedonia would be in flames and Asia Minor would be overrun.

Bosnia attracts the Sultan most. It is usual to say that his first consideration is for his fears, but his Majesty has a temper, too, and the loss of Bosnia is laid to Lord Salisbury's account, and Lord Salisbury has never been forgiven. The Sultan has always maintained, to his intimates, that he was led to assent to the Asia Minor Convention under false pretences, because he had not been told that England was going to propose at Berlin that Bosnia should go to Austria, an alienation of his territory which the Russians had not suggested in the Treaty of San Stefano. He says he had not been told that the territory was to be taken, and that still less would it have occurred to him that the proposition was to be made by England to the Powers. It is a curious fact that by giving Bosnia to Austria England offended equally the Slavs and the Turks.

Russia reassures the Sultan as to the probability of war, and for the present reassures him with some truth. In spite of the stories which have lately gone the round of the European press as to Russian mobilisation on the frontier of Roumania, it is probable that Russia will no longer pursue the policy of tearing off bits of Turkey, in order to set up small States which forthwith turn against her, but will support Turkey's life-interest in that property which she regards as her own in reversion. As I pointed out in the second chapter, the Sultan may become a dependent, like the Emir of Bokhara. The Russians at this moment desire most a friendly Turkey, which will keep England out of the Black Sea in time of war. I grant to Colonel Malleson that the Russians themselves think that we could harm them in the Caucasus and keep them out of Asia Minor by cutting their maritime supply-line across the Black Sea. The day to which they look forward, in which they could prevent our sending our troops to Kurachee by the Suez Canal, in a war in which France was not with them, and by their advances in Asia could prevent our making the Euphrates road, lies further in the future.

We have now to consider the direct bearing upon English policy of the subjects which have come before us in this chapter. England is free from engagements; for that to Turkey, as regards the Armenian frontier, is conditional, and the condition has never been fulfilled. We are free to select our alliances as we please. But we are so little prepared for war that no Power thinks our alliance worth having for a short war, and it is the first days of a war that count at the present time. Making a virtue of necessity, there are many in England who begin no longer to regard Constantinople as a British interest of the first magnitude, although they still talk of joining Austria for the purpose of defending the independence of the Balkan States. The Turk's disappearance, they say, should be as gradual as possible, in order to give time to the Christian States to consolidate their interests and form a confederacy. Bulgaria would have gone to Russia of herself, they think, as Servia has gone a long way towards Austria, if the Russians had not foolishly alienated, by their autocratic fashions, the affections of the Bulgarian people; but as they have done so we should take advantage of the sentiment, and while we should allow Russia to work her will upon Asiatic Turkey, we should protect the young States of the Balkans.

Russia could reach Constantinople through Asia, not so directly, but more surely and more safely than through Europe. There is this additional danger to England in her going by way of Asia, that she does not interfere with Austria, and that, on the other hand, she does interfere with the Canal route through Egypt. If Russia were once to establish herself in Palestine she could easily reach the Suez Canal by land, and although the distances are great, if we look to what has been accomplished by Russia in the Caucasus, towards Persia, in Central Asia, and towards China, in the last hundred years, we shall not feel that in the days of telegraphy and railroads such an advance is in the least impossible. By whatever route the Russians go, there are certain obvious drawbacks to this country attendant upon their possession of Constantinople. The military value of the Suez Canal, as I have shown before, may easily be exaggerated, and so may the importance, therefore, to us of our power of passage in time of general war through the Mediterranean. But there is one loss by a Russian occupation of the remainder of the Turkish dominions which no British Government would willingly face. It is the loss of trade. In the Asiatic provinces acquired by Russia at the end of the last Turkish war, where there used to be a considerable British trade, there is now none, for it has been killed by protective duties. Russia at Constantinople would mean our exclusion from the Black Sea trade, except the wheat trade out of Russia. Our commercial interests in

M

Asia Minor are very large, and they are placed in jeopardy by a further Russian advance.

There are many who declare that they would be willing to bring about an Anglo-Russian alliance upon the terms of giving Russia her head in the direction of Constantinople, on the understanding that our north-western Indian frontier should be secured and our temporary hold on Egypt regularised and made permanent. It is pointed out that the Emperor can have no great love for an alliance with French Republicans and ex-friends of Poland against his great-uncle and the military monarchies of Central Europe; and that what this new policy on our part would mean would be the adoption by us, under stress of circumstances, of the Russian policy advocated by the Emperor Nicholas to Sir Hamilton Seymour. In the present state of parties in England, where the pure Conservatives are unable to obtain a clear majority, and where the Liberals are supposed to have more or less pro-Russian sympathies, the opinions of Lord Randolph Churchill become of special interest, and, except as regards Egypt, he is supposed to incline in the direction which has just been indicated. He used to hold that Lord Beaconsfield's policy of 1878 was a mischievous and foolish policy. He was opposed at the time of the Berlin Treaty to any attempt to reconstruct the Turkish Empire. He always ridiculed the predominance on the Conservative side of the doctrine of the integrity and independence of the Turkish Empire; and, in short, he thought that in the days of Jingoism the English Conservative party had gone mad. There can be no doubt that the old-fashioned ideas

of English policy in the East are at a discount; and although
I do not myself agree in the novel views which have lately
been put forward with regard to the. possession by Russia of
Constantinople, it is impossible to deny that they have been
stated with much ability and by journals of great influence,
and that they have weight with an increasing section of
the public. Moreover, the English electors have a natural
and a growing dislike to war.

On the other hand, I am inclined to think that a
policy which would risk the loss of a trade which is almost
exclusively English, namely, the foreign trade of Asia
Minor, is not likely to be popular in the manufacturing
centres of the north of England. There are other points
which should be considered. If the Black Sea can be
forced by our fleet, or entered through the permission of
Turkey acting as our ally, the Russians in any future
war with England will have to keep in the Caucasus a
vast force which would otherwise be available for service
in Afghanistan and Persia. This would be the case even
though I should be right in my belief that we could not
succeed in harming Russia in the Caucasus; she certainly
must and would guard against the danger. The possession
by Russia of a magnificent military and naval base within
the Dardanelles would destroy our present power of using
the Suez Canal, even in a war with Russia in which France
was neutral, and would also make of the pick of the maritime
Greeks, who are now our friends, her servants. Russia once
at Constantinople, our future hold on India must be by the
Cape route alone, and it is a long way round by the Cape to

the points where we shall have to fight for India—the Helmund and the Persian Gulf.

The causes of difficulty between this country and Russia are worth examination, and those which have nothing to do with the continued existence of the Turkish Empire or with the possession of Constantinople are very numerous. One standing difficulty between Russia and all Liberal countries concerns the extradition of political offenders. The question has been very useful to Prince Bismarck in the past, because he has always tried to give full satisfaction to the Russian feelings upon this point, a satisfaction which never could be fully given by any other country. For many years this question prevented all chance of a Russo-French alliance, and maintained a close friendship between Germany and Russia. As regards ourselves, our laws have always been an enigma to Russian emperors since the days of Matveief's creditors and Whitworth's special embassy. After 1848 the whole of the European Powers united in making representations to us with regard to the proceedings of the foreign refugees, and from 1851 up to Mazzini's death, repeated representations, often menacing, were addressed to us with regard to supposed incitements to assassination. The fall of Palmerston on the Conspiracy to Murder Bill was not encouraging to future ministers in regard to interfering with the right of asylum, and no more was the verdict of "not guilty" returned by the jury in the case of Dr. Bernard and the Orsini attempt to assassinate the Emperor of the French. The Russian Government in the last few years has made repeated applications to the Governments of France and England for protection against conspirators who made Paris or London their residence, but the English Government has turned a deaf ear to the requests made for legislation.

A subject which has done more to separate the countries than the refusal to modify our law upon the subject of the extradition of political offenders has been the recent Russian action with regard to Batoum, and the confirmation given by that action to the English belief that Russia will never be bound by promises, however solemn. Those who pretend that Russia's declaration with regard to Batoum was really a spontaneous act can never have read the protocols of the Berlin Congress. The latter portion of Lord Beaconsfield's speech upon p. 208 of the English Blue Book, and the speeches upon the same and next page of the representatives of Germany, Austria-Hungary, France, Italy, and Turkey, show that the whole of Europe took the view that Russia had promised, rather than break up the Congress, to maintain Batoum as what Lord Beaconsfield called " a commercial port for all nations " by " the transformation. . . . of a disputed fortress into a free port." It is really idle for any friends of Russia to argue that a formal engagement has not been broken, indeed it is almost an insult to our intelligence that they should do so, and in the interest of Russia herself it would be wiser for them to admit that Russia has violated a binding declaration, only the more binding in honour because it professed to be voluntary in its nature.

Similar bad faith has been shown from time to time

by the Russians in Central Asia, and has exasperated English feeling. The first of the marked instances of the disregard by Russia of her own assurances to us concerned, oddly enough, the occupation of Herat by Persia, an occupation which forty years later an English Conservative Government themselves proposed. The deceitful conduct of Count Simonich was imitated in the disregard of Prince Gortscha-koff's assurances to Lord Clarendon in 1869 as to the evacuation of Samarcand, in the violation of the promises made to Lord Granville as to the Khivan expedition, in the disregard of the memorandum communicated to Lord Derby in 1875 as to advance beyond the then frontier of the Attrek, and in the disregard of the repeated assurances with regard to Merv.

The story of the successive steps by which Persia has been made to quit the Turcoman desert and has come more and more under Russian influence will never be fully known, but we have learned at least one fact, that it is not prudent for England to enter upon a game of secret treaties. In 1878 the proposals made to Persia to occupy Herat were at once made known to Russia, whereas the secret articles by which the territory down to Sarakhs was ceded by Persia to Russia were never made known to us. The fact is that Persia does not believe that we both can and will support her against Russia, and Turkey has now only become another Persia in this respect. Afghanistan, which was going the same way, has been secured by a direct guarantee of her frontiers, a fact which is not encouraging to those politicians who object to entanglements of the kind.

Another cause of difference between Russia and Great Britain lies in the unsettled condition of the Afghan frontier question, which has for a long time made little progress. The boundary between the Heri-Rud and the Oxus has not yet been settled, and that on the Upper Oxus is altogether in dispute, while Russia is giving trouble to the Ameer by intrigue at Balkh and throughout Badakshan. The feeling in Russia against England is strong, but not of extreme strength. It is nothing like so strong as the popular feeling in Russia against the Germans. It is not so strong as the permanent aversion entertained in France towards the English. Still as regards the armies and the upper classes of both countries, there can be no doubt about the mutual feeling. The national badge of Russia and of England is the George and Dragon, for St. George is a national saint of both the countries, but in Russia for the last fifty years the dragon has meant England, and in England for the last fifty years the dragon has meant Russia.

As regards the military situation between the countries, its dangers are both exaggerated and imperfectly appreciated here. The very same people will often be found to think that we could easily, if we would, act upon the terms of the Anglo-Turkish Convention and keep the Russians out of Turkish Asia Minor, that we could defend Constantinople, harry the Russians in the Baltic and the Black Sea and the White Sea, and yet that Russia could invade India without much difficulty. It may be confidently asserted that they are wrong upon both these heads.

England unassisted cannot keep Russia out of Turkey, she cannot get at her in Europe, but on the other hand she may feel assured that Russia is unable to effectively attack her in her Asiatic empire at the present time. It must be admitted that in the race for Herat Russia has undoubtedly beaten us, and that therefore we must contemplate the possibility of the ultimate occupation of Herat by Russia. But as she came on towards India from Herat the tables would be turned. She would be further and further away from the country where her government was established or where the people were friendly to her rule, and she would plunge into defiles inhabited by hostile populations.

It is a serious responsibility for a writer who is not a soldier to undertake to pronounce a confident opinion of this kind, for it is a point upon which the ablest and best-instructed soldiers differ. English officers as a rule maintain the possibility of a formidable Russian invasion of India, and on the other hand Russian officers as a rule deny that it is practically possible; but it must be confessed that, whilst military writers generally take a pessimistic view of the prospects of their own country, the indications afforded by the writings of officers belonging to neither of the two countries make against my personal view as set forth above. Foreign military writers, as a rule, do not so highly estimate the difficulties of a Russian advance upon India as do the Russians themselves. They maintain that forces advancing from the Oxus and from the Caucasus would meet at Sarakhs, and would easily occupy

Herat, and then bring the railway almost to Herat, before the English could have put 40,000 men at Quetta. Another Russian army would take the more difficult line of advance southward from Siberia through Balkh. They calculate that England, did she give up all idea of fighting in Europe and on the Pacific, and did she confine her attention to the advance on India, would only be able to place another 40,000 men in the field at the end of three months from the declaration of war. These would be troops sent from England, and the calculations of foreign writers may be affected by the promised reform in our arrangements for the prompt mobilisation of two army corps.

The continental writers assume that by the use of Goorkhas and other special native troops the native army could be kept quiet, that is kept from turning against us in the field, and even used for keeping up communications, but that its quality is not good enough to allow of its being used against Russian troops. They assume that the English position in India being perfectly known to the Russians, while the Russian position in Central Asia is not well known to the English, the Russians might be able by the use of money to produce some troubles which might lead to railway and other difficulties upon the lines of communication. It is assumed also that the English concentration would take place on the Helmund or at Kandahar, and that the Russians could advance, without serious molestation either from the English or the Afghans, up to near that point. The Russian numbers in the Caucasus being practically without limit, it is assumed that by the use

of the steam tramway* which they are rapidly making towards
their frontier over a very easy country the Russians could
place any conceivable number of men upon the Upper Mur-

* The following letter, founded upon this passage, appeared in the Fortnightly Review for 1st April:—

SIR,—Allow me to correct a statement made in the March number of the
Fortnightly Review in Part III. of the series of papers entitled, "The
Present Position of European Politics." The author, whilst speaking of
the Russian means of communication with Central Asia, calls the Transcaspian Railway a *steam tramway*, an expression which I cannot pass over in
silence for the two following reasons. (1) I published in the preceding
number of the same periodical a paper entitled, "The Transcaspian Railway," in which I tried to give a detailed account of the construction and of
the importance of this new iron link of connection between Russia and her
Central Asian possessions ; a road which deserves by no means the trifling
appellation of a *steam tramway*, being as it is a solidly well-built line of
three hundred and thirty-five versts in length, and having cost 40,050,000
roubles. (2) Without any right to inquire into the authorship of the said
series of papers which have excited so much attention throughout Europe,
there are many reasons for the supposition that the man who penned them
must have been or is intimately connected with State affairs, or at least
with State papers, which are not accessible to everybody. The author was,
or is therefore, a man of important position, and such a man cannot be
allowed to mislead public opinion by slighting a formidable arm in the
hands of your rival. The mistake evidently has arisen from the fact that
the first portion of the Transcaspian Railway, planned for the transport of
ammunition and provisions to the Russian army operating before Geok-
Tepe, was in reality a narrow-gauge railway built for temporary use
during 1880—81, and the calming words used in Parliament in 1882 by
the then Under-Secretary for Foreign Affairs were, as the present shows,
not quite justified. But since that time things have greatly changed.
The provisional line from Mikhailowsk to Kizil-Arvat has had to be totally
reconstructed, and, far from being a steam tramway, it is now a well-built
railway fully able to answer all expectations of Russia in a future war
against England.

Yours faithfully,
A. VAMBÉRY.

Professor Vambéry is wrong. I do not call "the Transcaspian Railway
a steam tramway." At page 150 I speak of "the Transcaspian Railway
now being rapidly constructed by General Annenkoff." Here I speak of
"the steam tramway which they are rapidly making towards their frontier
over a very easy country," and of "the Upper Murghab." The earlier
reference is to the line now being made from Chaharjui to Bokhara and

ghab,* where they would be faced by an English force of 80,000 men with 200 guns at Kandahar. Assuming that we were at war with Russia only, the troops would come through the Mediterranean, but if we were at war as one of a coalition with a coalition in which either France or Italy was against us, this route could not be used, and they must come round the Cape. If we were trying to hold Egypt against France the whole of these calculations fall to the ground, inasmuch as the force which could otherwise be sent from England to India would have to be kept in the Mediterranean or in Egypt. The foreign observers assume that the native army is not sufficiently trustworthy to allow those few regiments which are capable of fighting against Russians to be sent out of India, but that if the Goorkhas and the best of the Punjaub cavalry were to be sent to Kandahar the number of the army there must be diminished by an equal number of British troops left in India to take care of the communications and of the ordinary Sepoys. The Russian army advancing from Balkh, which would bring with it light guns only, would occupy Cashmere and threaten the Punjaub sufficiently to require an increase in the Punjaub frontier force and in the garrison of Peshawur, but the main struggle would take

Samarcand, which runs not towards "their frontier," or towards the "Upper Murghab," but away from both. The later reference is to the steam tramway which is being constructed towards the south-east from Askabad. This is at present a narrow-gauge, light, cheap line.

* The willingness of the Russians to spend money freely upon their Central Asian railroads is remarkable, as we may see from their laying down hundreds of miles of piping to bring water from the mountains for the engines which work them.

place in the neighbourhood of Kandahar. Foreign writers think that Russia, having in the eyes of the Indian people the advantage of the advance and of the attack against a Power remaining on the defensive only, would have the sympathies of the Oriental population on her side. They assume that the Turcoman cavalry, which are excellent, and which, while animated by strong Mahommedan feelings, are now enthusiastically Russian, would mask the Russian advance with a force which would conciliate the native population. They believe that the Russian organisation in Central Asia has been a marvellous success, and that the native princes of India think that the Russians would respect the usages of the people more thoroughly than we do. They assert that the late Maharajah of Cashmere was, as might be expected, in Russian pay, a fact confirmed by my own knowledge of recent Russian intrigue with deposed and exiled princes from the Punjaub.*

The whole of these views, though they are held by many foreign writers, appear to me exaggerated. I believe in the superior popularity of England among the native princes to any which may be thought to be enjoyed by Russia. I doubt whether the Russians have more than a few hundred Turcoman cavalry ready for a long march; but, above all, I think that Russia would have, for some years to come, far more difficulty in finding the enormous train which would be necessary for marching 100,000 men across from Herat to Kandahar than we should find in supplying an army of 80,000 men at Kandahar, which

* One of these intrigues has lately become public property.

would be sufficient to hold in check the advance of 100,000
Russians from the Caucasus and 20,000 from Turkestan.
The difficulties of obtaining camels and mules enough to
move large armies in such deserts are largely, no doubt,
money difficulties, but they are partly difficulties which
even money will not meet, unless the money is spent for
many years in advance in the formation of a permanent
train upon an enormous scale.

Real danger to India can only come after some revolution in Herat, or a dexterous use of Ayoub Khan, has
brought Russia there as peacemaker, after years of Russian
possession of the Herat valley have restored it to its former
fertility under irrigation, and Herat has been made a
secure base for an advance, connected by railway both
with the Caspian and with Turkestan. Herat will doubt-
less be taken one day by a sudden rush, for though
something in the way of fortification has been done
there of late, it is not properly protected by a sufficient number of detached forts, and cannot stand. But
the end will not be yet. The present ruler of Afghanistan,
in spite of his long residence in Russia, never was pro-
Russian, and may be trusted in the event of a Russian invasion. He, if still on the throne, would ask us to supply
his army with the newest arms, and would place a large
force in line with us at Giriskh or Kandahar, as well as do
something to defend Herat. He is a powerful and able
king. But he has an internal disease; his end may be
hastened by poison, and in any case he is not likely to live
long. Herat lies out of the Afghan country, and is an
Afghan post, a little in the air, which, with a "mobilisa-

tion" on foot, which takes six months to accomplish, the Afghan cannot efficiently defend. Our troops would reach Giriskh from England before the Ameer would reach Herat from Kandahar or from Cabul.

I shall, however, consider in the last chapter whether it has not become necessary for England to adopt a more modern military organisation, which, without imposing upon her heavier monetary sacrifices, would enable her better to perform her obligations—such as that defence of the Afghan frontier to which she is now resolutely bound. In the great efforts which England would put forth in the event of war with Russia, an attack upon Vladivostock could only be a matter of time. Even if we had to pour the whole of our available forces into India to be sent up to Kandahar, the embodied militia and the new forces raised in England would within a few months give us troops for an expedition of the kind. Those foreign observers who doubt the possibility of our holding our own upon the Afghan frontier admitted the significance of our occupation of Port Hamilton, and have been amazed at its abandonment. The Russians, creeping down the coast after the annexation of the district round Vladivostock, and of the island of Saghalien and the archipelago between Saghalien and Kamschatka, were casting eyes towards the Corea. Port Hamilton was wisely occupied as a base from which, with or without a Chinese alliance, Russia could be attacked on the Pacific. No doubt the occupation of windy and desolate stations is a nuisance to the navy in a time of peace; but to let Port Hamilton go, upon any promises,

unless with the clearest possible treaty understanding
that it would at once be strongly fortified by China, and
that China would continue to be friendly to ourselves,
was, in face of the difficulty of successfully attacking
Russia in other portions of the globe, simple madness. It
is vital to us that we should have a coaling station and a
base of operations within reach of Vladivostock and the
Amoor at the beginning of a war, as a guard-house for the
protection of our China trade and for the prevention of a
sudden descent upon our colonies; ultimately as the head
station for our Canadian Pacific railroad trade; and at all
times, and especially in the later stages of the war, as an
offensive station for our main attack on Russia. But it
must be, of course, a defended station, and not one to which
our fleet would be tied for the purpose of its defence.*

It is possible that Japan might be tempted, by the offer
of Saghalien, which we could easily detach from Russia, to
join us in the war, and her alliance would be useful. But
that of China would be essential, and whether she required
to be guaranteed in the possession of our conquests in the
Pacific and on the Amoor, or whether she asked for Upper
Burmah, her alliance ought at all hazards to be secured.
China and England have identical interests in Asia, and
they are menaced by Russia in an equal degree. They
trade together to an extraordinary extent, and are more
closely allied by trade than are any other two countries in
the world. Surely these considerations point to a permanent

* Sir William Dowell, referring to Sir Cooper Key's opinion in favour
of the occupation, says that if it were "made a first class fortress, I should
certainly advocate its retention."

alliance between the countries. England could have no objection to the increase of German influence in China; but the test of the success of English influence at Pekin will be found from time to time in the choice of Sir Robert Hart's successors.

The conclusion, then, to which we come is, that such is the patriotism of the Russian people, such the certainty that in the event of war Nihilism would disappear, and every Russian support the policy of his Tsar, such the defensive strength of Russia in Europe, such her offensive power from the Caucasus towards India, that not only is war with Russia to be deprecated as a terrible calamity, but that it would strain the powers of the British Empire to the utmost. At the same time I hold, as will have been seen, that even in a single-handed struggle we should ultimately win; that we should be able, although only by a tremendous effort, to hold our own in the neighbourhood of Kandahar, to prevent insurrection in India, and to check invasion; that we could not unassisted save Turkey, if Turkey were menaced in the war; that as against other Powers we could not hold Egypt or save the Mediterranean route; but that, holding India and the Mauritius and the Cape, we could carry the war into the enemy's country on the Pacific and destroy, at all events at any time during the life of those now living, Russia's power on the Pacific, and, indeed, probably tear away the Pacific provinces from her empire.

With all respect to Lord Randolph Churchill, this hardly seems the time for reducing the defensive power of the Empire. It was with Lord George Hamilton that at Christmas last he had his sharpest struggle. Now Lord George Hamilton was unduly optimistic in his recent speeches. The defences of the empire have for some time past been played with a little by the two great parties in the State. Taking the navy for example, when the Liberals are in, the Tories declare that the fleet is non-existent, but the moment their turn comes the Tory First Lord informs us that the British navy is equal to any three navies in the world. So too with the occupation of Port Hamilton and the fortification of our coaling stations generally. But the navy is not the only part of our warlike services which even Liberals should have in view. We may dislike the fact as much as we choose, but we are not now an island Power. By the, in my opinion, unfortunate prolongation of our Egyptian occupation we have increased our military responsibilities, and without that occupation they were none too light. Even disregarding the Anglo-Turkish Convention, as it is generally admitted we must, our responsibilities are still very great.

The defence of India we cannot disregard ; and the defence of India of itself will, as I have shown, in the opinion of foreign observers, prove too much for us ; and in the opinion of qualified English military judges at all events tax our powers to the utmost. There is cause for anxiety in the still unsettled condition of the Central Asian frontier question, on which Parliament has been kept in the dark since the appearance of "Central Asia, No. 5 of 1885." No. 6 was laid on the table and was ordered to be printed, but it was, I believe, afterwards withdrawn, and Parliamentary curiosity seems to have been confined to quarters nearer home. The Russians are at this moment strongly entrenched at Zulfikar * and at Akrobat, and the boundary is still unsettled. War, however, not between England and Russia only, but war generally is it may be hoped likely to be avoided. No sufficient cause has been shown for the coming upon Europe of so terrible a calamity; but war will not be made less likely by our weakly yielding to the other Powers upon such questions as that of the violation of engagements to us in the case of the New Hebrides; and the interests of the empire will not be best promoted by attempting to save sixpences upon the artillery or upon the navy. With regard to the army, we should be led too far if we attempted at this point to discuss the principle which ought to preside over its reorganisation. This may be left by me for treatment in the last chapter, that on the position of England. It is enough for the present to say that the reduction in the British horse artillery is not only the death-knell of British intervention for the preservation of Belgian neutrality, but constitutes in itself an increase of the standing temptation to Russia to attack us in Hindostan. Horse artillery is the most difficult of all arms to improvise under pressure.

* In the middle of April a Reuter's telegram announced in England that the Russians were advancing to Zulfikar, but they have been there for a long time, and in the month of March the commandant at Zulfikar was received in audience by the Emperor at St. Petersburg.

IV.

AUSTRIA-HUNGARY.

———

THE appearance of this chapter * is synchronous with the expiration of that compromise between Austria and Hungary as to customs duties, which lies at the root of the financial position of the Dual Monarchy. The resignation of the Hungarian Finance Minister and the fresh arrangements between the Cis-Leithan Empire and the Trans-Leithan Kingdom upon the basis proposed by the Hungarian Prime Minister form not only a victory of M. Tisza over Count Szapáry, but a gain of power to the former, which makes him master for the time being in the Empire. He holds, or virtually holds, for the moment as many great ministerial offices as the Duke of Wellington held at the time when "H. B." represented a meeting of the Cabinet at which all the ministers had the well-known nose. The Hungarian Cabinet appears to the world to consist of M. Tisza only, who when he came to power some twelve or thirteen years ago was expected immediately to fall, but who seems only to have become more powerful day by day. Both halves of the Empire have now adopted the measures of defence which the

* *Fortnightly Review*, 1st April, 1887.

Austro-Hungarian Government considered necessary. The fortifications of Cracow, upon which vast numbers of civilian workmen were employed in February and March, arc now complete. The Landwehr and the Honveds have been armed, and coats have been purchased for the Landsturm. The war preparations which have been made are such as ought to have been made some years ago, such as it was most dangerous to have been without, and the absence of which in the past was caused solely by the difficulties of the financial situation. Even under the terror inspired by the recent concentration of Russian cavalry upon the frontier of Galicia—a concentration officially denied in Austria, but well known to the Austrian Government to exist—the votes granted have been less in proportion than the votes secured by the Roumanian Government from the Chamber of Deputies in that country. Yet no one can suppose that the danger which menaces Austria is less than that which overshadows Roumania, for the Polish Jews, who according to Prince Bismarck were created by Heaven for the express and sole purpose of serving as spies on Russia, have done their work too accurately.

If we wish to obtain an authoritative view of the situation in Austria-Hungary, it is not so easy, as it is in the case of some other countries, to know whom to consult or where to turn. Strong as may be the Austrian and Hungarian statesmen who are in power; strong in the possession of parliamentary popularity and parliamentary majorities as may be the Hungarian President of Council; the Austrian President of Council, Count Taaffe; the Common Minister of Finance, M. Kállay; or the Common Minister for Foreign Affairs,

Count Kálnoky; they are all of them compelled by the difficulties of the situation of the Dual Monarchy to use temporising language, and to avoid anything like frankness of speech or expression of real intention. On the other hand, although Buda-Pest has at least one very powerful journal in the *Pester Lloyd*, and although Vienna is of all the capitals of Europe essentially the newspaper capital, yet there is a very marked difference of tone between the newspapers of the Austrian and those of the Hungarian capital. In the absence of guidance it is by no means certain to which we ought to look as indicating the probable lines of the future policy of the Empire as a whole. The *Fremdenblatt, Neue Freie Presse*, and many others that could be named of almost equal power, have, like the *Pester Lloyd*, an European fame ; but then, unfortunately, the great Hungarian journal and those well-known Vienna sheets contradict one another, not so much in words as in the general tone of their writing. Looking to the fact that some of the journals which write above all of the necessity to Austria of peace, and some of those which call at times for instant war with Russia, should she place a single soldier in Bulgaria, are equally supposed to enjoy official inspiration, it is useless to try to gather the policy of the Austrian Empire from the journals of the two capitals. One paper, indeed, there is in Vienna, the *Politische-Correspondenz*—if I may be permitted to speak of that most secret-revealing of all European sheets as a newspaper, as it is in fact in the highest possible degree, though hardly, perhaps, in form—which tells us much, and is always well worth reading, but tells us more of facts than of tendencies.

The difficulty is very largely explained when we remember that Austria and Hungary do not in reality agree, and that neither of them very clearly sees her way. Hungary, partly from old traditions, partly from the memories of '48-9, partly from her exposed situation in the middle of an enormous mass of Slavs, is bitterly anti-Russian, and therefore warlike. Austria is anti-Russian too, but with a distinct peace note, and with a certain desire to patch up matters of dispute, and to make ties of friendship, if they will not last for ever, at all events last some time. There is always a doubt which of the two policies is to prevail. Parliamentary control grows stronger in the Dual Monarchy year by year; yet this does but increase its difficulties. The Magyars are a military people, and proud of their king and of his army. The Croats of the Banat share these views, but detest their Magyar exponents, and the Diet of Agram is a thorn in the side of Hungary. The Tsechs of Bohemia and the Poles of Galicia also support the army and the Austrian Emperor, although with a desire to see the Emperor crowned king of the kingdoms of Bohemia and Galicia respectively, and a tripartite or a quadrilateral form given to the Dual Monarchy. But these feelings of loyalty to the sovereign and of glory in the army, which have hitherto held Austria-Hungary together, are greatly weakened by constitutional control; for even as matters stand Ministers are pulled both ways by combinations of minorities, forming what we may call scratch majorities without a common guiding principle. They are driven to attempt to meet their difficulties, like the Federalist Prime Minister of Austria, Count Taaffe, whose Irish extraction is perhaps too remote to account for his Home Rule views, by further concessions to nationalities and further divisions of Parliaments, and in any case the increase of parliamentary activity and power will tend to increase the existing division between Hungary and Austria. Count Kálnoky's concessions in the Hungarian Delegation, which have increased the constitutional element in the practical working of the Hungarian Constitution, are not, therefore, viewed with unmixed satisfaction even by the Constitutionalists of Austria.

The necessities of the situation which lie upon the surface are those which have been indicated in the first and third chapters. Austria-Hungary needs quiet; first and above all because of the state of her finances, and in the next place because, as has been seen in the last chapter, she is not in a military sense equal to the strain of war with Russia. But unfortunately for her she is in a domestic situation which further enforces the necessity of peace. The mixture in the Austrian Empire of the Slav and German races, and in the Hungarian Kingdom of the Slavs, the Magyars, and the Roumans; the strong Catholicism of a great part of old Austria and Croatia and Bohemia; the strong Protestantism of a large section of the Magyars—all these are securities against downright rapacity on the part of the two most powerful neighbours of Austria-Hungary. But on the other hand they enormously increase the difficulties of government. Germany cannot wish to tear from Austria the Archduchy of Austria or the Duchy of Styria, or Carinthia, or Salzburg, or North Tyrol, where there are altogether between four and five millions of Germans, on account of the violent Slav feeling in the Margraviate of Moravia and in the Kingdom of Bohemia, which separate German Austria from Germany. Prince Bismarck perfectly knows that the Slavism of the Tsechs would become Russianism if they were annexed to Germany, and he can hardly desire to increase his religious difficulties by annexing Cátholics so strong as the Catholics of German Austria and of the intervening strip, or his other difficulties by annexing the Socialists of the suburbs of Vienna.

Russia, too, which might easily swallow the Ruthenians of Eastern Galicia and of part of Bukowina, and possibly, although with more difficulty, the Catholic Polish Slavs and the Jews of Western Galicia, certainly could not digest the Magyars of the Hungarian plain, nor even the Roumans and the "Saxons" of the ex-Principality of Transylvania. Just as Germany cannot step across Bohemia and Moravia and a corner of Silesia, where there are seven millions of Slavs, to get to Central Austria, so the Russians cannot swallow up the Magyars and the Roumans to get to the Croats of the Banat and the Slovenes of the Kingdom of Dalmatia. When nationalities are considered from the annexing point of view, that excellent Berlin professor, unrivalled for his combination of map-making and ethnography — Dr. Kiepert — becomes a sort of saviour of the Austro-Hungarian Empire. But there is the reverse of the medal, and that mixture of races and religions, which in one sense secures the continued existence of a something which shall be called Austria, makes that Austria full of discordant elements, which have different sets of powerful friends outside her territory to whom they turn for advice and with whom they continually intrigue. The result is that Austria-Hungary is, of all the countries in the world, by far the most difficult to govern, and that as a necessity of her condition she must before all things long for peace. The German and Italian alliance was for Austria not a matter of choice but of absolute necessity, and however little direct advantage she may appear to gain from it, it may be confidently asserted that that alliance will continue. The more doubtful point is, given the fact that Germany, menaced on the one flank by Russia and on the other by France, is now only strong enough to hold her own, how far Austria will go in the direction of concession to Russia rather than draw the sword.

A few months ago some sanguine and belligerent Englishmen were disposed to think that the prospect of an English alliance, even standing by itself, was likely to put an end to the hesitation and the doubts of Austria. Now, an Italian alliance may be of great value to Austria, as I shall attempt to show in the next chapter. An English alliance, for those military reasons which I shall have to discuss in my concluding chapter, and which are perfectly known to Austrian statesmen, would, I fear, be regarded by them as of less instant value than an alliance with Roumania. The power of England at sea is absolutely useless in an Austrian alliance to save Austria from the immediate consequences of war. The power of England upon land, during the two months which probably would be sufficient for the Russian advance, may be looked upon as non-existent;

whereas the Roumanians can place 150,000 men in line, who are admirably officered and trained, and have the solidity of German troops.

The view which I have taken of the military power of Russia is looked upon as exaggerated. The subject is worth inquiry, as the chances are that we shall find ourselves at war with Russia one of these days; and the comparison of Austrian and Russian military forces is also of much interest, inasmuch as war between these two Great Powers is not likely to be long avoided. It is also personally important to ourselves, inasmuch as, if we have to look forward to the possibility of having to fight Russia, it would obviously be better to fight her with allies, that is with Austria, than to fight her alone. I fear that time will show that those who believe that Austria can hold her own against Russia are as wrong as are, I believe, those who hold, upon the other hand, that Russia is invulnerable by Great Britain in a single-handed war. Various military writers compute the real military power of the various countries of Europe in very different ways; and it is not easy to arrive at a common standard. When, for example, we discuss the military power of Italy we have to some extent to deal with the unknown. Italy pretends to have a number of " instructed men " far more than double that of Austria, and exceeding by 100,000 the number possessed by Germany; but this may be looked upon as a statistical romance; and we are obliged to consider in detail the speeches of General Ricotti, who is at least a competent authority upon military figures, and who well knows the real strength of that army which many years ago

he himself did much to create. He talks about the possibility
of mobilising twelve corps, and of putting in all 500,000 men
under arms, which is a very different thing from 2,862,000.
But in the case of Italy also there is another difficulty, which
is that the fighting power of the Italian army is in dispute.
I myself believe in the gallantry of her soldiers, which has
indeed been proved in their recent conflict with the Abys-
sinians; but there is more doubt about their heads. The
Italian officers are said by some high military authorities to
be wanting in steadiness, and to be the sort of men who
when beaten will always take their beating bravely, but
who are not likely to win their battles. This remains to be
seen.

On the other hand, in dealing with Russia, Germany, and
Austria, if I count the quality of the troops as equal on all
three sides, I shall be giving a little weight in the scale
against my own opinion. No skilled military observer
ventures now to assert that the army of the Dual Monarchy
is superior to that of Russia, man for man. Some think that
Russia is very short of officers, but they remember Inkermann,
and neglect too much what has been accomplished by Russia
since 1878. The Austrians do not now possess the advantage of having great generals who command the confidence
of officers and men. If we put aside quality, which in this
case may not unfairly be taken as being pretty equal, there
are tests of strength which are of value. We know the
expenditure upon the armies, and are certain, for example,
that Austria-Hungary spends a little more than Italy, and
rather less than two-thirds of what is spent by Germany,

upon the army. We know that she possesses a "Budget-peace-effective" rather greater than that of Italy, and rather less than two-thirds of that of Germany—that is in the same proportion as the expenditure. Austria-Hungary has rather more field-guns than Italy, and rather less than two-thirds of the field-guns of Germany, which is again in the same proportion. These tests are pretty sound ones so far as they go, and by all these tests Russia seems equal in military strength to Austria and Germany combined. As regards expenditure I cannot prove my case. Austria and Germany together spend rather over thirty millions sterling upon their armies. Russia, at the present rate of the rouble, appears to spend less upon her land forces; but as I pointed out in the Russian chapter, the charge of the War Ministry in Russia is very far from including the total army expenditure. If we look to the "Budget-peace-effectives," excluding constabulary and customs guards, but adding one-year volunteers, Russia has "850,000," or, as I think, 890,000, against 749,000 for Germany and Austria ; and while Russia in field-guns is slightly inferior to Germany and Austria together, she is superior to them in cavalry. I must maintain, therefore, the accuracy of my statement previously made and hotly contested, that Russia is as strong in numbers as Germany and Austria, and between two and three times as strong as Austria alone. No doubt her troops are scattered over an enormous territory, but it is chiefly a territory that needs no guarding, and she could put half her force in Austria and yet have plenty of men to garrison Poland and the Caucasus.

The Austrians, in spite of the rapidity with which they

have been spending money during the last few months, have
not yet taken all those precautions which they should have
taken considering that they share a very long common
frontier, which is purely arbitrary, with a tremendous military Power. Cracow and Przemysl are not even now fortresses
by which an army of inferior strength would be enabled to
defend Galicia against a stronger power. As a great foreign
military writer, Marga, has consolingly observed of Austria-
Hungary, in that which is the first of all the military works
of the day, "After several defeats she can retire into the
wooded Carpathians;" but, he adds, " the road to Vienna is
thus uncovered." Neither can Germany be trusted to defend
Vienna by menacing the long line of the Russian advance,
because when Germany ceases to be neutral the neutrality of
France in turn will cease, and Germany will have enough to
do to defend the Rhine. Italy, and Italy alone, can protect
Vienna, supposing that the Roumanians confine themselves
to defending their own neutrality, and Italy will have to be
paid for doing it. Paid, too, in coin more valuable than a
mere promise of help against the Pope and the Pope's friends,
in whose desire to regain the temporal power the Italians
now no longer believe. It is almost incredible that Austria,
whatever her financial difficulties, should not have fortified
herself in Galicia, with its seven hundred and twenty miles
of winding, artificial frontier towards Russia; unless indeed
she had made up her mind that she must lose Eastern or
Ruthenian Galicia whenever she goes to war, and that the
Northern Carpathians form the true frontier of her eastern
provinces.

So far from having under-rated the military strength of Austro-Hungary, I myself have been inclined to think that I have not set it low enough. There may be elements in the Austro-Hungarian ranks which may not fight heartily against Russia, as for example the Red Russians and Little Russians of Northern Bukowina and Eastern Galicia. There can be no doubt as to the unpopularity of both Austrians and Hungarians in Croatia and the Dalmatian Kingdom. Some observers think that the Croats, who are among the best of the Austro-Hungarian troops, would not, although Roman Catholic in religion, fight for Hungary against Russia unless a real federalism were promised them, and unless the King of Hungary were crowned at Agram. The Bohemian news-papers were some of them alarmingly pro-Russian not very long ago; but I believe the Tsechs may be counted on to fight for Austria, although, or perhaps because, Bohemia is an Ireland under limited Home Rule (and with a German Ulster). Count Taaffe has given extended suffrage, increased power to the clergy, the official use of the Tsech tongue, and a Tsech university, yet the Tsechs ask for more. One of the best executed of foreign works on European armies, that of Colonel Rau, points out that Austria-Hungary and England are, as compared with Russia or Germany, suffering from paralysis in military matters caused by a divided rule:—England through the division of responsibility between the Secretary of State and the General Commanding-in-Chief, and the Dual Monarchy (in a less degree, because it is a division which does not extend, as Colonel Rau shows, to the affairs of the "active army")

by the division of the control of the Landwehr and the
Honved militia between Austria and Hungary. There is a
joint War Minister, but there are also separate Austrian and
Hungarian Ministers of Defence.

The Emperor of Austria, who has given a great deal of
time and patient labour to the reorganisation of the Austro-
Hungarian army, is, it is understood, pleased with the recent
development of the powers of mobilisation of the Austrian
cavalry. But this is rather a case of shutting the stable-
door when the steed is stolen. The Russians had a very long
start, and it is probable they still maintain it. There was a
grave danger for Austria in the presence on her frontier of
an overwhelming force of the new Russian dragoons, which,
as I think, combine the best features of cavalry and mounted
infantry, and in the existence in Little Russia and the Don
Cossack Steppe of numerous Cossack reserves. There was, and
I think there still is, the danger that a few hours before the
declaration of war an immense horde of Russian cavalry will
swarm through Galicia, will cut the railroads and the telegraph wires, avoid the regular armies, but destroy the whole
mobilisation arrangements of Austria, and beat the less
numerous Austro-Hungarian cavalry, who are now stationed
in wooden barrack towns upon the line between Cracow and
Lemberg. The Austro-Hungarian cavalry have been increased of late for the purpose of meeting this danger, by
covering the mobilisation and the concentration of the army,
and by defending the strategic railroads of Galicia. But
they have not, I believe, achieved the first condition of
success—that of being able to present themselves on the

frontier with a superior force. The steps taken in Austria-Hungary have been to place a large number of independent cavalry divisions on the frontier and to give the regiments of which they are formed a peace-effective which is really a war-effective; also to arrange for sending forward all the cavalry towards the frontier immediately upon the receipt of the mobilisation order. The Austrian cavalry regiments will be able to start for the frontier at a moment's notice with nine hundred sabres each. But difficulty was till lately found in keeping a large force actually upon the frontier in time of peace. The climate on the Galician frontier is very bad. There are no large towns and few large villages, and the plains are extremely unhealthy in the spring. The Austrians have now, however, placed on the frontier two independent cavalry divisions, with fifty-four squadrons; and on the moment of the receipt of the order of mobilisation the railways will be employed for the purpose of carrying more cavalry to the front along the Vienna-Cracow line. On the other hand, the Russians have had for many years a large force on their frontier, and have lately, as the Polish Jews will have told the Austrians, greatly increased that force, although this fact has been denied. But the Austrians will not at present be able to place in the field more than a nominal force of 61,000 sabres, all told, and those who know the Russian army best must feel that such a force will be unable to make head against the regular cavalry of the Russians, even without taking the Cossacks into account.

It is not of much use to discuss what may be called the "grand possibilities" of Austria under circumstances such as those which I have attempted to describe. No doubt she should have been the "heir of Turkey;" the protector of a Greece extended to include Albania and Macedonia and the islands and the coast to Constantinople and down Asia Minor; the friend of Servia and Roumania; the president of a Balkan Confederation—and what not. But Austria is naturally slow to move, and under her many difficulties has become constitutionally timid. Moreover, to be able to look to such a future she would have to contemplate becoming that which her ethnic constitution ought to make her, but which both Germans and Magyars are determined she shall not become—a mainly Slavonic Power, in which the Tsechs and the Croats, if not the Galician Poles, would take their share of government with the Magyars.

The outlook for Austria then, is, in my opinion, far from promising. She will do all she can to avoid war with Russia, but if she avoids it she will probably be greatly humbled in the process. If she fights, I fear she will be humbled also, and humbled with the loss at least of Bukowina and the eastern portion of Galicia. Germany cannot save her, for Germany cannot interfere because of France. Italy, which could save Vienna, would have to be given South Tyrol as far as the language boundary, that is, up to within six or seven miles of Botzen; and nothing could exceed the pain to the Emperor and his Court and many patriotic Austrians of being saved by Italy. On the other hand, the idea of danger to Austria from any desire on the part of her German population to join their fortunes to those of Germany may be set aside. The interest of Germany, like the interest of Austria, is to keep quiet and let things alone. Germany does not desire the disruption of Austria, for the German provinces, Upper and Lower Austria, and the rest, do not lie next to Germany, but are, as I have tried to show, cut off from it by a district in which the most enterprising of all Slavonic peoples hate the Germans with a deadly hatred. The recent retirement from the Diet of Prague of the seventy German members of the Diet shows the present state of feeling in the Bohemian Kingdom between the Germans and the Tsechs. War now rages upon every point, and as the Tsechs are at present triumphant I suppose this book will be "seized" because I have not written *Praha*, though I have carefully avoided writing *Praag*.

It is difficult for any one except an Austro-Hungarian statesman to realise the difficulties of governing the Dual Monarchy. Cis-Leithania has, as is well known, a Reichsrath and seventeen Provincial Diets. The two Austrias, Styria, Carinthia, and Salzburg present no difficulties, but causes of trouble are abundant in the other districts. The Emperor will probably end by getting himself crowned King of Bohemia, although it will be difficult for him to lend himself to a proscription of the German language by the Tsechs as he has been forced by the Magyars to lend himself to the virtual proscription in parts of Hungary of Rouman and of various Slavonic languages, the teaching of Magyar in elementary schools being now compulsory. But how far is this process to continue? The German Austrians are as unpopular in Istria and Dalmatia as in Bohemia ; and Dalmatia is also an ancient kingdom. These territories were originally obtained by the election of the King of Hungary to the crown of the

tripartite kingdom of Croatia, Slavonia, and Dalmatia. Is
"Ferencz Jozsef" to be crowned King of Dalmatia? And
is Dalmatia to have its separate Ministry and its separate
official language, and its completely separate laws? And
what then of Fiume, the so-called Hungarian port? Then,
again, Galicia is also an ancient kingdom, although it has
at other times formed part of Poland; and the Emperor is
King of Galicia, as he is King of Bohemia and Dalmatia. Is
he to be crowned King of Galicia? And if so, is the separate
existence of Galicia to be a Polish or a Ruthenian existence,
or, indeed, a Jewish? for the Jews are not only extraordinarily powerful and numerous there, but are gaining ground
day by day. The Ruthenians complain as bitterly of being
bullied by the Poles in Galicia as the Croats complain of the
Magyars.

Even here the difficulties are not ended. The Margraviate of Moravia contains a large Tsech population, and
will have to be added to the Bohemian kingdom. Bukowina may go with Galicia or Transylvania, Austrian Silesia
may be divided between the Tsechs of Bohemia and
Moravia on the one part, and the Poles or Ruthenians or
Jews of Galicia on the other. But what is to become of that
which, with the most obstinate disregard of pedants, I intend
to continue to call *the* Tyrol? Trieste must go with Austria
and Salzburg, and the Northern Tyrol and Styria and Carinthia no doubt; but it is not difficult to show that Austria
would actually be strengthened by giving up the Southern
Tyrol, where the Italian people, or at least the Italian language, is gaining ground day by day. There really seems
very little left of the integrity of the Austrian Empire at

the conclusion of our survey of its constituent parts. Matters do not look much better if we turn to Trans-Leithania. Hungary has its Reichstag (which is also known by some terrible Magyar name), its House of Representatives, and its House of Magnates, and, although there are not so many Provincial Diets as in Austria, Slavonia and the Banat of Croatia possess a Common Diet with which the Magyars are far from popular; and the former Principality of Transylvania also possessed separate local rights, for trying completely to suppress which the Magyars are at present highly unpopular. Transylvania is now in fact an unwilling "integral part" of Hungary without Home Rule. The ex-Principality, although under Magyar rule, is divided between "Saxons" and Roumans, who equally detest the Magyars, and the Croats and Slovenes who people the Banat are Slavs who also execrate their Ugrian rulers, inscriptions in whose language are defaced whenever seen. Croatia is under-represented at Pest, and says that she goes unheard, and the Croats, who have partial Home Rule without an executive, ask for a local executive as well, and demand Fiume and Dalmatia.

If we look to the numbers of the various races, there are in Austria of Germans and Jews about nine millions to about thirteen million Slavs and a few Italians and Roumans. There are in the lands of the Crown of Hungary, two millions of Germans and Jews, of Roumans nearly three millions, although the Magyars only acknowledge two and a half millions, and of Magyars and Slavs between five and six millions apiece. In the whole of the territories of the Dual Monarchy it will be seen that there are eighteen millions of Slavs and only seventeen millions of the ruling races—Germans, Jews, and Magyars—while between three and four millions of Roumans and Italians count along with the Slav majority as being hostile to the dominant nationalities.

It is difficult to exaggerate the gravity for Austria of the state of things which these figures reveal. Count Kálnoky is a very able man; he has had a wide experience of men and things. He served his country first at Berlin and then at London; he has been ambassador at Rome and at St. Petersburg; and no one knows better than the Common Minister for Foreign Affairs how extraordinarily artificial is the existing state of things. The common army and the common navy are really controlled by the Delegations. The Delegations consist of a hundred and twenty members, of whom sixty are chosen by the Austrian Parliament and sixty by the Hungarian Parliament, which is thus vastly over-represented. Although Hungary only contributes a fraction over 30 per cent., Austria contributing 70 per cent., towards the joint expenditure, the twenty gentlemen selected by the Hungarian magnates and the forty gentlemen selected by the Magyar majority in the Hungarian House of Representatives hold in their hands half the power of the Empire. These gentlemen really represent only six millions out of the whole population of the Empire, and they are only 38 per cent. in their own half of it; while the Germans are only 38 per cent. in their own half. The Dual Monarchy is ruled by two minorities. All these figures may be contested. Austria and Hungary both habitually and purposely underestimate what may be called the foreign element in each of the two countries respectively. The Hungarians exaggerate the numbers of the Magyar population, which is undoubtedly gaining ground, and set it as high as 46 per cent., and the Austrians exaggerate the number of the Germans. It must be admitted also that the majority of the Slavs of the Dual Monarchy are Roman Catholics in religion, and are not in any strong degree, with the exception of the Ruthenians, pro-Russian. Still, whatever deductions may be made it is impossible to upset the main contention that the present state of things is artificial in an extraordinary degree and unlikely to continue.

All States are peopled by what may be termed, in an uncomplimentary word, mixtures. Just as, for example, the French, although a curious mixture, are a mixture that has been well mixed, so the people of Austria-Hungary are a mixture badly mixed. The Germans and the Magyars rule the country, but the Germans are not much more than a fourth, and the Magyars are not nearly one-sixth of the population, while the Slavs and Roumans have far more than a majority. There is a German park or German preserve in the two Austrias and their neighbourhood, and a German belt round the Tsech portion of Bohemia; but even in the Austrian Duchies there is a large population which is really Croatian-Slav. We are used to look upon the Duchy of Styria as German, but the southern portion of the Duchy is Wendish or Slovene. So, too, with the old kingdom of Illyria, which comprises Carinthia and Carniola, the latter of which provinces is mainly Slav, Wendish or Slovene. The Slovenes have an anti-German majority in the Carniolan Diet. In so-called Austria-Hungary upon the Adriatic there are neither Germans nor Hungarians. The Slovenes meet the Italians at Trieste, and the whole Dalmatian coast is Slav with an "Italian" upper class, itself Croatian by race. In Central Bohemia the German language is being now proscribed, and German judges have to enter at an advanced age upon the study of Tsech. Moravia, which is three-quarters Tsech, is likely to follow suit. In some parts of the lands of the Hungarian Crown the Slavs and in other parts of the Hungarian provinces the Roumans are gaining ground. In Croatia the present "language compromise" is that all public documents shall be written both in Croat and in Magyar, tongues which are about equally unintelligible to Germans or other peoples of the West. In Galicia, while the western half is Polish and Catholic, the eastern half is Little Russian and Orthodox. The Ruthenians call themselves Russians and their country the Russian land; and they are, in fact, a very good representative specimen of a Little Russian people. "It is difficult to be a patriot in Austria," said a distinguished Austrian to me, the other day, "for one does not know to the representatives of what race, religion, tongue, or principle one's allegiance is due."

No solution of the ethnic difficulties presented by Austria considered from a nationality point of view, is really possible at all. If Germany should ever come by Bavaria and the Bohemian Highlands to Vienna, Tsechish Bohemia would drive a Slav wedge into the German Empire of the future. But, on the other hand, if Slav unity should ever be contemplated, the German rim round Bohemia would prove a terrible difficulty in the way. Both German concentration and Slav concentration seem impossible. The Germans of Transylvania are far indeed from the Fatherland. The

Roumans and the Magyars cut off the Serbs and Bulgars, and cut in half the Wends or Slovenes or Croats even according to the Pan-Slav maps of Moscow.   The Roumans, in cutting the Slavs in half, only fulfil their duty as the forgotten outposts of ancient Rome.   They were put there on purpose.

According to one's fancy one may look at Tsechish Bohemia as a Slav arm thrust into the side of Germany, or upon the German part of Moravia and upon the German Duchies of Austria as two German arms thrust into the side of Slavdom. No ethnographic frontier in these districts can be good or lasting.   The difficulties are insuperable.   Many of these countries, the disposal of which is difficult, were ruled once by Poland.   If you look at the map of Cromwell's Europe, in which France and the United Kingdom are alone of the territories of the Great Powers substantially unchanged, you see a gigantic Turkey as diverse as the Austria of to-day; a tiny Prussia under another name; a vast Poland ruling Red Russia, White Russia, Lithuania, and half of Little Russia. For reasons given in the preceding chapter, I regard the reconstitution of Poland as impossible.   Certainly, a reconstitution of a Poland which might be friendly to Germany and form a barrier against Russia is out of the question altogether.   I know something of the sad years that followed the repression of the last Polish insurrection, and I have a strong opinion in regard to their events.   I have crossed Siberia from Perm with the long lines of Polish exiles, and on my return have met their endless chain still going on their eastern way.   But I frankly admit that in Russian

Poland in the present day the German is more hated than the Russian, and that the Pole, like every one else who is of Slavonic race, seems born with an instinctive hatred of the Teuton. Were there any possibility that Slavonic unity would be achieved, it certainly would be a formidable matter for all Europe. There are at least one hundred and twenty millions of Slavs in Europe—that is, of Slavs who are still Slavs in sentiment, without counting the Germanised Wends of Styria or of Prussia. Moreover, the Slavs are gaining ground. The progress of the Tsechs has been extraordinary. I once saw Palacky at Moscow, and assisted, as it were, at the new birth of the Tsech nation. The Tsechs re-entered Parliament in 1879, after having for some years abstained from taking any part in its deliberations. In 1880 they obtained the right of equality of language; but by 1886 they had got so completely their own way that the Germans quitted the Bohemian Diet.

A great French geographer has described Austria-Hungary as being a personal union of fifty-six States. Historically it is no doubt a Christian union against the Turk, but in modern times it has become an attempted Magyar and Jewish union against the Russian. This pretended union is mined by violent hatreds—Italian against German, Slav against German, Slav and Rouman against Magyar. The Tsechs, who are the best of all the Slavs, habitually describe their German fellow-countrymen in Bohemia as the "bugs," whilst the Germans of Bohemia style the Tsechs the "liars" or the "reptiles." The favourite memories of Bohemia are memories of a civil war, and celebrate the national rising under a leader whose name the Slavs pronounce as " Goose," whilst we insist upon talking of the Hussites. These uncompromising Tsechs are gaining ground even outside Bohemia. There are at the present moment more Tsechs in Vienna than in Prague itself.

In the Adriatic, Italy is faced by an Italianised Slav country in Dalmatia, just as Greece is faced by a Greek country on the Asia Minor coast; for, while waters such as great rivers and arms of the sea are commonly taken as frontiers by modern statecraft, waters fuse just as mountains divide ; and whilst mountains commonly separate civilisation from barbarism or one civilisation from another, you generally find the same race or the same manners on the two sides of a great river or of an easily traversed sea.   There is hardly a German or Magyar in all Istria and Dalmatia who is not a mere official temporarily there.   Hungary, which is ruled by one of the most interesting of peoples, which ought to be preserved under a glass case as the only powerful non-Aryan race in Europe—Hungary is torn by the dissensions caused by the hatred which these Christian Turks provoke in the minds of Roumans, Slovacs, Croats, Serbs, and Slovenes, who all oppose the Magyar policy, whilst the Germans themselves are not hearty in its support.   At the same time, the Hungarians will fight to the death for their own views, because, as they say, they are not like the Roumans, the Slavs, and the Germans, who have all of them a possible existence outside of the Dual Monarchy.   The Roumans have their brothers of Roumania to look to ; the Germans have the German Empire ; the Slavs have Russia, or their dream of a great Slav Power ; but "we Magyars have no relations in all Europe; we have nothing but the rag of soil which our ancestors conquered by the sword ; outside the plain of Hungary there is nothing for us but death, and we will not perish. Hungary fought throughout the Middle Ages to defend its existence against the Turks, but fighting for itself at the same time saved Europe. Hungary will fight again to the death to defend its existence against Russia ; and again in so doing she may save Europe, and at all events we shall know we have played our historic part."

After surveying the whole field of Austrian politics, I fear we must conclude that the Dualism of the Monarchy is very nearly dead, and that if Austria is to exist at all she must rapidly become tripartite, and ultimately resolve herself into a somewhat loose confederation. The probability is that both the Austrian statesmen and the wearer of the Imperial Crown will favour the nationalities (as Count Taaffe does already) against the Germans and the Magyars from day to day more and more ; but there are other dangers unfortunately besides the ethnic dangers by which the very existence of Austria is menaced. Austria is exposed to all those dangers of the unknown which exist in constitutional countries with a very limited electorate. The Taaffe Government policy of decentralisation and encouragement of nationalities is a wise one, although M. Tisza will not follow it, and the Empire can only be maintained at all by such means; indeed, the autonomy of the provinces is likely to be still further increased. But the weakening of the Central Government increases the danger from Socialism, and Socialism is perhaps a greater and more present danger in the Dual Monarchy than in any other country. A few years ago the Vienna police had a very unpleasant surprise in the information with regard to Socialistic activity and organisation in Vienna which reached them from London. Socialism, too, thrives in Hungary, where it has only been driven underground by the new anti-Socialist law. At Grätz in Styria, at Klagenfurth in Carinthia, at Wiener Neustadt, at Florisdorf near Vienna, at Reichenberg in Bohemia, and at Brünn in Moravia, Socialism is almost universal among the working men. The Socialism of Austria is not, indeed, in its public expression very violent. The writings of Austro-Hungarian Socialists are conscientious, heavy, and dull; but there seem to be two sorts of Socialists in Vienna—the reading and thinking Socialists and the party who answer to our dynamite conspirators. It is a curious fact that whilst all Europe has been occupied with Russian Nihilism, though the number of militant Nihilists in that country is small, Socialism has been making extraordinarily rapid progress in England and Austria, as well as progress, steady but more moderate in nature, in the German Empire. Of all the great European cities, it is in Vienna that the Socialists are strongest at the present moment; but even there as yet they are within control. It is a question, however, whether the loose cohesion of a federation can deal with them effectively.

I have nothing to add to what I said in my first chapter in regard to the nature of the Austro-German alliance, and it will be seen from what I have said in the present chapter that I think the most Germany can do is to keep France neutral, and to allow Italy, if she will, to help Austria for a price. Of course, Prince Bismarck has not bound Germany to espouse all the quarrels of Austria no matter where and with whom. Of course he will not bring Russia and France upon himself by threatening Russia, or by heading or leading the European opposition to Russia in matters in which Germany is not the Power most concerned. Austria, therefore, is left to bear the brunt. To use Prince Bismarck's phrase, he "gives Austria the preference." He explains that he yields to Austria because, while he wishes to uphold the sanctity of treaties, he must leave it to the Powers who have the most direct interest in their strict observance in each case to enforce the necessary respect for their provisions. We have seen, in the course of the present chapter, what are the reasons which make the honour which Prince Bismarck offers to the Austro-Hungarian Empire so embarrassing. Military weakness; race quarrels; Socialism; financial difficulties: these are the reasons why Austria-Hungary is unable to move in war.

In the first chapter I briefly considered the question whether, owing to her inability to fight unless absolutely attacked, the Dual Monarchy would be driven to accept from Russia that territorial compensation which she does not want, and of which she is in fact afraid. The occupation of Bosnia is already a sufficiently troublesome matter, although it has, among many drawbacks, the incidental advantage of keeping Montenegro quiet, and of preventing Prince Nicholas from attacking King Milan of Servia, in order to make himself prince of that country as a Russian satrap. By going forward to Salonica, Austria

would increase her military weakness; she would deeply
offend the Servians and the Greeks and the Bulgarians ; and
she would by increasing the number of her Slavonic subjects
only hasten her own break up. The country which some
think she covets, but which as a fact she fears—Macedonia—
is the battlefield of races. Even if we put aside Great
Albania as a dream, and agree in the, I think, reasonable
view that, as there are already great numbers of Albanians
who are contented subjects of King George, Albania might
well join Greece under a personal union, yet Macedonia is
claimed by the Greeks, the Servians, and the Bulgarians.

It is an unfortunate fact that while the young peoples
of the Balkan Peninsula have each of them a splendid vision
of the future founded upon the memory of a more or less
glorious past, their ambitions are terribly in conflict.
There is in Transylvania, Bukowina, and Bessarabia, a
Greater Roumania enshrined in every Rouman heart, and
the Bulgarians, the Servians, and the Greeks respectively
have their Greater Bulgaria, their Great Servia, and their
Greater Greece. But while each of these ideas has
admirers among us in England, their admirers must
admit that it is difficult to reconcile them. Roumanian
ambitions are chiefly disagreeable to the Hungarians and to
the Russians ; but the Bulgarians and the Serbs and the
Greeks lay claim to the same territory. All of the four
small Powers may be regarded as equally hostile to the
great ones. Montenegro is, of course, an outpost of Russia,
but the other Balkan States hate Austria and Russia
pretty much alike, although their anger from time to time

is turned against one or other of the two Powers whom they look upon as the great confederates.

If we examine the conditions of the four smaller Powers one by one and look first at Roumania, we find that the position of the King and of the Government of Roumania is one of refusal of a regular alliance with Austria-Hungary, but of determination to refuse a passage to Russia and firm intention of fighting in defence of neutrality should that neutrality be attacked. There would be a good deal to say in favour of the policy of Roumania making common cause with Austria-Hungary in any event—that is, for the policy of a defensive alliance. Should Russia annex Bukowina, a large portion of Roumania would be absolutely uncovered and left standing in the air; and the result might be that Austria having been beaten first, Roumania would then be plundered in her turn. On the other hand, if Roumania were to ally herself to Austria she would probably be the first invaded, and the Russians might content themselves with the occupation of the Lower Danube without attempting to cross the Southern Carpathian chain. In other words that would happen which generally happens in alliances, namely, that the weaker Power in the end would pay the piper. The real consideration, however, which has dictated the refusal of an Austro-Hungarian alliance by Roumania is the natural resentment which is felt at the manner in which Roumania has been treated by Austria-Hungary in the past. Austria, in the hesitation of Roumania as to making common cause with her, reaps her reward for her foolish and aimless opposition to Roumania's Danube policy, which in her own interest she ought to have supported. If from the moment of the termination of the last Russo-Turkish war Austria had made common cause with Roumania, she would have had without cost or damage to herself an all-important and permanent ally. There have even been Roumanian statesmen who have considered the possibility of Roumania voluntarily joining the Austro-Hungarian Power. Nearly one-half of the Rouman race inhabit the dominions of the Dual Monarchy, and the Roumanians would make great sacrifices to unite their ancient people under a single rule. Russia has incurred the lasting hatred of the Roumanian race by stripping them of Southern Bessarabia, a country inhabited almost entirely by Roumans; but the feeling of the Roumanians as regards the two Great Powers has been recently expressed by one of their most distinguished statesmen thus : " We detest the Russians, but the Austrians we both detest and despise." Roumanian feeling towards the Dual Monarchy has not been improved by the suppression of Transylvanian autonomy by the hated Magyar.

When Austria asked at Bucharest and at Berlin for a distinct Roumanian alliance, the Roumanian Government made a counter request for a distinct guarantee of Roumanian neutrality. The formal treaty of neutrality having been refused, Roumania immediately began to spend money on fortifications. She has now determined to depend upon herself alone, and her army is so remarkably powerful that for a short war it stands sixth in Europe ; so that it is possible her neutrality may be respected. It is now certain through Russia's action that if Russia occupies Bulgaria without intending directly to attack Austria-Hungary, she will have to conduct her operations by sea, and of course with the consent of Turkey. The spirited policy of the Roumanian Government is popular in the country, and instead of shooting their Prime Ministers as though they were partridges on the 1st of September, which was the recent diversion of the Roumanians, they are now supporting them by almost unanimous votes in the Chamber. It is a point I think in Lord Salisbury's favour that he has secured the representation of Great Britain at Constantinople at the present time by an ambassador who has had great experience of Roumania, and Sir William White, indeed, is fortunate in having served in Warsaw, in Eastern Germany, and in Servia as well; although it is perhaps a pity that he has not through his past services learnt to know the Greeks personally as well as he knows the Roumanians and the Slavs. That the Sultan should have refused to welcome so distinguished a diplomatist and a man so free from anti-Turkish prejudice as Sir William White only shows his blindness or the strength of Russian influence at the Porte. When the Sultan made difficulties about receiving Mr. Goschen he had a particular object in view; but when he at first objected to receive Sir William White he can have had none, and all that his Russian prompters wished was to show their influence to the world and to make England look ridiculous.

One of the several insuperable difficulties which lie in the way of a Balkan Confederation is the personal dislike of the King of Roumania for the King and Queen of Servia. The King of Roumania is every inch a king, and no more able

P

and accomplished sovereigns sit upon their thrones than King Charles, and the remarkable writer, Carmen Sylva, whose poems and novels and maxims go the round of the literary world, and who is his Queen. On the other hand, King Milan and the Queen of Servia are what may be styled third-class sovereigns, and unfortunately for them the King's mother and the Queen herself were both originally connected with Roumania and with what may be called the Roumanian Opposition. The feelings of King Charles of Roumania towards the King and Queen of Servia might be imagined if one were to try to picture to oneself what would be those of the King of England towards the King of Holland, if the latter's father had married into the family of Cobbett, and he himself into that of Mr. Labouchere. The isolation of Roumania from her neighbours is, as will have been seen, complete ; but she is isolated by the very fact of her existence. Whether the Roumanians are as they assert, and as I believe, the actual descendants of the Roman legionaries, or whether they are, as Moscow professes to believe, Slavs who have been partly Romanised, they at all events are entirely separated from their neighbours by language and by race or fancied race, and are connected with them only in that religion which comes to them from abroad in a Slav form. Isolated as they are, cutting as they do the Slavonic world in half, the Roumanians need to be a tough race ; and they are a tough race. I fancy that in toughness and permanency of national characteristics they are equal even to the gipsies or the Jews.

A very different people are the Servians next door, who

are much the same people as the Croats of Hungarian Croatia, though belonging to the Eastern instead of the Roman Church. Dreams or memories of Great Servia led them to attack the Bulgarians, as we know, and led to a defeat which was all the more pleasing to those who dislike aggression in that, owing to the better organisation of the Servians, it was unexpected. The Servians claim a large portion of Macedonia in their Great Servia, and parts of it, indeed, are looked for by the Bulgarians, and others are included by the Greeks in their Greater Greece. Unfortunately for the future, these Greats and Greaters overlap. The King of Servia is supposed to be the tool of Austria, and is known to be disliked in Russia. It is a curious fact that Russia turned the Karageorgevitch family off the Servian throne and restored the family of Obrenovitch because the former were too Austrian, but is now suspected of an intention to perform the opposite operation for precisely the same reason. King Milan is unpopular in his own country, and sooner or later will probably be displaced by Prince Nicholas of Montenegro or by the latter's son-in-law, who is, however, a feeble youth. At the end of 1883 there was a rising in Servia, which threatened the existence of the Servian throne, and which was the outcome of discontent produced by unconstitutional acts of the King. There was also much feeling with regard to the great pecuniary loss to Servia through the Bontoux railway contract and the failure of the *Union Générale*, and on account of the increase of taxation and of the subservience of the King to Austria. It was urged by the Radicals of Servia that the King was practically

212 THE PRESENT POSITION OF EUROPEAN POLITICS.

leading the Conservative party in that country, and that the
Radicals in the Chamber were improperly excluded from all
voice in the Government. The Radicals had obtained a
majority at the general election, and the King had followed
the example of the King of Denmark and refused to listen
to the Skuptschina. The mode in which the insurrection
was stamped out in 1883 was one of the principal causes of
the complete and deserved defeat of King Milan's forces by
the Bulgarians in the recent war.

There is some doubt as to whether the majority of the
Macedonians are Serbs or Bulgars. The probability on
the whole is that the Russians are right in their contention
that they are Bulgars; but the various races speaking the
Southern Slavonic tongue which exist in the Balkan Peninsula
melt imperceptibly the one into the other. The future of that
portion of Eastern Macedonia which is still Turkish probably
lies with the Bulgarians, although the Turks might have
continued to rule it with the assent of all, had they been wise
in time. The King of Servia recently expressed to the
representatives of Bulgaria his desire for a personal union,
which only shows that King Milan is even more blind to the
signs of the times than his worst enemies could suppose.
The notion that the Bulgarians would willingly select as
their ruler a prince who had violated the constitution of his
own country, who had shown a complete disregard of all
constitutional traditions, and who had also been conquered
in the field by an inferior force, was a singular one; but had
the Bulgarians listened to King Milan's suggestion, there
can be no doubt that its adoption would only have hastened

the coming of the inevitable day when he himself will be driven from the Servian throne. To place King Milan on the throne of Bulgaria and to make him governor of Eastern Roumelia would be impossible without a general war, and if they are to have a general war, the Bulgarians would prefer some one more popular than King Milan. These Bulgarians are the Japanese of Europe. Pleasant, courteous to strangers, all apparently young like the Japanese statesmen, prudent and yet full of ideas, the English-speaking men of Robert College certainly inspire one with confidence.

Greece, like Roumania, has this remarkable advantage over Servia and Bulgaria, that whilst Bulgaria has a monarchic constitution but cannot find a king, and Servia is provided with an unpopular ruler, Greece and Roumania have kings of real ability, and, I may add, equally charming queens. Not that the King of Greece is "popular." Greece is perhaps too intensely democratic for any king to be personally much liked in Athens, but that he is able there can be no doubt. Lord Beaconsfield once said of him, " He will be a remarkably clever fellow who can teach anything to that young man," and this was said, not with regard to book learning, but with special reference to the power of governing.

To estimate the progress of Greece it is only necessary to compare, for example, Thackeray's picture of Athens in 1844 with Athens to-day ; but what the Greeks have done within their terribly contracted boundaries is hardly a sufficient guide to what they would do were they given even Epirus and the wholly Greek part of Macedonia. No doubt the Greeks have obtained Ossa as well as Pelion, but they naturally want Pindus and Olympus too. The rest of Epirus with the completely Greek town of Janina and the Islands they are certain to get, and would obtain, as I think, even at the hands of that Austria of which they are so deeply jealous. Just as the Servians, the Roumans, and the Bulgarians have no friends among their neighbours, so too the Greeks. It is difficult to say whether they more dislike the Austrians or the Italians, and their latest fancy is to declare that not only does Italy covet the Albanian coast, but that she has fixed her view on Rhodes.

One great difficulty of the Greeks is in Albania. The Albanians are a separate people, with a language unlike any other, and they have a strong sentiment of nationality; but I repeat that the Albanians might well accept of their own free choice a personal union with Greece under the King of the Hellenes. No Greeks fought harder for the Hellenic cause against the Turks than did the Albanian Souliotes, and the Albanians are not numerous enough in the coveted position which they occupy, to stand alone.

The Greeks have already become prudent in their policy. Their present able minister, M. Tricoupis, reduced the number of their Chamber from, roughly speaking, two hundred and fifty members to about one hundred and fifty, and this proceeding has met with extraordinary success, for it has made of their Parliament a practical and working body. At the same time it is impossible for them to rest content within the boundaries of the present kingdom. There are only about two million Greeks in Greece. There are three millions in the Greater Greece outside, without counting those in Asia Minor, which is fast becoming completely Greek. There is every reason why England should view with pleasure the rapid development of Greece. An enlarged and strengthened Greece would be a maritime Power, almost an island Power, dependent upon English favour, trading chiefly with Great Britain, and the glad servant of the policy of the United Kingdom. The Greeks are sanguine of their ability to accomplish the process of which I spoke just now— the Hellenising of the Albanians. They say that the southern Albanians are not only largely Greek in religion and in dress, for they wear the Greek *fustanella*, but that they are Greek in their leanings, and would very easily become completely Hellenised.

But the Greeks are afraid of Italy and of Austria. They declare that an Italian squadron has of late been continually at Rhodes surveying and landing parties, and of course all remember the Italian intrigues in Albania not very many years ago. As regards Austria, they try to make Austrian statesmen understand that if Austria goes to Salonica, without wishing to go there, under Russian pressure, because she desires to satisfy national vanity by a show of compensation for the Russian advance, it will be only a weakness to Austria in the future. What Russia gives, Russia will some day take away. The extension of Austria would, they point out to us, be damaging to British trade, and the division of the Balkan Peninsula between Austria and Russia almost disastrous to it. On the other hand, the Greeks, who are commercial, would be good traders with us even if we should ultimately fail in keeping Russia from Constantinople. The Greek islands, which mask the Dardanelles, produce 50,000 of the best sailors in the world— certainly the best sailors in the Mediterranean ; and if the Russians should, by confining Greece within narrow limits, ultimately cause her Government to break down, and should gradually absorb these islands, it would be disastrous to British trade in the Levant.

The Greeks in the past have made enormous sacrifices for the Greek idea. They have borne well the heavy blow of the denial to them of Janina after it had been promised to them by the collective voice of Europe; but Austria at Salonica, or Italy in Albania, would be a blow to the Greek idea which the Greek monarchy could not bear. Austria, they point out, has made herself as unpopular in Bosnia as has Russia in Bulgaria. She has called down upon her the detestation of the Slavs by cutting through the old Servian land. Bosnia is not happy under Austrian rule ; all except the Roman Catholic people there are discontented ; but this long strip of territory is apparently held by Austria because it is the road to Salonica and to prevent Austria from being cut off from the south. In the Turkish provinces which Austria administers there lurks still that brigandage from which Greece has succeeded of late years in absolutely ridding her own territory, and Greeks proudly contrast the progress which has been made in the recently occupied parts of Thessaly with what they think the failure of Austria in Bosnia and Herzegovina.

Nevertheless, if Russia should advance in the Balkan Peninsula or should occupy Bulgaria, Austria will be driven to fight, and even with such help as she may receive is likely to be beaten; or else she might advance to Salonica as a necessary compensation for the wound to her national vanity, Greece getting the rest of Macedonia behind her, and either Greece or Italy the Albanian coast. This advance on the part of Austria might mean, however, her ultimate destruction through the predominance of the Slavs; but should she go to pieces, no very great change can be expected in the countries out of which the Dual Monarchy is at present formed, inasmuch as no power can hold down the Magyars, and no rearrangement of boundaries can, as I have shown, meet the case of the Southern Germans and the Slavs of the surrounding districts. It has been of late suggested that the whole question of Bulgaria and the dangers which grow out of the Bulgarian situation should be referred to an European Conference. It has also been suggested lately that the Conference should meet, but should be more general and should consider the question of the disarmament of Europe. I believe that when England was "sounded" in February upon the meeting of the proposed Conference on Bulgarian affairs she objected on the ground that it was useless to have such a Conference unless the Powers knew pretty well beforehand what it was they were about to do. It is generally somewhat dangerous to go into conference unless the basis of discussion is clearly defined beforehand. To meet without a defined basis is always more likely to provoke war than to lead to the preservation of peace.

It is useless to read the translations of the Turkish native papers, as they are not allowed to publish anything except obvious lies, or such items of news as that the Queen of Spain has a cold. But there have lately been some interesting articles in the *Levant Herald* upon the future relations of Austria to the territories now comprised in the Turkish Empire, and on the possibilities of forming a Balkan Confederation. These articles, besides being of value in themselves, should be also looked at for other reasons, as their publication under a severe censorship may reveal something of the secret opinions of the Porte. It must be remembered that the censor sits in the office of the *Levant Herald* whilst the paper is being "made up," and acts as a sort of editor. As the statements of the articles are made under so sharp a censorship, they must clearly be articles which the Turks think it wise to have seen and read. In these articles it is pointed out that the advance of Russia on Constantinople by Asia is more likely and more dangerous than the advance by Europe. In Asia Russia has no enemies behind her. As regards Europe, the "pure and patient patriotism" of the Bulgarians gives ground for hope in the possibility of the formation of a powerful Balkan Confederation under Turkish headship, but England has cut the future Balkan Confederation in half by presenting Bosnia and Herzegovina to Austria at Berlin. The vast number of Serbs in the Banat and in Bosnia, and the vast number of Roumans in Transylvania point, in the opinion of the *Levant Herald*, to the necessity of some rearrangement of boundaries between the Balkan Confederation of the future and the Dual Monarchy.

The weakest point in the suggestion of the *Levant Herald* for a Balkan Confederation under Turkish headship, is that Roumania, expecting the brunt of any attack to fall upon herself, would probably prefer to keep clear of any such arrangement. In the second place, the Servians would not improbably be stirred up by Austria to resist it; and in the third place, on the side of Greece, the proposal of such a confederation at the present time would virtually constitute a request to Greece to guarantee Turkey in her present dominion, and to give up all hope of receiving Janina itself. I fear that a Balkan Confederation, whether under Austrian or Turkish headship, is a dream, and about as little possible of realisation as that union between Servia and Bulgaria for which King Milan longs, and which would only lead to his deposition in favour of some one else—as, for example, the Prince of Montenegro, who could unite all Greater Servia and Slavonic Macedonia, and thus overshadow Greece. Of all the Balkan States, Bulgaria is the only one which would be inclined to come into confederation at the present time; and it is of no use to even talk of such a scheme at a moment when the Continent is bristling with bayonets. The only real question worth asking is the one which I have asked before, namely, Will Austria resist Russian pretensions; and will she, if in danger of conquest, be supported by allies, or will she yield and take her share of the spoils?

Much fault has been found with what I said on a former occasion as to Russia at Constantinople, and as to whether

Constantinople is a British or an Austrian interest. A good deal depends upon how Russia reaches Constantinople. From one point of view it may almost be said that if Russia gets to Constantinople by Asia it will be a great blow to England, and that if she gets there by Europe it will be the destruction of Austria. Some are inclined to argue thus: What does any present influence at Constantinople give us that an understanding with Russia would not give us? The answer is, that the history of the past, and indeed of the present, will show that understandings with Russia are not worth much.

The fact that Turkey is pro-Russian at the present time, that the Levant trade is not just now very profitable, and that the Turkish railways are not paying and are not being pushed forward—all these considerations concur to make the English taxpayer and the English investor inclined to be neutral, and he has come to think that it would be better to agree than to fight. Germany will not fight to keep Russia from Constantinople, and we are told we should be as practical. We are also told of our want of power to carry on the struggle, which is a somewhat dangerous argument. As a matter of fact we are not in numbers relatively weaker now than we always were, though I admit and have shown that we are more vulnerable. There is, however, less danger of a mere rush for Constantinople at the present moment than there has been for some time. The small peoples of the Slav races which were expected to help Russia towards Constantinople are now alienated from her, and as long as she remains a military autocracy that alienation, once provoked, is likely to continue. On the other hand,

she cannot advance through Asia as long as she professes to
be friendly to the Turks. Why not, then, wait and watch,
and without exaggeration on either side keep our hands free
for the future ? We are not bound to make up our minds
upon this particular case, irrespective of the considerations
of the moment. We are not here bound by treaty obligations ; for the conditions of the Anglo-Turkish Convention
have certainly not been fulfilled. Let us only avoid inviting
Russia to Constantinople, as some of our writers and speakers
do, to the possibly great detriment of British trade.

Two views have been taken of Lord 'Salisbury's speech of
November last : the one that he expected at that time that
Austria would play the main part in barring the approach of
Russia to Constantinople ; the other that he already knew
that Austria would avoid war by all means in her power.
The latter is the true view, as I showed in the first
chapter. There is nothing new in this shrinking back on
the part of Austria. Lord Salisbury has experienced it once
previously in the course of his career. An arrangement was
discussed by Lord Beaconsfield and Count Andrassy, at the
time of the Treaty of Berlin, by which Austria and England
were jointly to guarantee the integrity of Turkish territory
—Austria in Europe and England in Asia Minor. Turkish
territory, it should be remembered, at that time meant
practically, as it does still theoretically, Eastern Roumelia
and the Balkan line. Moreover, there was behind this the
understanding that England was to come to the assistance of
Austria in Europe, and Austria to make common cause with
England in the event of Turkey being attacked in Asia

Minor. But this offer of an English alliance to Austria fell
through in the same way in which the suggestion of England
in October last failed to receive encouragement.

If the Austrians would adopt a policy of friendliness and
consideration towards the Greeks, the Roumanians, and the
Servians; if they would abandon all idea of advancing under
any circumstances towards Salonica; if they would strengthen
the internal condition of the Dual Monarchy by converting
it into a loose confederation, with equal rights conferred on
Bohemia and Croatia and Polish Galicia, while holding fast
to the Italian alliance, to be paid for, when the time arrives,
by the Southern Tyrol—if they did this, they would be able
to maintain themselves as a Great Power. Very naturally
as matters stand they are in mortal fear of Russia, and the
result is that Count Kálnoky and all the leading ministers of
the country, great as are their abilities, get a reputation for
weakness which they do not deserve. The courage and
energy of the Magyars are a very important point in
Austria's favour, and so also under a tripartite or federative system would be the energy of the Tsechs; for the
Austrian Slavs, with the exception of the Little Russians
of Ruthenia and Northern Bukowina, do not sympathise
with Russia to any great extent. At the same time they
detest both the Germans and the Magyars; and Slavs,
Germans, Magyars, and Roumans cannot be permanently
held together in the Empire except by the adoption of the
federative system.

Here lies the danger of the Eastern Empire, which many
used to think was menaced by Prince Bismarck, who as a

matter of fact is, of all men in Europe, the man who most desires to keep Austria alive. It is a necessity to him that she should continue to exist. Once destroy Austria, and Germany is left to fight it out with France and Russia without assistance; for in this case Italy would not move. Austria gains on the one side by this feeling in Prince Bismarck's mind, or let us say in the German mind. She gains on the other by the existence of a somewhat better feeling towards her of late in the minds of the Bulgarians and of the Balkan Slavs, and by a thorough and clear conception on the part of the Hungarians that their very existence would be menaced by the downfall of the Dual Monarchy.

After the division of the respective spheres of influence of Bulgaria, Greece, and Servia in Macedonia, Austria might gradually increase her influence in the Balkan States; and if she would take the bold step of making an arrangement for evacuating part of Bosnia and the Herzegovina, so as to show she had no intention of going southwards to Salonica, she might bring together in a general understanding with herself the small States and the Turks; but this unfortunately is impracticable, as Austro-Hungarian pride will effectually prevent the abandonment of any portion of Bosnia. While Balkan confederation is out of the question, Balkan alliance is possible, and will offer the advantage of helping to prolong Austria's existence. The division of the Balkan Peninsula between Austria and Russia would, on the contrary, only make the downfall of Austria the more certain. For Austria to go to Salonica would be for her to embark in the most irritating kind of warfare with the whole people of Macedonia—Greek, Servian, and Bulgarian; and when she got there she would only have increased her unwieldiness and the number of her Slavonic subjects, and could not after all maintain herself in Macedonia one day longer than Russia chose to allow. The ultimate result would only be her downfall and the establishment of Russia upon the Adriatic.

V.

ITALY.

It seems to Englishmen an extraordinary fact that a Ministry with a bare majority, and that majority itself disappearing so fast that Parliament had to be twice prorogued to give time for bringing new men into the Cabinet, should be able to sign a treaty of alliance involving obligations the extent of which is not fully known. This is what has been lately done in Italy, where a feeble Ministry directed a falling Minister to sign a treaty of strict alliance with Powers so unpopular with the unrepresented mob that effigies of Prince Bismarck were carried about the streets of the Italian cities at the Carnival. This treaty was signed, too, at a moment when a majority of the principal organs in the Italian press were in favour, not of reversing the previous policy, but of keeping the hands of Italy free.

How comes it that such temerity is possible? In England it would be impossible. England is far more directly menaced in her interests, at all events in her Indian Empire, by Russia than Italy is menaced by France or Russia, yet no weak English Ministry could enter in time of peace into an alliance with Austria and Germany against

Q

France and Russia, and assuredly no Ministry could do so without facing Parliament. The Opposition in Italy is not wanting in vigour, but it would seem at first sight as though Signor Crispi must be singularly inferior in offensive power to Lord Randolph Churchill for the conclusion of such an alliance to have been possible. It is difficult to understand the phenomenon unless we remember that weak as may have been the late Government in Italy they were faced by a divided Opposition, and unless, also, we trace at length the effect upon Italian foreign policy of the occupation of Rome in face of the continual protests of the Vatican. To attack the Government upon their failures in Abyssinia was an easy task, but to incur the wrath of Prince Bismarck was too much for the courage even of the " Lord of the Rats and Mice," as Signor Crispi, the most powerful man until last month in the Opposition, and the most powerful man since last month in the Government, is called by those respectable politicians of the Italian Right who look upon all the Southerners as bandits, and upon Signori Crispi and Nicotera as the leading brigands. While there are no true parties in the Italian Chamber, but only a number of personal groups, so, too, there are no real parties in Italy as regards foreign policy, and until a great change shall be publicly known to have taken place in the counsels of the Roman Curia, almost the whole Italian electorate will remain united in support of a pro-German policy.

So far as they can be said to exist at all, the Italian parties going by the name of the Right and Left may, roughly speaking, be said to be the successors of the

Cavourian and Garibaldian sections of Italian Liberals The advocates of Italian unity having been divided into two parties, whose adherents were respectively in sympathy with Constitutional Monarchy under the house of Savoy and with republican institutions, the old names adopted in former days have been retained while the distinctions between Right and Left have disappeared, and are now applied to agglomerations of groups which have personal rather than political significance. For many years after the death of Cavour power continued in the hands of the moderate men who held his views. Between the Right represented by Signor Minghetti, and the extreme Left which contained the adherents of Mazzini and Garibaldi, there gradually arose a kind of third party, the Left Centre, of which Signor Rattazzi was a prominent member. From this group, when the Left itself came into power, it took the present Prime Minister, Signor Depretis, in whom Italy found that it had obtained a Parliamentary leader who possessed the tactical art of Parliamentary government in a high degree, and who has been willing to constitute at various times Governments of the most diverse elements, supported in turn by every section in the chamber, from the Right to the extreme Left.

It cannot be too strongly or too often stated that in Italy nominal adherence to the Right or Left does not necessarily imply the holding of any definite set of views. The Right is in general supposed to contain the more Conservative politicians, but leaders of the Right like Signor Bonghi habitually describe themselves as Liberals, and on not a few questions are in fact more Liberal than are many members of the Left. There are Unionists to be found both in the Right and in the Left. There are Federalists divided in the same manner, and free traders and protectionists are not confined to any one group. The only section which contains a complete body of adherents to any set of views is the extreme Left, but then it is a very small section, and naturally the groups contained in it are smaller still. The extreme Left contains at once the uncompromising Irredentists, and the mere handful of peace-at-any-price Radicals who are their bitterest opponents. That which ought to be the real Right is absent from the Chamber although present in large numbers among the town councillors of municipalities—the Clerical Conservative party. The most Conservative of the Right who sit in the Italian Chamber we should call Whigs, or high and dry doctrinaire Liberals, and they closely resemble the Belgian Liberals, with whom many of them agree in their strongly anti-clerical feeling.

Much confusion is caused, of course, in foreign countries n the minds of those who attempt to follow Italian politics by the use of the phrase " The Left" for a body of politicians who form the vast majority of the Chamber, and who are in part supporters and in part opponents of the present and of all recent Ministries, and who contain representatives of the most opposite classes of opinion. Among the Left are to be found some Radicals, some Socialists, some Republican Anti-socialists, and even some Conservatives. Composed as it is of heterogeneous elements, the Left is broken up into personal fractions, and it is high time that a new division of the Italian Chamber should be attempted. Want of distinguishing principle leads to the most curious apparent changes of personal grouping. For example, when Signor Depretis first came into power with a Cabinet representing the moderate Left, Signor Cairoli, another of the leaders of the Left, saw no reason why he should not make a coalition with the Right, but finally decided to give a general support to the Depretis Ministry. After this Signor Depretis brought into his Government representatives of the Right, and obtained the support of the greater portion of the Right, while he lost the support of a large section of the Left. Later again, the opposition to Signor Depretis was led by the "Pentarchy," or alliance of five leaders of the Left. This combination brought together at the head of the majority of the Left Signori Cairoli and Crispi, who had often opposed each other; but later still Signor Depretis has taken two of the Pentarchs to his side in the persons of Signori Crispi and Zanardelli. The three other Pentarchs have been considering during the last few weeks whether they shall ask for embassies as supporters of the Government (it being understood that Signor Cairoli would like to come to London), or shall lead a re-constituted Opposition. It will be seen that in spite of the coalition between the moderate Left and the Right, which is known in Italian politics as "The Transformation," the transformation of parties and party names, unfortunately for the cause of clearness, is not yet complete.

It was after the fusion of the chief part of the Right with that portion of the Left which was represented in the Depretis Ministry, that is, after the elections of 1882, that

Signor Depretis began to take what may be called a strongly
Conservative line, and to adopt as the cardinal points of his
policy those main objects for which the Italian Right had
all along contended.   These were the support of the Monarchy and of the law of Papal guarantees, and the maintenance of the alliance with Germany and Austria.   At the
same time, the Pentarchic Left which was opposed to him,
although containing elements really hostile to the Monarchy
and elements opposed to friendliness or ·neutrality towards
the Church, was not willing to frankly attack Depretis on
any of these grounds.   We may conclude, then, that whatever
may be the party names in Italy, the great majority of
Italians, or at all events the great majority of their
representatives in the Chamber, are really united upon all
the larger questions that are likely to come up.

Along with the existence of a great and predominant mass
of good sense, there is a little eccentricity in Italian politics,
shown by the occasional return of swindlers, libellers, lunatics,
and murderers to sit at Montecitorio.   The special local
causes which tend towards these peculiar elections are
aggravated by that very absence of direct party issues
and of parties, in the English sense of the term, of which I
have just now spoken.   While parties and distinguishing
principles are wanting, men are plentiful.   The deaths of
Minghetti and of Sella were a tremendous loss to the Right,
but these statesmen left behind them Signor Bonghi, and
Italy was able to find in Depretis and Magliani Ministers of
remarkable ability, and in Cairoli an Opposition leader of
high honour.

The recent reconstitution of the Depretis Ministry will, it is understood, make no change at the Consulta, for foreign affairs have passed into the hands of the Prime Minister himself, who is not likely to reverse a policy which was in fact his own. In taking back Signor Zanardelli, whom he had lost once before, his Ministry may seem to have become less Conservative, for when Zanardelli and Baccarini left him to become two of the Pentarchic chiefs, the former Depretis Ministry was transformed into a Conservative Ministry, resting upon the support of the Right and of the Conservative section of the Left; but while taking back his more advanced ex-colleague Zanardelli, and taking also Crispi from the ranks of the Opposition, he has also taken in a Minister of War who belongs to a very different section, so it cannot even be said to be clear that Signor Depretis has once more turned back towards that Left from which he came. The difficulties of his Government before the change were caused, not by differences of opinion upon points of policy, but by the withdrawal of active support by a portion of the Right, owing to the unpopularity of the Abyssinian campaign. The personal nature of Italian politics is clearly seen from the manner in which the Italian Prime Minister " sheds off " his colleagues instead of making common cause with them; and Italy will never find Ministerial stability until the English and Belgian system of standing or falling together is rigorously enforced.

While the great majority of Italian politicians support the Austro-German alliance, for reasons which we shall presently consider, they have to face a minority which, though as small among the electors relatively as it is in Parliament, makes nevertheless a great deal of noise. The more numerous opponents of the Austro-German alliance are those who declare for the policy of "free hands," and who are really supporters of the very "German policy" which they denounce; men, that is, who, while refraining from signing treaties in time of peace, would, were war to break out, enter for themselves into the same alliance. On the other hand, some of the young men burn Bismarck in effigy, and profess friendship for France. These are mere "savages" or "wild men," as the Germans would say, and are not worth counting, any more than are the ultra-Irredentist faction, who would quarrel at one and the same time with England about Malta, with France about Savoy, with Austria about the Tyrol, with Switzerland about the Ticino, and with Turkey and Greece about Albania. They have received, however, few as they are, a certain amount of practical support from some Opposition newspapers, which are continually asking very disagreeable questions about the amount of good which the Austro-German alliance has wrought. It is difficult to explain that, besides working good, this alliance may have prevented mischief in the past and may bring tangible benefit in the future, because it would be equally inconvenient to have to explain what had been the dangers averted and what were to be the benefits received.

Besides the Austro-German alliance, there is a feeling in favour of close friendship with England which is also popular with the electorate. Lord Palmerston's assistance in the Garibaldian expedition to Sicily; England's steady

friendship continued for many years to the young kingdom ;
Mr. Gladstone's offer of a joint occupation of Egypt, have all
contributed to make this feeling strong. Not long before his
death, Signor Minghetti complained most bitterly of the
refusal by Signor Mancini of the English proposal for the
co-operation of Italy in arms with England with regard to
Egyptian affairs. There never was a greater surprise than
that refusal. At the time when the proposal was made, not
only the English Government but the whole of the Italian
Embassies were under the impression that it would be accepted. But the good was done by the offer itself, for it is
always gratefully remembered. No doubt the Italian statesmen are abler men as a rule than the Italian diplomatists, but
some of the latter are clever, and Count Corti, if he, as
Signor Bonghi, I believe, once told him, can hardly think
himself the equal of Prince Bismarck, is a man of remarkable ability. But on the occasion of which I speak, the
diplomatists were right, the statesmen were wrong, and an
Italian alliance with England would have given to Italy
without risk that position which the Red Sea expedition was
intended, but has failed, to gain.

In August, 1884, there was a development by England of
the policy of consulting Italy with regard to Egypt. The
French always defend their claim either for exclusive
influence or more often for joint influence with ourselves in
Egypt by pointing to the large number of subjects and
"protected subjects" they possess in that country. But
there are more real Italians than real French in Egypt, and
the proper way to meet undue French claims is to point to

those of Italy and Greece. I cannot but think that it must have been Germany which warned Italy to keep out of Egypt, for Italy in recent years has taken her policy as submissively from the German Empire as in 1866 she took her policy from France. Still, the refusal of the offer and the subsequent regret at the refusal have not made the Italians angry with us but only with themselves; and if Germany did give bad advice, that advice has not had seriously bad results.

It is then clear that not the slightest modification of Italian foreign policy may be expected to result from any changes which may occur from time to time in the occupancy of the Consulta. Since Signor Depretis has been Prime Minister, there have been as many changes at the Italian Foreign Office as there have been in the constitution of the Government majorities; but the foreign policy of Italy has not varied, and will not vary. The attitude of the Italian Government towards the European Powers is not affected whether the Foreign Office is presided over by a politician like Signor Mancini, who was Foreign Minister when the Austro-German alliance was first made, or by a soldier and diplomatist of very different views, like General Count di Robilant. Count di Robilant, in spite of his early training, borne witness to by his armless sleeve, which is I believe a reminiscence of Novara, is said to have been very Austrian in his sympathies since his residence at Vienna and his marriage with an Austrian lady; but the least Austrian of Italian politicians, were he to replace the General at the Consulta, would carry out the same, that is the Bismarckian policy.

Italian foreign policy may be said to be so thoroughly accepted by the electorate as to be independent of Parliamentary groups or parties, and no variation in the policy is to be looked for because any given politician is at the head of the Cabinet or is Minister for Foreign Affairs. The proceedings in the Chamber, after the recent disaster at Saati, may be taken to exemplify this. The Government of Signor Depretis demanded a vote of confidence. Signor Bonghi and other influential members of the Right consented to vote with the Government on the Abyssinian question, although they withdrew their support in the next division, not as approving or disapproving of the African policy, but merely because certain personal modifications in the Ministry had not taken place. The news of the disaster came upon the Chamber while it was in the midst of a stormy discussion on the votes for public works. The suddenness of the news could not fail to call forth a great deal of demonstrative rhetoric in an assembly of Italians; but although the Minister obtained eventually only a diminished majority, the speeches which were made on the reception of the news all breathed identical sentiments of patriotism, though pronounced by men belonging to all the different groups. The money asked for was voted almost unanimously in the Chamber, and quite unanimously in the Senate. The subsequent demand for a vote of confidence prevented a unanimous manifestation of patriotism, but the African policy was never really in question. Like all divisions in the Italian Chamber, this one was determined on personal grounds, and it was Generals di Robilant and Ricotti who were personally attacked.

The colonial policy of the Italian Government, as well as its foreign policy, is likely to maintain its continuity. notwithstanding the changes in the Cabinet. A military disaster of course always brings down upon the ministry in power more or less popular indignation, and the satirical prints of Rome have been full of pictures displaying Signor Depretis with a background of skeletons in Italian uniforms bleaching in the African desert. The disaster in Abyssinia will, however, probably not seriously check Italian colonial enterprise. The Italians have hitherto emigrated to the colonies of other nations rather than colonized for themselves. There are said to be at present two millions of Italian subjects abroad. Many of them, of course, are only temporary emigrants, who have left Italy for France or for Egypt, in the hope of making a fortune with which to live at home. In the South American republics, however, there are a vast number of Italian permanent settlers. In the Argentine Republic there are one million, and more than one-third of the inhabitants of Buenos Ayres are Italians. The tide of emigration, too, is increasing. Two hundred thousand people left Italy last year, of whom the greater portion went to this part of South America, and the Argentine Republic is rapidly becoming an Italian state.

Irish, British, Scandinavian and German settlers thrive only in temperate latitudes, in which there are no new countries left to annex ; but the Italians are able to endure hot climates, and it is not impossible therefore that, late as it is in the day, an Italian policy of colonization may succeed. This is the reason which induces them to persevere in their

Red Sea policy. The main motive which the Italians have in attempting to open up a portion of the African coast is commerce. Italy wishes to establish important posts which will bring into its hands the commerce of central Africa, which is now diverted to the north, to the Congo, and to Zanzibar. But Italian designs on Africa are not confined to the Abyssinian coast. I spoke in the first chapter of the promises with regard to Tripoli, as well as to Tunis, which were made to Italy at Berlin. The French protectorate of Tunis still rankles in Italian breasts, and the desire to obtain Tripoli as a set-off is only checked by the fear of extending the common frontier of Italy and France in a district where it would be more difficult for the Italians to defend themselves than it is in the passes of the Alps. The possession of Tripoli would only weaken Italy in the event of a conflict with France, by increasing the already onerous duties of her fleets and armies.

Italian intrigue in Albania has been during the last few years so little heard of that it is perhaps only necessary to mention that in 1879 intrigues were rife, and that they must be expected to be set on foot again in the event either of the disruption of the Austrian Empire or of an Austrian advance upon Salonica. The future of Albania must depend upon the wishes of the Albanians. The Albanians are not numerous enough to be likely to form an independent power of themselves, but they are a tough race of fighting men who will be able to make their voices heard in the ultimate decision of their destiny. There are so many of them in Greece that I should have thought that they might

have joined Greece in personal union with less loss of
national characteristics and of dignity and self-respect than
would be involved in their accepting Italian conquest. My
strong sympathies with Italy do not prevent my being glad
that the intrigues of the Consulta were divulged to the whole
world by the publication of the famous letter dated from the
Roman Foreign Office on the 6th of April, 1879, by Signor
Corte, the Italian consul at Prevesa, and addressed to Moukhtar Pasha. In it Signor Corte explained the agreement of
the Italian Ministry with Moukhtar's project of colonizing
Greek Epirus by Mahometan Albanians and of opposing the
occupation of Novi Bazar by Austria. These intrigues
are, I hope, matters of the past, and probably came to an
end when Count Tornielli resigned the general secretaryship
of the Italian Foreign Office. I repeat the expression of my
hope that the future of Albania may depend less upon the
Italian Government than on the wishes of the Albanians
themselves.

A movement which indicates the same desire for expansion,
but which is supported by wholly different and much more
sentimental pleas, is the Irredentist agitation. Generally
considered, the "Italia Irredenta" movement is declining.
The feeling which exists in France for the restitution of
Alsace has no counterpart in Italy, and the circumstances
of course are wholly different. In a sense it is true that
as Italy represents the principle of Italian race history, Nice,
Corsica, Malta, the Italian cantons of Switzerland, the
Trentino, Trieste, the Dalmatian coast, and others of the
former possessions of that Republic of Venice of which

Italy believes herself the heir, must sometimes tempt Italian politicians. So long, moreover, as the house of Savoy rules Italy, the cradle of the kingly race cannot be forgotten. On the other hand, it is admitted by all Italians who know the facts, that the Italian cantons of Switzerland and the Duchy of Savoy do not desire to be Italian. The Italian cantons desire to remain Swiss. Lakeside Savoy, which smokes Swiss cigars and had sooner not pay double duty on them, and which dislikes the blood-tax, may desire to be Swiss rather than French, but Italy has no hold on the affections of the people. In the county of Nice there is a great deal of anti-French, and some little Italian feeling, and in the event of the destruction of the French army at the hands of Germany, it is just conceivable that Nice would once again become Italian without armed resistance.

When I read under the title of "England and Europe," an article on the foreign relations of this country, by a thoroughly competent judge, whose remarks upon many points are full of wisdom, I was amazed to find that his account of Italy is comprised in less than a single page, and concludes with the statement that if war should break out, Italy, as the price of her adhesion, would "look first to the restoration of Nice." If it is possible to make any confident prediction with regard to foreign affairs, I should have thought that it is certainly clear that, whatever else Italy may ask for, she never will go out of her way to ask for Nice. For Italy to take Nice from France would be for her to repeat the folly of Germany in taking Alsace-Lorraine, with the difference that Italy is obviously inferior to France in military strength, and with the certainty that from that time forward, France, unless destroyed, would strain every nerve to take the country back. There never was much in the Irredentist movement as regards the Ticino. In Savoy, I repeat, there is a good deal of local Savoyard feeling, but no Italian feeling proper, and those in Savoy who are anti-French mainly incline towards Switzerland. In the county of Nice there is a great deal of local independent feeling, but Nice never was Italian in its sympathies, and if called upon to choose between France and Italy would, by a large majority, unhesitatingly again choose France. Corsica, also, is Corsican rather than either Italian or French. There is a good deal of Greek and other non-Italian blood in Corsica, and Italy does not find her islands so easy to rule as to make it wise for her in any event to seek to burden herself with more. In certain circumstances the Italian movement with regard to the Dalmatian coast might become formidable, but for the moment it may be disregarded. Germany does not wish that Austria should ever cede Trieste, and Hungary will cling to her Adriatic port. The local feeling in Malta, England, were she wise in the matter, could easily content. There remains, however, the question of the Southern Tyrol.

The question of the possible annexation of the Italian Tyrol to Italy involves two sides of Italian policy, the Irredentist policy and the policy of *pourboire*. The Trentino in my opinion will probably one day pass to Italy, and its ultimate destiny is already practically accepted by its inhabitants and by the voice of Europe, as was that of Lombardy and of Venice long before they fell to the Italian kingdom. In the autumn of 1869 Napoleon III. made overtures to Austria and Italy with a view to an alliance against Prussia, but Signor Minghetti held out against some of his colleagues and, it is said, against the king. It was then proposed that France, Austria, and Italy should guarantee mutually their possessions, and that, in the event of war with Germany, Austria should be given territory at the expense of Prussia, and that Italy should take the Southern Tyrol. It is believed that the negotiations then broke down because Signor, Minghetti insisted on the evacuation of Rome by France and, indeed, went further in declaring that it was not for the partizans of Italian unity to oppose the foundation of German unity. Napoleon III. then sought a merely Austrian alliance, which, with all respect to the memory of Count Beust, he certainly thought he had obtained, and the Southern Tyrol had a respite from proposals of Italian annexation. That territory, in my belief, Italy sooner or later will undoubtedly receive from the necessities of Austria. There is probably no thought of Nice or Savoy or even Corsica in the minds of those members of the Italian Right who are the most strongly inclined towards an Austrian alliance. They know that to take advantage of any difficulties of France, however grave, for the purpose of reannexing Savoy or Nice, or of seizing Corsica against the wishes of the population—for the Italian party are a small minority both in the county and the duchy and the island—would be to cripple Italy for ever, inasmuch as she would from that time forward be forced to

R

be continually armed to the teeth against the French. But
the friends of Austria and the enemies of Austria concur
in desiring, and in expecting to obtain the Italian Tyrol.
The friends expect to get it as a free gift for helping Austria
against Russia, and the enemies expect to get it as a prize
upon her downfall. It is just possible that although the
Italian franchise has been greatly extended, the foreign policy
of the majority of the people, that is the foreign policy
of the Catholic *contadini*, might prove to be different from
the policy of the majority of the existing electors, although
I do not think so, but supposing that ultimately, when the
suffrage is again extended, the pro-German policy should
disappear, the Southern Tyrol will not less surely, but in a
different way, be lost to Austria.

I sum up, then, my view upon both the Irredentist and
the *pourboire* policy by asserting that practical politicians in
Italy would no more think of rousing a feeling in favour of
the cession of Malta by England or of Corsica by France
than would practical politicians in Germany or France raise
a similar cry for Heligoland or for the Channel Islands.
The different feeling which exists with regard to the Trentino
is due to the plain fact that in that direction there is, on
the borders of Italy, a population which desires union with
Italy, and also that in that quarter Italy knows that she
has a wretched frontier. Sentiment and the desire for
security concur in this particular instance, and Italians of all
groups are united in a desire to obtain from the Austrian
alliance the Tyrol so far as Botzen. Looking more generally
to Italian foreign policy I should explain that, in desiring

the maintenance of the *status quo* upon the Mediterranean, Italy not only hopes to protect herself against any desire to re-constitute the temporal power, but also hopes to hold Russia's ambition in check. Italian public opinion, supported, as it believes, by that of England, strongly resists the expansion of Russia in south-eastern Europe. I must frankly admit that the language with regard to the maintenance of the *status quo* is pushed farther in Italy than the facts would warrant. All sections of Italian politicians repudiate the desire to ask for the Trentino as the price for services rendered. But in private they frankly hold language very different from their public utterances.

The only Italians who are warm in their friendship for France are a remnant of old Garibaldians deeply attached to Republican institutions. The lack of friendliness for their great western neighbour does not arise from ingratitude or from Irredentist tradition, but from a series of irritations; one of the earliest of which was the continued occupation of Rome by French troops so long as men could be spared for the purpose, and one of the latest of which is the ridiculous pleasantry of finding in the imaginary Khroumir a pretext for the sudden occupation of Tunis. That there is bad blood between the two nations is seen in the disturbances which occur in all great centres of population where French and Italian workmen are brought into contact. The old feeling of irritation towards Austria has almost subsided, and Italy, or, to speak more accurately, the present electorate of Italy, seems very willing to enter into alliance with its former foe.

As to Germany, moderate politicians in Italy decline to be irritated at expressions of gratitude addressed by the Imperial Government to the Pope for his aid at the recent elections. The phrase in the Pope's letter which seemed to point to a hope of the restoration of the temporal power has been explained away as having been written, during the illness of the Pontifical Secretary of State, by a juvenile hand, and, although the explanation need not necessarily be believed, it is an interesting fact that it has been offered and accepted. But what is perhaps more important is, that Italy at once demanded an explanation at Berlin, and received from Berlin the strongest possible denial on the part both of Germany and Austria of any dream that, under any circumstances, the position of the Supreme Pontiff would be regarded by those Powers as a matter calling for their interference. Although Italians outside the Government are hardly aware that these completely satisfactory explanations have been given, they take Prince Bismarck's speeches in a very friendly spirit. They say that the German Government could not do less than publicly express gratitude to the Holy Father for his co-operation in the triumph of Imperial ideas. They smile at the recollection that the first great interference of the Pope in modern times in Europe has been an interference in support of the policy which the kingdom of Italy strongly desires to see prevail. They point out that this very interference on the part of the Vatican in an important internal question in a foreign country is a patent proof to all Europe of the complete liberty of action which the Supreme Pontiff enjoys, though, or because, deprived of temporal power. The successors of Cavour and of Minghetti declare that the Pope's action is a triumph for the Italian Government, and that it is a realisation of what that party have always affirmed, that the power of the Papacy would become far more effective if delivered from the trammels of a temporal kingdom.

Italy might, of course, by avoiding an Austro-German alliance, and by keeping her hands free for eventualities, abstain also from maintaining so large an army as she has, at all events nominally, to support at present. I doubt, however, whether in any circumstances she could with prudence reduce her armaments. The Italian army is very numerous on paper; it is not very large in fact: and the Italian fleet is a cheap one considering its power, and it needs to be strong when we remember that Sicily and Sardinia have to be held, that an enormously long and very narrow kingdom has to be saved from being cut in half, and that Italy is directly menaced by the French positions at Carthage, in Corsica, and on the Riviera. Italy thinks, moreover, that a great European war is inevitable soon, and that owing to her geographical position she will be forced to take part in it as the permanent ally of one side, or else to sell her co-operation to the highest bidder. Italy has in her King a cavalry officer with a strong desire to distinguish himself in the field. She is nervously anxious about her generals. Perhaps the most important feature of the proceedings consequent upon the disaster at Saati is the censure passed upon the general commanding at Massowah. The Italian Government expressed its disapproval of the actions of General

Genè, and his position becoming untenable he has been replaced by General Saletta, who initiated the occupation and who knows the country well. At first sight this seems to bear out the suggestion made by me in the last chapter that while the Italian soldiers may be as brave as they appear to have proved themselves at Saati, their superior officers are not to be depended upon for head work in difficult circumstances. Against this view, however, it should be remembered that all Governments, when overtaken by sudden military disaster, are inclined to make scapegoats of the unfortunate commanders. General Genè has not yet been heard in his defence, and should he be proved to be incompetent it does not follow that there are no capable commanders in the army. We have had our own reverses in Africa frequently within the last fifty years, but we have no lack of competent generals who might be trusted to retrieve all errors. Be that as it may, however, there is an impression abroad that Italian generalship may have some difficulty in regaining the reputation lost in 1866. King Humbert is an enthusiastic soldier and may be trusted to see to the efficiency of his troops so far as lies in his power. The Italians are quick in learning their drill, they can subsist on very little, and their Alpine regiments are unequalled for mountain warfare. In that excellent work, *Military Italy*, which is, I believe, written by Captain à Court, of the Rifle Brigade, the author makes perhaps his only mistake when he states that the French Chasseurs, the men who would have to meet these splendid troops, are " selected " from " gamekeepers, hunters, and foresters." The French, in my opinion, are utterly unfit to meet them, and it is probable that even if Italy were engaged with France in a single-handed contest the French could not, without great efforts, force the passes of the Alps.

The real value of the Italian army may, perhaps, be best ascertained from a careful consideration of the debate in December, 1886, in which the then Minister of War, General Ricotti, explained the exact force which, after the 1st of April of the present year, Italy would be able to put into the field. He did not for one moment pretend that the enormous nominal force which Italy possesses, exceeding by 100,000 the number of instructed men possessed by Germany herself, would really be found when wanted; but he gave figures which would go to show that the Italian army can put into line about such a force as we should expect from the Italian war budget, namely, a force somewhat inferior to that of Austria. It is the combination of a large army and a powerful fleet, which really makes Italy formidable; for if Italy has only the fifth army it has the third navy of all the Powers.

Captain à Court has admirably pointed out how, for a young country, and a country with an overburdened budget, it was not possible to build ship for ship against France, and not within Italy's power to create a fleet numerically equal to that of France, but that what was possible was to build a small number of enormous seagoing ironclads of the first class, "larger, stronger, swifter, and more heavily armed than any afloat." Were Italy not protected by a powerful fleet, such as might have some chance of holding its own against the French in its own waters, the French fleet could be used to destroy Italian mobilization if Italy had joined an alliance against France. The Italian railway lines could be cut at many places from the coast. Not only from Toulon and Ajaccio, but also from her new port at Biserta, on the Tunisian coast, France could keep watch and could pounce on Italy. The great difficulty, however, in the way of Italy is caused by her want of coal, for Italy may be said to have no coal for her ships, and the difficulty of getting coal to her southern ports in time of war would be immense if she had not command of the seas.

In materially increasing the number of her large ironclads Italy has been aiming at nothing less than the command of the Mediterranean as against France ; but supposing that France were sufficiently free from the risk of maritime attack elsewhere to be able to concentrate her naval strength in the Mediterranean, it would be a delusion to suppose that the Italian naval forces could hold their own against the French. The Italian material is excellent, no doubt, but the results of Lissa are not encouraging. To judge from naval expenditure, Italy seems to get a great deal for her money. If we were to look at the figures we should suppose that there were five navies in the world worth counting, the British and French of the first class, and the Russian, German, and Italian of the second class ; but as a matter of fact the Russian and German navies are not worth counting by the side of the Italian navy of to-day. I doubt, however, whether the Italian, German, and Austrian navies could possibly hope to hold the Mediterranean against those of France and Russia, weak as is the Russian navy, in a general continental war, so high is the estimate which I form of the power of France at sea. Russia, indeed, spends more upon her navy than does Italy; but Russia probably does not get her money's worth. Italy at the present moment, in addition to the two splendid ships which she has at sea, is building or equipping eight first-class sea-going ironclads as against seven being built by France and eleven by ourselves, and she certainly seems to have, as regards the material of her fleet, achieved remarkable results at a low rate of cost.

The Italian fleet, in the event of war, would not have those scattered duties to perform which would fall to the lot of the French and English navies. The fleet of Italy would have to defend the Italian coast against attack, and if possible to keep up the communications with Sicily and Sardinia. Massowah would have to take care of itself, and the Italian fleet would be concentrated, whilst that of France, in some degree, would have to be dispersed over the whole world; but unless France had to put forth on land such efforts as to need the men and guns of her navy for the defence of her own fortresses, the time of concentration in the Mediterranean would arrive, and a great strain would be imposed upon the Italian fleet. Those who look upon the Italian navy as being a navy of offence because it consists chiefly of ironclads of the first class capable of holding the seas, forget the necessity imposed upon Italy by her shape and geographical position. It is impossible to defend the coast of Italy by fortifications, and there is no country so vulner-

able.   The mountains run down the centre of a long narrow
strip, and the strategic railway lines are easily reachable
from the sea.   On the south, too, Carthage once more threatens
Rome.   The Italian monster ironclads are certainly not too
numerous for the defence of the Italian coast, and in my
belief the naval policy which has been pursued by Italy is
one which was necessary to her existence, and she is to be
congratulated upon the low price at which she has succeeded
in obtaining her splendid ships.

The recent fall of the War Minister will be productive of
as little change in the military policy of Italy as the fall of
the late Foreign Minister will produce change in the foreign
policy of that country.   Count di Robilant was directing the
colonial as well as the foreign policy proper, and the two
chief ministers who have gone out are the two who were
responsible for the conduct of the Abyssinian expedition.
Still, not even the Abyssinian policy will be changed, or if
any modifications should take place in it, they will be wholly
independent of the recent alterations in the ministry.

Power at present in Italy is vested in the hands of the
Prime Minister, "the old Parliamentary hand" of Italian
politics, "the fox," as he is usually called, both by his
opponents and his friends, the man without a policy, but
supreme in Parliamentary management, able to work either
with the Right or with the Left.   Although Italian policy,
especially perhaps Italian foreign policy, is so far removed
from the hysterical as to continually remind one of the
calmness and calculation of Machiavelli, yet the impression
which a stranger carries away from a sitting of the Italian

Chamber is that the methods of expression of Italian politicians are, to say the least, emotional. Persons not familiar with the energy of Italian rhetoric would imagine that a dozen duels next morning must be the result of a heated debate in the Chamber, unless indeed they were anticipated by a free fight on the floor of the House. The scenes which took place on the reception of the bad news from Massowah were of this description, and Count di Robilant, trained amid the discipline of soldiers and the calm of diplomatists, is hardly the man to cope with violent rhetorical onslaughts.

Very different is the Prime Minister, "the old Stradella," as he is called from his long association with his Lombard constituency of violin tradition. He is told every morning in journals representing every shade of opinion that neither the country nor the Chamber is with him, but newspaper criticisms disturb him as little as do turbulent scenes in Parliament. It is confidently asserted, and, more than that, it is believed, that had he failed in forming his new ministry, which contains a preponderating representation of the Left, he had ready in his pocket a second list, for presentation to the King, of a Cabinet containing a predominant element of the Right. For more than twenty years, ever since he first entered "the Cabinet of conciliation," he has been, with short intervals, a minister. After Rattazzi's death he became leader of the Left, and a few years later he succeeded in upsetting the Minghetti Government, and was called upon to form a ministry. In 1882, after the death of Sella, he parted from his old colleagues of the extreme Left and became the leader of the two centres, having arrayed against him a combination of the Pentarchs, or five leaders of the Opposition Left. By taking into his Cabinet two of the Pentarchs he has divided the two southern Pentarchs, Crispi and Nicotera, and taken one of the three northern Pentarchs away from the two others. Much more interesting to the Italians than any question of foreign policy, is the discussion as to the line which will be taken by the two principal of the three Pentarchs who remain outside, Cairoli and Nicotera. Although, as I said, it is understood that Cairoli would accept the withdrawal of Count Corti and the gift of the embassy in London, there may be English difficulties in the way.

Although the fact that Italian politicians of all groups pursue practically the same foreign policy may in one sense tend to the preservation of the peace of Europe, yet the lack of stability in successive Italian Governments must prove a certain weakness to the country itself. This defect in Italian politics cannot but be regretted by Englishmen, as Italy, of all the nations of Europe, is our one warm-hearted, and I may add disinterested, friend. In all quarters, in the journals representing every shade of opinion, England is always spoken of in terms of cordial affection. Italians frequently abuse one another, attack the Russians, attack the Greeks, attack the French, and even attack their Austrian and German allies, but their references to us are always more than courteous. It is to England that they look for historic guidance as well as for modern advice. During the late difficulties in the formation of an administration an important pamphlet appeared at Rome which, after pointing out the defects in the existing groups, strongly urged the formation

of a coalition Government in which politicians of all views
should sink minor differences in face of the grave condition
of continental affairs. To strengthen his argument the writer
quoted all the coalition Governments of England for more
than a century past. English Parliamentary institutions are
reverenced in Italy, and the record of the last few years in
the English House of Commons has not yet destroyed the
good tradition.

The reconstitution of the Cabinet throws little light upon
the future of Italian politics, for it has failed to bring to the
front what are called coming men. Crispi has been styled
the Gambetta of Italy, but, except that Gambetta came from
the south of France and Crispi comes from the south of Italy,
I see little resemblance between the men. Crispi was an active
politician in 1848, when Gambetta was a child, and now,
within two years of seventy, he is not likely to rise to a
higher position in Europe than he commands at present.
Zanardelli is his contemporary. General Bertolè Viale, who
has succeeded General Ricotti at the War Office, was previously in office as long ago as 1869, before General Ricotti
was at the War Office for the first time. He is nearly sixty
years of age, and, representing as he does the moderate
element among the new Ministers, is not over popular with
a large portion of the Left. The strongest of the old members of the Cabinet who did not go out are Signor Brin,
the Minister of Marine, and Signor Magliani, who has never
been a deputy, but who, on account of his great financial
astuteness, seems likely to sit on the Government bench in
perpetuity as Minister of Finance.

The Socialist party is of no great account in Italy.   In the large towns of the north there is an ultra-Radical element, and in Rome there is a section of the population inclined to Republican views, but the Italians themselves seem to think that they are more free from difficulties either with the Socialists or with the Republicans than are the other Powers.   A Roman satirical paper lately published a cartoon representing the great Powers parleying and bickering about armaments and alliances, while in the background the dangerous elements in the respective countries are depicted as 'jackals waiting for their opportunity.   Thus in Russia there is the Nihilist, in Germany the Socialist, and in France the Anarchist, but many will think that the artist is hardly well acquainted with the politics of the United Kingdom, for he labels our corresponding beast of prey as " Orangist."

The most interesting and the most difficult of all the problems which Italy presents is that of the future relations of the Italian Government and the Vatican.   These are not, of course, a matter of merely domestic interest, and indeed there is an inclination on the part of the English, French, and German press to overrate rather than under-estimate the importance of the question of the Temporal Power.   There is a section of Italian politicians represented by journals of some influence, which adopt an irreconcilable tone to all pretensions of the Holy See.   For instance, after commenting upon the recent utterance of Prince Bismarck, a leading Opposition journal asks if Italy can regard with indifference this alliance on the part of her ally (Germany) with her " worst enemy " (the " Papacy " or the Vatican).   There are, however, in Italy, a great number of sagacious politicians who do not consider the Pope to be the natural foe of modern civilisation, and who follow Cavour and Minghetti in hoping to establish good relations between the Holy See and the Italian Government without giving up one atom of the principle of Italian Unity.

Cavour, of course, did not live to see even the removal of the capital from Turin to Florence, but in his last days he expressed the hope that it would be his fortune to still live to date from Rome a treaty of peace with the Vatican, which would have singular importance to the future of human society. Minghetti, for whose death Italy still mourns, followed Cavour in the desire to give the Church greater liberty than it had ever enjoyed, while maintaining unimpaired Italian Unity. The followers of this eminent man advance two propositions: the first, that it was not merely the Italian Government which took possession of Rome, but the entire Italian nation which occupied it; the second, that the nation though not ardently Catholic is profoundly Catholic. They differ from Machiavelli's opinion, that the Italian nation by the fault of the Papacy is the least religious in the world. There is indeed, in Italy, none of that aggressive antagonism to the Church which is characteristic of modern France. The number of parents who will not permit their children to be baptized, or who are in favour of purely civil marriage and burial, is very small. On the other hand, while the nation is imbued with Catholicism, it is a Catholicism of a much calmer type than that of the Catholics of France and Belgium. The nation, moreover, is one which understands the spirit of compromise, and it has no taste for religious persecution. " Death to Priests " may be written up occasionally on the colonnade of St. Peter's, but meanwhile the most uncompromising Liberals send their children to the schools of the Fathers.

It is important to understand this attitude on the part of the Italian nation, amid the apparent or outward war to the knife which is supposed to exist between the Vatican and the Government of the King. It has been wittily observed that Protestantism has made no progress in Italy because the would-be proselytizers try to persuade the Italian to give up opinions which he does not possess, for others which he does not understand. The Italians at present look upon churches and the priesthood as they do upon their blue sky and sunshine, as part of Italian life, but moderate men are throwing out warnings, which have not yet become threats, that unless the Vatican will step forward to a solution which will put an end to the political antagonism existing between the Papacy and the Catholic masses of the country, the anti-Papal feeling will develop into an anti-Catholic movement which, once set going, will become as national as is now the recognition of the Church. It is certain that the Kingdom of Italy has no intention of ever admitting the sovereignty of the Pope over even a particular quarter of the city of Rome. Under no circumstances would any portion of the population consent to the possible withdrawal of absolute liberty of the press, of religion, and of education. It is certain also that no European power will find it expedient to wage war upon united Italy for the purpose of imposing restrictions upon the unity of the kingdom. In justice to the Holy See I ought, however, to state that nothing can be stronger than the private declarations made, that the Holy Father would not accept of armed intervention on his behalf. The Pope's own view is supported in Catholic circles by remembrance of the humiliations and disasters which have been brought upon the Holy See by the armed support of foreign powers, and on the other hand by evidence that the Pope, deprived of temporal power, is at the present moment a more considerable figure in the councils of Europe, with Protestant as well as with Catholic governments, than he could ever hope to be were he again invested with some merely territorial sway. The political influence of the Vatican has risen higher lately than the highest point at which it had stood since the Reformation, and it will rise yet higher as the temporal power recedes into the mists of the past.

We have seen that among the leaders of public opinion in Italy there are two sets of views in regard to the future of the Papacy. There is the view of the irreconcilable party who treat the Pope as a pretender to a portion of Italian territory; and there is the moderate view, which, while it will not concede anything whatever to the supposed territorial pretensions of the Holy See, not only professes the greatest solicitude for the complete liberty of the Supreme Pontiff, but also expresses the liveliest satisfaction at the increased power of the Vatican in Europe now that it is unfettered or freed from foreign influence.

It is not very easy to state the view which the Vatican itself takes of the situation, because there are two opinions among the Cardinals, as there are two opinions among Italian politicians. Persons whose acquaintance with the Sacred College is confined to social intercourse with certain of its members during a brief stay at Rome are frequently struck by the limited scope of the ideas of those Princes of the Church with whom they are thus brought into contact. On some matters not entirely ecclesiastical the Roman Cardinals are no mean authorities. On musical criticism, on the culinary art, and even on the science of philology, an almost perfect knowledge is sometimes met with, but the questions of the day interesting to public men are treated by the eminent Church dignitaries at Rome either with a limited apprehension of their bearing or with childlike simplicity. The society Cardinals, however, are not the men who are admitted into the intimate councils of the Pope. They represent His Holiness admirably well in ceremonials of the Church, in which they make an imposing figure, but they have no part in suggesting the policy of the Holy See.

The Vatican, which in the minds of most foreigners is a magnificent cluster of galleries, gardens and libraries, in the recesses of which the Holy Father sits a captive, is as a fact the most wonderfully organized collection of public offices in the world. No capital in Europe has the advantage of finding under one vast roof all its departments of State as is the case at the Vatican. India alone in part shares with the Holy See this advantage, if we consider as the capital of India the dark and dingy building in Charles Street, Whitehall. But the Vatican has that which India cannot find, polished diplomatists who are familiar with the life of Courts,

astute statesmen and men of the world, who every morning
read the leading journals of all Europe, as well as a host of
skilful permanent officials well versed in office work and
equally competent to indite a despatch in ecclesiastical Latin
or in diplomatic French. To the Piazza di S. Pietro there
come daily the representatives of all the nationalities, not
only priests, not only Catholics, but politicians also, whose
governments do not officially recognise the Papacy.

The diplomatic relations of the Holy See with those
Powers which have official dealings with it, are maintained
at Rome by four ambassadors, those of France, Austria-
Hungary, Spain, and Portugal, and by Envoys Extraordinary
from Prussia, Belgium, and Bavaria among others. The
representatives of the Vatican abroad are Nuncios at Paris,
Vienna, Munich, Lisbon, Brussels, and Madrid, if we leave
out the less important capitals. It will be seen that the
sending and receiving of representatives is for the most part
mutual, but there are exceptions in the case of the Protestant
countries which have relations with the Holy See, Prussia,
for example, sending an Envoy Extraordinary and not
receiving a Nuncio. Holland receives an inter-Nuncio—
a diplomatist of the second class—but does not send an Envoy.
The nunciatures are the chief training ground for the highest
offices of the Vatican. Leo XIII. himself was Nuncio at
Brussels. Cardinal Franchi, his first Secretary of State, was
Nuncio at Madrid; Cardinal Nina, who succeeded Franchi,
was, like the Pope, formerly at Brussels; and Cardinal
Jacobini was called from Vienna to be Secretary of State.
Several of the present representatives of the Holy See in

European capitals are men who are likely to be heard of in the future beyond the limits of the diplomatic body; as, for example, Cardinal di Rende, who holds the most difficult post, that of Paris; and the brothers Vannutelli, who are at Vienna * and Lisbon, and who are both remarkable men. Cardinal Rampolla, the Nuncio at Madrid, is one of those who have been spoken of as likely to succeed to the office of Secretary of State; but there are rumours as to his health not being sufficiently good. He is one of the youngest wearers of the scarlet biretta, being only forty-three, and he was himself trained in the nunciature at Madrid, when Cardinal Simeoni was the apostolic representative there. It will be seen that the persons who mainly direct the Vatican affairs are all Italian, and I may add that all the members of the Papal Secretariate, from Monsignor Mocenni, the accomplished pro-Secretary of State downwards, are Italians to a man. A waiting game is at present being played upon both sides. The Quirinal waits for the Vatican to formulate some proposition which will recognise that the seat of Italian government must remain at Rome; and the Vatican likewise waits, declining to make any move whatever. At the same time the Vatican undoubtedly has no illusions, and does not expect, either from Italy or from abroad, any concession of territory or of temporal power.

The Italian clergy are not without national feeling, and the disaster in Abyssinia brought it out in calling forth pulpit commendations of the soldiers who died for their country. The irreconcilable Italian politicians discount this

* A change has recently been made at Vienna.

patriotic action by urging that the Holy See has every reason
for encouraging Italian colonial enterprise, inasmuch as its
successful accomplishment would involve the establishment
of Italian missionary bishoprics, which would be under the
direct control of the Vatican; but the priestly patriotism is
none the less real for all the gibes and sneers.

The Pope never sets foot beyond his so-called prison.
Every now and then a paragraph appears in the Italian and
French papers which states that the Holy Father has been
recognised taking a drive in the streets of Rome in disguise,
or at all events not in Pontifical attire. Such statements are
probably not intended to be inventions, but they have been in
each case the result of a glimpse of his elder brother, Cardinal
Joseph Pecci. The imprisonment of the Pope has had an
effect in Rome and in Italy wholly different from that which
it has had in foreign countries. Abroad his captivity invests
him with a mystery which has increased his influence. Even
people who are well acquainted with the real surroundings
of the Pope are impressed with the idea of the captive figure
of the Vatican not only directing the affairs of what they
look upon as the Church Universal throughout the world—
for Westerns know little of the Eastern Church—but also
influencing the policies of European powers from his self-
imposed prison. On the Roman people his withdrawal from
public view has had an entirely different effect. The Italian
nature is not spiritual or mystical. Moreover, the people,
though accepting the Catholic religion as a part of their
daily life, do not trouble themselves about polemical discussions on matters of belief or of ecclesiastical polity. It has

been unfairly said of them that they would be a nation of freethinkers if they had ever been known to think, but there is a certain measure of truth which underlies the epigram. The simpler portion of them are, however, moved, as no other people is moved, by gorgeous pageantry and the rich colouring of bright processions. The Pope enclosed within the Vatican walls to them is nothing; but a Pope making a progress through the streets of Rome in his chariot of state, and attended by the noble guards, is an embodiment of all they admire and revere. The Pope's advisers ought to know their own business best, but it cannot be doubted that if the Holy Father had been permitted to make himself visible to the Roman people, each drive he took through the city would have been a triumphal progress. The King and the Queen would have been the first to pay him marks of reverence, and the spectacle of the popular rulers of united Italy yielding public homage to the successor of St. Peter would have had a result difficult to over-estimate. It has not, however, seemed good to the majority among the Cardinals that this policy should be followed, and the Pope is unknown to the younger generation of Italians.

Although the Cardinals take the view that I have put forward they have no belief in the restoration of any form of temporal power, and, on the other hand, not the slightest intention of leaving Rome, to which they are attached by large money interests and by every consideration which makes life endurable to highly civilised old gentlemen. They are well aware that even supposing the impossible, viz., the future existence of an Italian Government which would consent to abdicate in any degree the position attained in 1870, there would still be the population of Rome itself to reckon with. The city has undergone an extraordinary change since the occupation by the Italian troops. It has enormously increased in size since it has become the capital, and not only are the new inhabitants strongly opposed to the restitution in any form or degree of the temporal power, but the great bulk of the old Roman population is now, if not ardently attached to the Royal Government, at all events greatly disinclined to return to the former state of things.

The policy of the Vatican in prohibiting good Catholics from taking any part in Italian political affairs, either as electors or as candidates, has been much discussed of late. The *contadini* could possibly be greatly influenced at the ballot boxes by the priests. But the Pope could only return a Catholic chamber by frankly giving up the temporal power; otherwise only those who were traitors to their country and ready for civil war would support his men, and these are very few. The policy, though probably foolish and mistaken from what ought to be the Vatican point of view, is a mere corollary of the Pope's attitude to the Italian Government. Those who talk about the Vatican having it in its power to make constitutional government impossible in Italy show an entire misapprehension of the situation. What the Vatican has it in its power to do is to strengthen by a mild and friendly exercise of its influence both the Italian Government and its own position, to the advantage of Conservative interests in Italy and throughout the world. In July, 1880, there was considerable discussion at the Vatican as to the attitude to be adopted. Some of the foreign Cardinals were at that time most anxious that conditional support should be given to the Italian monarchy, but the majority of the Cardinals held and still hold the opposite view. The "inexpedient," on which ground the Church, after a fierce debate in council, decided not to take part in Italian politics, has, I am sorry to say, in the recent prevalence of reactionary views, been explained as meaning "unlawful," so that there is now direct prohibition. On the other hand, Italy swarms with active bishops of vast influence, and the Church, in my opinion, has it in her power to make modern Italy into a citadel of the Church, provided she frankly accepts Italian unity and takes a completely patriotic attitude as regards the few home affairs in which she ought to make her influence felt. The reactionary party among the Cardinals make use of modern weapons. They point out to the Roman Pontiff, what no doubt is true, that the Church must not be Italian but world-wide. If, however, the Church is not to be Italian, it might be well to begin by so changing the constitution of the Sacred College as to make that body cosmopolitan and not Italian. One Cardinal for Canada and one for Australia may be enough for the present, but it is ridiculous to say that one Cardinal is a sufficient representative in the Sacred College for the Catholic population of the United States. In my opinion both changes might be wisely made. The government of the Church might be made non-Italian, and really placed in the hands of the whole Church, to select without regard for nationality the best servants that she can find ; and, on the other hand, Italy might become a sure haven, as free from foreign influence as Switzerland herself, and the most peaceful and contented of possible homes for the seat of a great Church. The Church has it in her power to aid the Italian patriotic view in favour of the creation of a modern state which should have something of the glories of ancient Rome. The Mazzinian and Garibaldian forms of the Italian revolution may both be weak in Italy, but patriotism and the sentiment of unity are strong, and the Church is supposed by the people to be non-patriotic if not hostile to unity. When once it becomes clear, as sooner or later it must, that Italy can have Catholic unity, a really world-wide Church may find in Italy, without any temporal power, a true independence.

If we look to the religious side of the question, surely from the Catholic point of view the decision that it is unlawful for good Catholics to take part in Italian elections seems open to exception, for it leaves the majority of Italian Catholics to be legislated for in all home matters by representatives of the minority of non-Catholics, and nominal Catholics who reject the authority of the Church. The reactionary party at the Vatican are, therefore, apparently not only doing that which is unwise from the point of view of the political interests of the Church, but also that which may be wrong from the religious point of view.

Even the most extreme among the reactionary party at the Vatican do not expect a restoration of temporal power. They keep out of Italian public life the most Conservative element in Italy, and they profess to wait for that which

they well know can never come.   There are many who think
that the Church is wise to maintain the interdict on voting,
because the removal of the interdict would only reveal the
fact that the Church cannot control the voters.   Certainly it
cannot control the voters in a sense hostile to the Italian
kingdom, and certainly it would be foolish to remove the
interdict with the view of making war on Italy.   On the
principle of the grandeur of the unknown, it is no doubt
true that the hostility of the Church in abstention produces
more effect than would be produced by the hostility of the
Church coupled with an ineffective exercise of the voting
power; but my contention is that the time has come for a
patriotic exercise of the voting power by Catholics, and for
the abandonment of an attitude which may be dignified but
which is contrary to the real interests of the Church.

The Pope and the working Cardinals take pleasure in
dealing less with the masses than with "sovereigns and
statesmen," to use Lord Beaconsfield's expression.   For this
work they have a marvellous aptitude, and were they less
fettered by the attitude of the reactionary majority there
is hardly any limit to the influence to which the Holy See
under modern conditions might attain.   There are, however,
certain subjects upon which the cleverest intellects of the
Vatican take as cramped a view as do the most prejudiced
priests who have no dealings beyond their own limited
horizon.   There is the question of Freemasonry, for instance.
Nothing will persuade the Supreme Pontiff and his most
accomplished advisers that Freemasonry in England has
no dealings with Freemasonry on the continent, and has

nothing in common with anti-religious secret organizations.
It is useless to point out that English Masons are merely
a collection of non-political convivial people who, whether
rightly or wrongly, like to combine feasting with charity,
that the heir apparent to the throne is at their head, and
that it so happens that all or nearly all of the chief officials
are past or present members of Conservative administrations.
It is useless, also, to ask where, if the mere use of secret signs
and passwords is to constitute a wicked crime against the
Church, the line is to be drawn, and if the Foresters,
the Oddfellows, the Druids, the Free Gardeners, the Buf-
faloes, the Bisons, the Caledonian Corks, and what not, are all
equally enemies of religion. The only reply which can be
obtained from the Vatican is that the distinguished individuals who countenance such societies in England err
through ignorance of the real nature of the societies to which
they belong, perhaps because they are mainly members of
the "stupid party." The question of English Freemasonry
would be too trivial to introduce into a serious political
article were it not that it shows that the acutest intellects
of the Vatican, who are far in advance of the rest of the
priesthood, have need to widen some of their views before
they can deal with popular movements in modern times.
The recent action of the Holy See in regard to the Knights
of Labour in America is held by some to be the first dawn
of a broader policy; but it seems odd for a Conservative
body to bless the Knights of Labour and continue to condemn
the English Masons.

The present Roman Pontiff is not only a statesman well-informed as to all that is going on in the capitals of Europe, but also an administrator of the greatest industry. He not only frequently writes his own despatches, not only super-intends an enormous correspondence with all parts of the world, but the trick of his style is sometimes said to be recognised in the official organ of the Vatican. Everything that appears in the *Osservatore Romano* may be taken as having been sealed with the Fisher's Seal. The *Moniteur de Rome* is not recognised as official, but its articles are often meant as feelers, and are, in consequence, well worth reading. Monsignor Galimberti was at one time intimately connected with this journal, and he is now the envoy of the Vatican who is always employed on delicate missions which require tact and adroitness. The arbitration between Germany and Spain in the matter of the Caroline Islands is said to have originated with him. His recent journey to Berlin, which has been much commented upon, and which has caused irritation amongst some Italians, related solely to the interior policy of Germany and the relations of Prince Bismarck with the Centre.

The Pope's intervention was probably a matter of actual bargain, a certain amendment of anti-clerical laws having been first promised; but of course the Jacobini letters were also defensible before the public on the ground of the popular belief that the vote of the septennate was indispensable to the preservation of peace. If this latter point of view is taken, however, it ought logically to lead to a direction to the faithful to vote at Italian elections in favour of the pro-German policy of the Italian kingdom. Some scoffers may be disposed to think that Herr Windhorst's speech upon the Pope's interference really amounted to a declaration in the following terms: "The Pope is infallible, no doubt, but when he knows what we have to say he will see that he has made a mistake." But it is still more curious to observe that Bismarckian Protestant papers in Germany declare that for so saying the German Catholic leader is "worse than Martin Luther." I am told, however, that Herr Windhorst still remains on the best of terms with the Vatican. It will be seen that I take the view that the Pope's action was directed solely to German internal affairs, although no doubt he was pleased to be consulted by Prince Bismarck and to play a great part in Europe. Some, however, have taken the terms of the Jacobini letters to suggest that he received, or at least asked for, some promises upon the subject of the temporal power. The phrase made use of has, as I have said, been explained away, and that it was an unfortunate one is proved by the fact that Italy received from Berlin full and immediate satisfaction upon the subject. It has, however, been suggested that Germany is now about to undertake to bring about a permanent understanding between the Quirinal and the Vatican. The base of such an understanding would be that the temporal power in every shape has gone for ever without the slightest hope of its restoration by any means, and that King Humbert was justified in calling the Roman settlement "a conquest that cannot be touched."

It is difficult to see what concessions the Italian kingdom can make to the Pope, at Prince Bismarck's wish, greater than the concessions which are contained in the Law of Guarantees. The law of 1871 declares that the person of the Sovereign Pontiff is sacred, and that all attempts, direct or indirect, against his person, are punishable in the same way as attacks against the person of the King, while offences and insults against the Supreme Pontiff are similarly dealt with. Royal honours are rendered to him, and the Italian Government declares that it maintains the pre-eminence of honour recognised by Catholic princes as belonging to the Sovereign Pontiff. It allows him to keep up guards; it gives him a magnificent endowment and the whole of the apostolic palaces and their dependencies; it provides that the Conclave shall be absolutely free, by forbidding any judicial or political authority from placing any limit to the personal liberty of the Cardinals during periods when the Holy See is vacant. It forbids public officials and the police from entering any palace of the Sovereign Pontiff, or any building in which is assembled a Conclave or an Œcumenical Council. It frees from all responsibility to, and all investigation by, public authority all ecclesiastics, whether Italian or foreign, who, by reason of their office, participate in Rome in sending forth the acts of the spiritual ministry of the Holy See. It gives to all envoys to the Holy See the same prerogatives and immunities as are given to all envoys accredited to the Italian Government. It gives absolute freedom of correspondence by post and telegraph, and the power to maintain in the Vatican postal and telegraph offices worked by Pontifical clerks. It gives to the couriers of the Supreme Pontiff the immunities of the Cabinet couriers of the Italian kingdom and of the couriers of foreign Governments. It

provides for the freedom from charges and taxes of the letters
and telegrams of the Vatican, and it gives virtual extra
territoriality to the seminaries of Rome and those of the
suburban secs. It abolishes all restraints upon the right of
meeting on the part of the Catholic clergy, restrictions which,
be it remembered, were maintained by the former Catholic
Governments of Italy. It exempts Popes from the oath of
allegiance. It may be safely asserted that by this statute
greater freedom and power are given to the Catholic Church
in Italy than it possesses anywhere else, and that the Church
obtains by it the advantages, very difficult to combine, of the
power of establishment together with actual freedom from
State control. Of course a good many legal difficulties are
created by the Act. Jurists who are also jocular have
asked whether, for example, in the event of a siege of Rome
the Pope and Cardinals would be liable to be expelled by
the military authority as *bouches inutiles*. I fail to see,
however, what the Pope can hope to obtain better than that
which he has been given. On the other hand, there is
some danger that if he does not come to terms there may
arise popular agitation in favour of a repeal of the Law of
Guarantees, and the abolition of that portion of the Constitution which declares the Catholic Church to be the State
Church of Italy, and also a demand for the secularization
of all Church property. There have already been some
signs on the part of the Left of an inclination towards petty
persecution of the Church. These acts only bring down upon
the kingdom the drawbacks of war without gaining any of
its possible advantages.

Some have thought that the Jacobini letters and the

Galimberti mission had to do less with German internal politics and with the dignity of the Holy See, or, on the other hand, with the temporal power, than with the Pope's project that he should become the moderator between France and Germany. This report, with all the fanciful details of a neutralized Alsace, is imaginary. Arbitration by the Pope is out of the question. "Arbitration" implies in diplomatic language that you must take the arbitrator's opinion or risk war. What is probably meant is rather in the nature of "mediation" or "good offices," but the whole story is without foundation.

The Pope has only himself to blame for the false impressions that have got abroad with reference to the Galimberti mission, and the phrase as to the future help of Germany was unjustifiably ambiguous. The explanation that it was written by a young man, ignorant of the world outside Rome, is a mere excuse, which means that those who offer it now know that the phrase was a foolish one. The threat of foreign interference has the same effect in Italy that Spanish interference on behalf of the Pope used to have in Elizabethan England, and this unfortunate sentence has done harm which it will not be easy to undo. The support, even when we put the temporal power out of view, which the Pope can receive from Prince Bismarck is of a limited kind. The May Laws, according to Prince Bismarck's own account of them, were passed as an act of war against the Church; "but while melinite is a useful thing when you are at war, it is undesirable as an article of furniture in time of peace." The May Laws, therefore, can be completely repealed, the position

of the Church in Germany may be rendered as good as it
is in any other country, almost as good as it might be in
Italy, if the Pope would frankly accept the position created
by the Law of Guarantees.   Moreover, the Pope's situation
in Europe may be improved by great personal deference
being attached to his declarations and his actions.   He may
be treated as a king, and as something more than a king.
He may be applied to to mediate in unimportant matters, or
on occasions when mediation is only intended to be offered
and not accepted.   Further than this it is impossible for
Prince Bismarck to go; and, in my belief, further than this
the Pope knows Prince Bismarck cannot go.   On the other
hand, it is quite possible that the Pope may be anxious to
make peace with Italy and to accept the Law of Guarantees,
and may find it easier to take this course with dignity through
Prince Bismarck, than by means of direct negotiations with
the Quirinal.   He may also wish that the Law of Guarantees
should receive dignity and permanence from European recognition of its terms.

   I have discussed in previous chapters the question of the
French protection of Catholic missions in the East.   Should
peace ever be made between the Quirinal and the Vatican,
it is possible that some day Italy may become the protecting
Power of the Church, and may aid the Pope in guarding
Catholic interests throughout the world.   That France should
be the Power protecting Catholics in China is positively
hurtful to Catholic interests.   Why, as the Chinese ask,
should France insist upon protecting the Christians in China,
whether the local Christians desire that protection or do not?

To oppress or expel in France, and to protect and guard, not only in China, but also even nearer home—in Morocco —is too sharp a contrast. "Clericalism! that is the enemy!" is printed outside Gambetta's books; but Paul Bert, who taught him the doctrine, himself became the protector of the Clericals in the far East, though retaining his militant atheism at home.   The better view will continue to be that no State should be the protector of Christian interests in general, but that, while each should help its subjects, spiritual Christian interests can best be looked after by the spiritual heads of each Church, that is, in the case of Catholics, by the Pope.   It is possible, however, that Italy may one day become the Pope's right arm.   It is certain that the relations of the Church with France are less good now than they were in November, 1885, when the encyclical which declared that the Church was not attached to any special form of government was taken as an intervention in favour of the Government of France.   The Chinese question made these relations very much worse in 1886.   M. de Freycinet's threats have not been forgotten, and the intervention in favour of Prince Bismarck has further widened the breach, although France, indeed, was far from desiring the rejection of the German military law.

There are, of course, causes for anxiety in Italy, as there are in all States at the present day.   As Great Britain has her enormous responsibilities and her military unreadiness to meet them, as Russia has Nihilism and corruption, as Austria has Socialism and race difficulties, as Germany has her weak military position between two first-class military

Powers, as France has her traditions of financial wastefulness and the want of statesmen, so Italy too has her difficulties. Of these difficulties the backwardness of Sicily, and of the southern provinces generally, is perhaps the greatest. I think that, on the whole, Italy has fewer dangers to face than any other of the great Powers. I am convinced that she is making more rapid progress than any of them, with the exception, of course, of Russia, which has the advantage of being, territorially considered, almost a second United States. A vast advance has been made of late in education, in manufactures, and by the suppression of brigandage, and while a great deal remains to be done, more has been done in Italy in the last sixteen years than is generally acknowledged or believed.

VI.

THE UNITED KINGDOM.

In the five preceding chapters, in which I have examined the relative positions of the great Continental Powers of Europe, it has been shown that Germany and France, notwithstanding their extraordinary armaments, are unlikely to provoke a breach of the peace. Germany is under the apprehension that Russia might join with France in case of an outbreak of hostilities; and in France the really peaceful tendency of the majority of the electors rules the country, notwithstanding the Chauvinism of a certain section of journalists and politicians. Austria-Hungary, from its internal difficulties and the uncertainty of obtaining an effective alliance against Russia, is equally interested in maintaining the peace of Europe; and Italy is also, in spite of the strength of her naval and military forces, in the highest degree unlikely to provoke a war. Russia I have treated as the one uncertain factor in the European situation, and, unfortunately, Russia is the Power with which England has to reckon.

There remains for consideration the United Kingdom, which, under its various titles, has been incidentally mentioned from time to time in these chapters. We have seen that England is past her fighting days, unless moved by a very powerfully irritating cause ; in the first place on account of her admitted military unreadiness, and in the second place on account of her strong desire for peace. In speaking of England's unreadiness it has been pointed out that, though in a long war England, on account of her vast resources and the courage and energy of her people, would display greater power of endurance than any other nation, yet, in these days of rapid mobilisation, it is the first few weeks of a war that count, and England, being unable to rapidly mobilise large forces, could do nothing in the first months of a Continental conflict. This view was illustrated by showing that, in the case of a war in which Austria was engaged, a Roumanian alliance, which would provide 150,000 admirable troops at the very spot where they would be most wanted, would be of far greater immediate value to Austria than an alliance with England. It may be noted, however, that the wide-spread love of peace in England to a great extent arises from the very reasons which would make us formidable in a war of long continuance : our immense wealth and resources, and that concentration of energy upon business which every-where indisposes to war. This strong desire for peace, which arises as much from reserved strength as from immediate unreadiness, has stood the peace of Europe in good stead of late years, in face not only of irritating attacks by Continental journalists, which it is easy to disregard, but in face also of exasperating acts of policy, such as the treatment of British subjects in Madagascar during the war, and the occupation of the New Hebrides. England has, moreover, refrained from justifying the common Continental imputation that she is a plundering Power, for, with the exception of the annexation of Burmah, the movement upon which country was caused by the action of a French consul at the capital, England has made no recent annexation, down to that of Zululand, except in self-defence, as, for example, in New Guinea, against the annexation policy of Germany, and has successively declined to annex Egypt, Zanzibar, the Cameroons, and other countries in different parts of the world. That this policy of self-restraint has been in some degree a self-denying ordinance is seen by the fact that wherever owing to our abstention a territory is annexed by France, we are, sooner or later, made to suffer in common with the inhabitants of the territory itself by the imposition of differential duties upon foreign goods. With regard to the subject of British trade we have also seen that it suffers by annexations which have nothing to do with colonial enterprise ; every territory annexed by Russia is closed to our trade by means of heavy protective duties, and this we have found to be the case with Austria also, in a district the occupation of which by Austria was actually proposed by England, our Government forgetting then to make stipulations, which would probably have been accepted, in favour of British trade.

In respect to our relations with the Great Powers of the Continent, we have seen that with Germany they are on the whole friendly. The comparatively small differences that have arisen over colonial matters have failed to cause any serious friction between the countries. Prince Bismarck does not approve of our sentimental methods with regard to Turkish Christian subjects; but in the more practical question of keeping our road to India clear and maintaining order in Egypt, we have his general support. We have seen that our relations with France have been somewhat strained owing to the hostility to England of a certain section of French journalists, but that the good sense of the majority of both peoples is a great security against serious consequences ensuing from estrangement. Our chief difficulty with France being the Egyptian question, we have found nevertheless reasons for deciding that it is clear France does not intend that war between the two countries shall arise thence. We have seen that the present position of France in Egypt is owing to her own policy of standing aloof; that England, during her single-handed occupation, has been moderate in her actions, and that our chief interest in Egypt is admittedly free transit. We have also seen that it is easy to exaggerate the importance of Egypt to us, as, in a war in which France was against us, the calls upon our fleet would be such that the Suez Canal would be practically closed against British troops or trade carried in unarmed ships, and possibly closed to British traffic or passage in any form.

As to Russia, I have suggested reasons for thinking that although one day the fight between the elephant and the whale will probably take place, single-handed war between England and Russia is unlikely at the present moment, chiefly because the Russians have powerful military reasons in the condition of their Asiatic railroads for wishing to postpone it.

We have seen how the whole fabric of our policy of 1878 has collapsed, and how necessary it is that England should make up her mind with regard to the extent of her interest in the future of Constantinople. We have seen how the old doctrine of British concern in the integrity of the Ottoman Empire has been thrown over by Lord Randolph Churchill and other powerful politicians, and how numerous are the causes of difficulty between this country and Russia which have nothing to do with the existence of the Turkish Empire or with the possession of Constantinople. We have noticed the recent repudiation of solemn promises by Russia with regard to Batoum, and the exasperation of English feeling by Russia's bad faith in Central Asia and by the unsettled condition of the Afghan frontier question. We have seen how immense are the resources of the Russian Empire, and how, in spite of what is said of her finances, she comes next to England in power of endurance for a long war ; while on the other hand, a careful examination of the facts led me to suggest that Russia would be unable effectively to attack England in her Asiatic empire for some years to come.

It has been seen that the feeling of Austria-Hungary as to an alliance with England must continue to be regulated, as it has been in the past, by her calculation as to the immediate utility of such an alliance in the case of a war with Russia. Although I have no belief in the accuracy of the opinion that Austria, unaided by Germany or Italy, could hold her own against Russia, I have nevertheless pointed out that as the chances are that we shall find ourselves at war with Russia sooner or later, it would perhaps be better to fight, if we have to fight, with allies than alone. Austria, however, is terrified at the prospect of a war against Russia, even with an English and Italian alliance, on account of the inability of such allies to rapidly assist the Austrian army in the field upon the side of Galicia. In the case of Italy we have noted her consistent friendship with England, no matter what other combinations she may have entered into.

Of minor questions which have been discussed, the most important, perhaps, to ourselves is that of the neutrality of Belgium, to which I shall have in the present chapter to return. I have dwelt upon the unreadiness of Belgium to resist an infringement of her neutrality; upon the standing temptation to the German staff to invade France by way of Belgium; upon the impossibility of England, even if she wished to do so, opposing by force any serious invasion of Belgian neutrality; and upon the probability of the other Powers declining to join us should we propose to them to come to the assistance of Belgium. This paragraph may not be pleasant reading either to the Belgians or to ourselves, but in these matters the truth is seldom palatable to the parties concerned. I expected when I began to write these articles, that everyone would be displeased with them, and I am no more likely to be disappointed by the effect of this one in the United Kingdom than I was by the reception in France, Russia, and Austria-Hungary of the second, third, and fourth.

Just, indeed, as there is much in the previous chapters which is necessarily displeasing to the inhabitants of the Continental countries discussed, so I fear that there is a good deal in this chapter and the others which cannot be made altogether pleasant reading at home. For example, it is not satisfactory to us to hear of the real strength of Russia, with whom we may at any moment find ourselves at war; but at the same time, it is better to face the facts than to live in a fools' paradise. We are too much in the habit in this country of attending only to one subject at a time, and when we are thinking about Ireland, which is very commonly the case, we are apt to forget all else, and both our relations with foreign Powers and those between ourselves and our dependencies drop into the background. Yet, grave as is the importance of the condition of Ireland for many reasons, that which in the highest degree constitutes its gravity is the additional embarrassment it causes in our dealings with the world at large. It is too much the case with us in England that when we are occupied with the consideration of the Irish problem, or dealing with the circumstances which most often lead to the rise and fall of Ministries, we allow the foreign affairs of the country to be transacted in the dark, with an absence of control that, owing to the efficiency of our Foreign Office, may produce no ill, but also with an absence of knowledge which cannot be advantageous. On the other hand, when some awkward circumstance arises, a disproportionate weight is attached to it by those who have wilfully remained in ignorance of the true position, and the diplomacy of the country is suddenly unduly hampered by criticism which rests upon no foundation of fact. While home affairs are watched with the closest attention, and conducted by all parties with high skill, foreign affairs pass from periods of contented but ignorant calm to periods of discontented or violent, but often equally ignorant, panic. There is not, it must be admitted, the same consistency in the foreign policy of Great Britain which is to be found in the foreign policy of the autocracy of Russia, of the constitutional monarchy of Italy, or of the Republic of the United States. It varies under the influence of the personal views of leading statesmen, but more than this, it even undergoes extraordinary modification from time to time while remaining under the influence of one and the same party in the State.

In the present reign of force in Europe, of which in the first chapter I investigated the cause, England is of all Powers the most unprepared for war, but then on the other hand she is of all the Powers the one which through her insular position can, some tell us, afford to be the least prepared. I have already pointed out, however, that it is easy to push arguments for economy, drawn from the insularity of our position, much too far, and that our enormous carrying trade and also our position as an Asiatic Continental State, make it impossible for us to adopt with impunity the practice of the American Republic. Much harm has been done to the cause of sense and truth by the exaggerations of the most violent members of the anti-Russian school among English writers and politicians. I have tried in these chapters, and especially in that on Russia, to sift the wheat from the chaff and without giving way to the counsels of pessimism, to show exactly how far Russia is, and how far she is not, a danger to our State.

It seems sufficiently established for any who may have gone along with my arguments, that it is impossible for the United Kingdom to adopt a policy of disarmament or of effacement in Europe without the gravest danger for her future. It is impossible to treat the necessity incumbent upon us of defending India against possible attack as though it were an isolated obligation. That necessity in itself forces us to closely watch European combinations, even if we give up as main objects of our policy the defence of Belgium and the keeping of Russia away from the Mediterranean. I should be sorry, however, to limit the necessity of our watching Continental politics, and of our remaining armed, by considerations relating to India alone. No doubt our chief colonies are able to defend themselves; no doubt our carrying trade can be protected by naval means without a great resort to additional expenditure upon the services; but I cannot honestly pretend that we are at present in such a perfect position of defence at home as to be under all circumstances safe against the possibility of invasion. We have to face the fact that we are one of the least popular of Powers, and that if we alone were attacked no hand would be raised in our defence. There are, moreover, considerations which go wholly beyond those of the selfish order, and which equally direct us not to abdicate our place in Europe.

If it were possible to conduct the foreign relations of a democratic country, such as England has now become, with secrecy as well as with firm devotion to a fixed line of conduct, no doubt it would be better to leave the consideration of many questions until they actually arise; but at the present moment we suffer from the disadvantages of both systems. We do not fully discuss foreign relations in advance, and make up our minds as to our best course; we do not even take steps to inform ourselves thoroughly as to the facts; but at the same time we encourage our public men to make rash and hasty statements founded upon imperfect knowledge, and we "go wild" from time to time in various directions. In 1878 the country appeared to be as deeply committed to the opinion that it was necessary at all hazards to keep Russia from Constantinople, as it had in 1870 been deeply committed to the opinion that it was necessary to save Belgium from annexation by either Germany or France; yet, in 1887, Constantinople and Belgium alike are given up, and given up in public with much demonstrative earnestness, by many of the same men who but a few years ago were strongly urging upon their countrymen the exactly opposite view. The last debate which occurred in the Imperial Parliament upon foreign affairs was, I fear, calculated to harm the interests of peace by encouraging Russia to take steps which would produce a general conflagration, or at least bring about results damaging to this country. The responsibility incurred by those who initiate such debates is great. Parliamentary summaries are telegraphed to the foreign newspapers in a very imperfect form; they are read by foreign statesmen with minute attention, but sufficient allowance is not made either for the mistakes of the telegraph and of the translators, or for the exaggerations of party politics. In the time of Castlereagh the true declarations of this country upon her foreign policy were made in secret letters, and despatches were written for publication with the view of throwing dust in the eyes of Parliament; but nowadays foreign statesmen are apt to read the debates at Westminster as being the real revelations of our policy, and the despatches and memoranda of our Foreign Secretaries and ambassadors as being of a less solid nature. Again, attacks of the class of those which one or two members of the House occasionally make now upon Sir James Fergusson, but which a few years ago were made by a handful of Conservative members with more violence upon Lord Edmond Fitzmaurice, are productive of unmixed harm. Questions too are often put which, as Sir Henry Maine says, are "deliberately intended to work public mischief." On the other hand, questions sometimes are not pressed which should be pressed, as for example, the questions recently put about our threats to Hayti. Every Government, or at all events every Government of England, looking to the complexity of the interests which it represents, must, if it takes part in foreign affairs at all, from time to time receive rebuffs. It is, I suppose, only human nature that Oppositions should desire to call the widest possible attention to the fact that 'the Government of their country has been, as they would style it, "snubbed" by one or other of the Great Powers. Because we are wont to see Oppositions (or rather individuals in opposition, for the great majority of the Opposition do not countenance the attacks of which I speak) taking advantage of the temporary humiliations of our foreign policy, it by no means follows that it is for the good of the country that attention should be called to those rebuffs. It is undoubtedly real weakness which they indicate, and weakness for which we all are in part responsible, because we know that we are not equipped to discharge the duties which we take upon us, but it is a bad thing for the country that this weakness should be revealed abroad. As, however, we cannot hope for secrecy, let us at all events draw from the publicity of our times the advantage which should attend publicity, of fully informing ourselves upon the facts, of speaking only from real knowledge, and of doing all that is in our power to bring the masses of the electorate to recognise their responsibilities, and to fit themselves for their station in the world. It is not perhaps impossible that that general acquiescence in an uniform foreign policy, based on knowledge, which is found even in the democratic and somewhat violent assemblies of Italy and of the United States, should one day be met with here. We can all do something towards the attainment of the end in view, if we abstain from approving in our friends that parliamentary course which we blame in our opponents, and if we all speak and write on foreign affairs in such a way as to show that we are aware that playing with them in a party sense is playing with the fiercest kind of fire.

When I find myself compelled to write, in answer to official optimism, of our unpreparedness for war, I must at once admit that it is not in expenditure that we fall short. We spend, indeed, more upon war services than does any other empire in the world, and perhaps more not only absolutely but even relatively in proportion to our enormous responsibilities. Considering, indeed, how much we spend and how little we can show for our money, I cannot but feel inclined to ask those who are giving at present so great a portion of their time to the discussion of the Irish question, whether they could not afford to turn a little of their energy to inducing their countrymen to consider for themselves a problem which is as pressing, as lasting, and, as it seems to me, still more grave. A great many are prepared to meet it roughly and impatiently up to a certain point. They say, we are an island, we can reach India by sea, we can practically defend England and our colonies from the sea; and they content themselves with the expression of a desire that our navy should continue to be of transcendent strength. But then I have shown in my article on Russia, that as against Russia, at all events, we cannot wholly contend by naval means. By pointing out how we could, in the event of war, bleed Russia to death on the Pacific, until there comes the inevitable day when her Trans-Siberian railways shall be made, I have gone as far as possible in the direction of concession to those who attach sole importance to our strength at sea. But when we prepare for fighting in defence of India (and no one can say that the risk is not, at all events, so great that we should prepare to meet it), it must be as a Continental power against a Continental power. There has lately been published in the pages of the *Fortnightly Review* an article[1] by a most distinguished officer, which puts, as strongly as it can be put, the optimistic

(1) The British Army : Past and Present. By General Sir John Adye. *The Fortnightly Review*, April, 1887.

side. Another most optimistic document is the memorandum
of the Secretary of State for War relating to the Army Estimates. The triumph of complacent optimism is, however,
reached in a little pamphlet lately published by Mr. Howard
Vincent, the title of which, *Through the British Empire in
Ten Minutes*, shows us that the writer has "beaten the
record," and excelled the "performance" of Jules Verne.
In it Mr. Vincent states "the approximate military defensive
strength of the British Empire" at 2,250,000 men, without
telling us anything of the time that it would take to place
even a tenth of this force in line near London, provided with
a sufficient field artillery, and ready to engage even a much
smaller Continental force, for the defence of the heart of the
Empire itself. I have no desire to put the pessimistic view
before my readers; all that I wish to do is to get as near as
may be to the truth.

Now what is the most scientific foreign opinion with
regard to our present military position? If we collate the
statements of the leading foreign writers upon the subject,
we find that they point out that our colonial garrisons are
singularly small; for example, in Trinidad, we have 106 men
(they take no account of the volunteers), in the Bahamas,
93 (black), in Honduras, 226 (black); on the other hand
the French keep in French Guiana 1,000 French soldiers
(white men), while we keep in British Guiana 163 (black
troops); the French have in their West India islands more
men than we have in ours; and furthermore the French
have strongly fortified their chief colonial positions, Fort
de France, in Martinique, and Dakar, in Senegal. It is

U

pointed out that we have talked a great deal about the fortification of our coaling stations, but have not as yet at most of
them accomplished much, so that our fleet would have a
heavy task in guarding, for example, Thursday Island, King
George's Sound, and our Crown Colonies against attack from
French or Russians in time of war. It is also shown that
in now beginning to fortify our coaling stations we seem to
forget that the places will need garrisons; that we are
under obligation to defend Belgium, but that we are unable
in fact to do so ; that upon our Indian frontier we shall have
to fight the Russians, and that it is "impossible to prophesy
the result of this inevitable struggle ; " that our army is
sufficiently supplied with possible infantry forces to form
eight army corps, but that not more than two such corps
could be used abroad on account of the want of cavalry
and artillery. This is an allusion to what even Mr. Stanhope
calls "the abortive scheme of the eight army corps in 1875:"
yet this is the moment which Mr. Stanhope chooses for the
reduction of that portion of the forces which it needs the
longest time to set on foot. The highest foreign scientific
military opinion informs us that a great war in which
England is engaged will not end without an attempt at the
invasion of this country; that the fleet cannot be certain of
being able to prevent invasion; that, while it is useless to
land in Ireland or Scotland, or in the north of England,
it is a possible operation, and one which would undoubtedly
be attempted, to land in the south of England suddenly
and by surprise, and to march on London. It is assumed
that we should concentrate—and concentrate too slowly and

too late—at Croydon or in its neighbourhood, but that we should be attacked not only from the south, but also from the side of Harwich. Our fleet would be embarrassed by the necessity of defending positions which are important to our future, but easily attacked, such as Kingston, in Jamaica. The Channel Islands would also be attacked, and could not be held without protection from the fleet. Plymouth, we are told, is so unfinished as to be easily open to bombardment from the sea between Rane Head and Fort Tregantle, as well as from points between Saltash and St. Germans; Portsmouth is unfinished upon the Fareham side, and both the Hilsea Lines and the Portsdown forts are somewhat out of date. Sir E. Hamley's proposals for the defence of London are contemptuously dismissed as a suggestion that after the enemy have landed they are to be asked to pause in their march until the metropolitan volunteers have thrown up earthworks that are satisfactory. We are told that Sir E. Hamley's "volunteer guns of position" would be useful if the enemy were kind enough to attack the selected position in front, not otherwise. Altogether, the scientific summary of our position is far from favourable to the views in the direction of retrenchment which have been expressed by the last three Chancellors of the Exchequer, although undoubtedly it is difficult to maintain that we at present get the greatest possible return for our expenditure.

About the possibility of running the gauntlet of the Tilbury forts and attacking London from the Thames, foreign military opinion is, on the other hand, not calculated to frighten us. No doubt submarine mines and torpedoes should be employed to reinforce the Tilbury forts, but Woolwich is close at hand, and the supplying of the apparatus needed would probably not be delayed in the event of war, provided that it has not been " economised " away. Sir Edward Hamley's remarks on this point are thought sound, but while it is well to guard against danger by taking the various steps he has advised, they are easily taken, and this Thames risk is small by the side of the other risks which London runs. The difficulty in our present position is that we are not impregnable at any point, and that the nervousness of the capital would greatly hamper the action of our fleet. If the Thames were safe, if our force for home defence were sufficiently well organised and sufficiently provided with field artillery to make us feel easy about coping with sudden invasion by a small force, then the fleet would be free to concentrate at points which the general interests of Imperial defence were supposed to advise; but as matters stand there would be a tremendous outcry in the press that London should not be left defenceless, and practically the large ships would find themselves forced to parade backwards and forwards between Harwich and Dover, or to mount guard as it were over London at the mouth of the Thames. At the same time, if our navy is not free to move in all directions, our Crown Colonies and our sea-going trade are at the mercy of our enemies. If the British navy is to have its full efficiency to act against the navies of our enemy, and to defend our trade, let alone the necessity of making, for the best defence, a counter-attack against those who have in the first place attacked us, it is essential that our ports should be safe, and that London should be secured against a sudden attack: it is not in these days possible to be certain that we shall be able to defend ourselves upon the opposite principle of blockading every conceivable enemy in his own port. The advice of a great naval officer which was given through Sir Peter Scratchley to the Australians upon this point, applies exactly also to ourselves: "To call on ships to protect the ports, instead of the ports the ships, is to invert the obligation, and prevent them performing their proper duties."

Not, indeed, that it is likely that we shall have to face what is called by naval men an ironclad attack. No doubt our antiquated forts, unsupplied for the most part with guns fit to pierce the armour of the most modern ships, or mounted upon one of the systems by which they could be worked against modern quick-firing guns, are not in a condition to enable us to contemplate with calm the possibility of an ironclad attack. Even supposing that melinite has been a failure, it may be taken as an admitted military axiom that provisional works lack the requisite powers of resistance to the most modern guns. I do not, however, myself believe that the next war will reduce itself merely to a conflict between the powers of roburite and those of melinite. We heard as much of the marvels of the mitrailleuse before August, 1870, as we hear now of those of the new shells; yet, although the mitrailleuse contained the germ of the machine guns and of the quick-firing guns of the present day, it was a failure in the first war in which it was used.

At the same time we are not prepared to protect ourselves even against sudden light attack. We may regret as much as we please the progress of destructive weapons, and the fact that since we built our fortresses they have virtually gone out of date, and we may lament the growth of the military power and of the rapidity of mobilisation of our neighbours; but it is a fact that quite apart from our obligations in India, in Asia Minor, and in Belgium, which I shall presently discuss, we are not in a condition to diminish, and probably may have to increase, our expenditure upon home defence. Our commercial ports are at present virtually undefended even against the lightest of light attacks, and we are far indeed from having reached a point at which the insurance of our national existence can be looked upon as complete.

I hear that something has been done lately to increase our stock of arms and ammunition; but it is believed abroad, and I fear with reason, that even within the last two years our stock of rifles was so small that there were only enough guns in store to arm the first-class army reserve, so that in fact there was from the military point of view no reserve at all of rifles, and that our ammunition stood at about a similar point of exhaustion. Although, as I said just now, there are some who think that our insular position enables us to remain "the least prepared" of Powers, it seems to me, on the contrary, that, given the fact that our army must be small, we should be, as far as readiness goes, the best prepared. No doubt we could only be successfully invaded by means of a rapid incursion by a small force, but this very fact shows that the invasion would take place without necessarily involving even the number of days' delay of an ordinary Continental mobilisation. Sufficient troops for a rush on London could be prepared in France, for example, without a sign, and the blow might fall on us with extraordinary suddenness. It would seem, therefore, that our army, though small, should be not worse but better prepared than that of any other Power, and for this purpose it is essential that we should not be exposed to a reduction of stores whenever the humour takes a Chancellor or an ex-Chancellor of the Exchequer.

In his April speech at Paddington, Lord Randolph Churchill claimed credit for having been the cause of a saving of a certain number of hundred thousand pounds. So far as I could understand him, he seemed to think that there was reason for congratulation in the fact that he had driven the Government to spend so many hundred thousand pounds less than they thought necessary for the safety of the country. But, with a still weaker Government, a Chancellor of the Exchequer of equal boldness might on this principle claim credit for saving the whole amount of the army and navy expenditure. He would, indeed, possibly be borne in triumph for it, although also possibly afterwards hanged when the country found that he had been wrong in his calculations. Lord Randolph Churchill appears, in his speeches about the army and navy, to take much account of pounds and of pence, but no account at all of the still more important matter of what the safety of the country needs. He is too, I must say in passing, open to the remark that he is more careful of the money of the represented English voter than of the unrepresented British-Indian taxpayer. When he was Secretary of State for India he did not decrease the military expenditure of that portion of the empire, which stands, no doubt, in need of defence precautions, but not more so than the rest; the Burmese business was costly, and generally speaking it must be admitted that Lord Randolph's Indian administration, while marked by great efficiency, was not especially economical. But surely the English democracy, which gave so wide and deep a popularity to Professor Fawcett for his insistence that the English and Indian taxpayer should be treated upon an equal footing, will not support Lord Randolph Churchill in the combination of zeal for economy without efficiency in England, and zeal for efficiency without economy in India. As I have named Professor Fawcett in connection with the Indian side of Imperial defence, let me hasten to say that it is my opinion that he pushed his excellent principles much too far, for he was always prepared to resist the imposition on the Indian taxpayer of any portion of the charges for wars which, if they were defensible at all, were very largely Indian wars. But Lord Randolph Churchill out-Herods Herod in the opposite direction, and when charged with financial carelessness by Mr. Goschen in the House of Commons (on the 25th April last), replies only, "India pays!"

The impatience of the country with regard to its military expenditure is largely caused by its very reasonable doubts as to whether it gets full value for its money. I think that it does not, and I hope to be able, in some small measure, at a future time to put forward considerations upon this subject; but the votes themselves are not, I think, excessive, looking to the responsibilities which we have voluntarily incurred—responsibilities which are greater than those of any other Power in the world. Let us have just taxation, which shall press upon those who are best able to bear it, and which, spent as it is for national insurance, shall chiefly be contributed by those who have a good deal to insure. But because the English people are brave, do not let us neglect precautions which every instructed observer, home and foreign, assures us to be necessary. Let the taxation, I repeat, fall on the right shoulders; let us take every conceivable means of securing that it is rightly expended, but do not let us congratulate those who take for their sole principle the mere reduction of amounts. This is not a time when the public are upon the one side and the army upon the other; the public as a whole have not responded to the invitation addressed to them by the last three Chancellors of the Exchequer in favour of a mere blind reduction of estimates; on the other hand, the most capable men of the army do not pretend that we get the most for our money at the present moment; they tell us very frankly that they are almost in despair at the condition of the army, and they ask us to co-operate with them in restoring its efficiency in comparison with the armies of the other Powers. I need not do more than mention the various points upon which they agree in telling us that money must be spent—the adoption of a new infantry arm; the more rapid increase of the heavy ordnance for the defence of the coaling stations, the Thames, our mercantile ports, Portsmouth, Plymouth, and our other fortresses; the wider adoption of cupolas, and, in other places, of the hydraulic machinery for mounting disappearing guns; the equipment of the volunteer force in such a way as to enable it easily to take the field in England; the completion of the defence by fortification of the coaling stations on a scheme which, greatly cut down as it was by Mr. Gladstone's Government from the report of the Royal Commission, and further cut down since Mr. Gladstone's time, has nevertheless not been fully carried out, even upon the thus reduced estimate; the garrisoning of such stations; all these are matters upon which there is a universal consensus of opinion among all who have considered the subject.

It being assumed for the moment that we are to give up all idea of acting upon the Asia Minor Convention, or of defending Turkey in any manner upon land, and that we are to put Belgium out of sight and think only of the defence of India and of England, and the protection of our colonies and trade, it is nevertheless the case that, even upon this reduced estimate of our responsibilities, in the opinion of all competent men we fall short of power to accomplish our task. Moreover, it is impossible to meet even the smaller duties which we now seem to set ourselves, upon the same expenditure as that which was sufficient to provide for the larger ones but a few years ago, and it is idle to attempt to limit present and future expenditure by the standard of our expenditure in the past.

Some indeed of our military advisers appear to have resigned themselves to the inevitable, and to now readily and willingly accept the policy of confining the army to the defence of India and of England. On the 23rd of April Lord Wolseley made a speech at a dinner of the Press Club, in which he began by explaining how the heads of the army had been organising the army for a great number of years, but had never done so much as they had done within the last few months. All this organisation seemed, to judge by the words of his speech, to be for the purpose only of producing "two army corps and a cavalry division," and it was clear from what Lord Wolseley said about "getting rid of the theatrical" element, and reducing the units of cavalry, infantry, and "batteries" (? artillery) into a proportional number of units as regards the various arms, that he approved of that reduction of horse artillery of which almost every other soldier disapproves. On the 27th April Lord Wolseley made another speech, in which he plainly took the defence of the reduction of the horse artillery upon himself. The two army corps and the cavalry division are intended, according to Lord Wolseley's speech, for the defence of England, "because no sane man would for a moment undertake the defence of this country with any smaller organised army, in addition to the auxiliary forces, than the two army corps to which I have referred." He went on to say that the country was "open to invasion," and that we must "have such a defensive force in this country that we may be able to sleep quietly in our beds at night, knowing that we have an army able to defend the country should it be attacked." It certainly seems an extraordinary thing that we should have been spending a far larger sum every year on the army than any other country spends, and spending indeed a larger sum if we make every deduction from the figures which is involved in the absence of a conscription, and yet should be able to produce by an expenditure of about thirty-eight millions sterling a year only 70,000 troops in India and two corps in England—or say four strong army corps in all, besides a little over 20,000 infantry in Malta, Gibraltar, and other portions of the world. The great majority of native regiments in India could not with safety be used against a European foe ; certainly not so long as they go into action with about four European officers each, and are liable to be commanded, as in one case in Afghanistan, by a subaltern just arrived from England. Less than five corps in all, prepared to take the field, appears to constitute the actually available army upon which nearly forty millions sterling are expended by the Empire, for only a small portion of these millions is expended upon the militia, yeomanry, and volunteers ; and the volunteers, without the support of mobile field artillery, are not much more useful than the inferior Indian troops.

So far as I know, this speech by Lord Wolseley, taking the plain meaning of the words, is the first declaration from a high military quarter that the two army corps in England, to which the ambitious eight army corps of 1875 have fallen, are intended simply for home defence. It causes painful reflections that this position of despair should apparently be taken up by the man who, but a short time ago, was the military hope of youthful England. After the reduction of the eight army corps to two as a possible standard, we were

told that the two were to be always ready for instant movement to any part of the world where their presence might
be needed ; now we seem to be told that the two are only
to be ready for home defence. I doubted when I read it
whether Lord Wolseley's speech was to be taken literally,
and felt that he would probably stay for the present at a half-
way house, and if pressed would tell us that he meant that we
could not hope to do much for the defence of Belgium against
either Germany or France, or for the defence of Turkey
against Russia. If on the contrary we were at war, not
with Germany or with France, but with a Power which could
not hope to invade us, as for example Russia, this force,
which as against Germany or France must be kept at home
to resist invasion, would be available for distant expeditions,
as for example against the Russian positions on the Pacific.

I am not left, however, to rely upon my own fancy as to
what Lord Wolseley really meant, but have had the opportunity of hearing, from those who are in a position to know
it, what is his own explanation of his speech. His friends
admit that military opinion is hostile to the reduction of the
horse artillery, but say that the opinion of any number of
soldiers who have not the whole of the facts before them,
ought scarcely to weigh at all against that of the few who
are working with full knowledge of the facts, and with their
hearts set earnestly on securing the utmost possible increase
to our effective fighting strength. The case for the reduction is as follows, according to their defence. "The great
danger that has hitherto threatened us does not," they point
out, " lie in India, however real our danger in India may be,

nor does it lie in direct invasion of Great Britain, although if there be not an adequate force at home that invasion is a possibility." The greatest danger is said to lie in the undefended condition of our trade. It is pointed out, however, that we possess an enormous advantage for the protection of our commerce in the possession in every sea of coaling stations of our own. "The *articulus stantis aut cadentis* " *Imperii* is at present their defence. For if defended so " that no cruiser can assail them, our fleets have the security " everywhere, in pursuing cruisers, of being able as often as " they need it to re-supply their bunkers, while the cruisers " cannot, except at their first start, get coal at all. If these " harbours are undefended the cruiser, on the other hand, has " the command of all this coal, and by setting fire to all that " it does not use, can pass on to the next coal depôt and do " likewise, preying the while upon our commerce, and making " pursuit impossible. Now the defence of these coaling " stations is mainly, though not wholly, a question of an " adequate force of trained artillerymen, supplemented by " an adequate number of auxiliaries. In other words, the " essential condition of the moment is the rendering effective " what at present is the most inadequate in point of numbers " of all parts of our army, the garrison artillery. Relatively " to the needs of the empire, its importance as compared with " the horse artillery, at least as compared with any excess of " horse artillery, is beyond all expression. An increase of " the garrison artillery is absolutely indispensable. Where " shall the money come from ? The armament is there, or " very soon will be, at each station, and is useless without

" men. Of course, if some means can be found by which an
" army equipped with all the improved conditions of modern
" life can be had for less money than we are now paying,
" new necessities may be met without curtailing other ex-
" penses. But of this I am sure, that we cannot afford to
" reduce our slender force of regular infantry, which at this
" moment, thanks to the calls of Egypt, does not provide the
" necessary strength of *cadres* for training our recruits, the
" very pith and marrow of our system ; and I think no one
" will say that our cavalry could be lessened. To lose any
" force so trained as our Royal Horse Artillery is of course
" a very serious matter, but the batteries reduced were always
" stripped of men and horses in the case of war; and in the
" event of future war their fate would be (what it has been
" in each campaign that we have had, when guns and supply
" waggons were required), to be reduced to absolute ineffi-
" ciency by all their drivers and horses being taken to make
" up other batteries and the supply train. It is all very
" well to talk about keeping a nucleus of the second line of
" waggons, but we absolutely require, and shall far more
" require with magazine rifles, to have a body for regimental
" transport and ammunition-supply almost as perfectly
" trained as the horse artillery itself, as to being able to go
" anywhere and do anything."

Another friend of Lord Wolseley's whom I have consulted says, "Lord Wolseley often uses expressions about the
improved state of our army, which those who are anxious to
improve it further wholly misunderstand. He has had a most
difficult game to play, and has, despite all difficulties, done

more for our actual increase in strength than all other men put together. When he speaks of improvements he has not the slightest dream that finality has been approached, but he believes that we have been moving in the right direction, and, in order to prevent our simply being stranded in obstruction, he speaks out as to the value of what has been done." No doubt Lord Wolseley is a soldier who, if given a free hand, could and would organise an army for us which would be of value, but his own speech at the Press dinner, if words have meaning, is the best of proofs that we do not possess such an army at the present time. It was confirmed by him at the United Service Institution on the 20th of May.

In one point I fully sympathise with Lord Wolseley, and agree in the language of another speech of his at Fishmongers' Hall. It is necessary for the statesmen, or, if the statesmen will not, then for the public, to lay down for the soldiers a basis of military policy. It is impossible for the soldiers to be satisfied that they are giving us what we want till we decide what it is we do want. At the present moment our policy is merely a hand-to-mouth one, and, until we obtain something like a certainty for the future, the army expenditure will continue to be wasteful on the one side and unduly influenced by the Treasury upon the other. At the same time it is humiliating to remember that in the last eleven years our military reformers have steadily lowered their tone, and constantly proposed to give us less and less for our money. While we have had an ever-increasing army expenditure, rapidly growing from thirty millions sterling a year to nearly forty millions at the present day—nearly sixty millions sterling being spent in one year, and always now nearly fifty, upon the Imperial army and navy—we have been promised a constantly decreasing force able to take the field. No doubt the reason is that in former days there were hardly any British soldiers who knew what constitutes an army fully equipped for the field, and that now this experience has been acquired. Still, whatever the reason, the fact is as I state it. When Mr. Gathorne Hardy, in my opinion the greatest of House of Commons speakers, moved the Army Estimates in 1875, I heard him explain that the militia, the volunteers, and the yeomanry would constitute our army of defence, while "we must look to the regular army as the offensive army"—offensive because offence is often, according to the military axiom, the best, or even the necessary, defence. Can we fight Russia, for example, by remaining on the defensive both at home and in India while Russia over-whelms Northern Persia and Eastern Afghanistan, and once, her base of attack secure, proceeds to hammer at us upon our Indian frontier? It has been pointed out over and over again that we can only meet the Russian attack upon our defensive line by pounding at her upon some other line, chosen by ourselves, and this is exactly that from which we are now debarred by the apparent policy of Lord Wolseley's earlier speech. In 1876, on the second night of the debate on the Army Estimates, I heard the same Secretary of State for War declare that the regular army was intended for the defence of India and the Colonies, "but for offensive purposes also, should the necessity unhappily arise." Between 1875 and 1876 had been developed what Mr. Gathorne Hardy's successor, Mr. Stanhope, now calls "the abortive scheme of the eight army corps." But what did Mr. Gathorne Hardy say of it at the time of its invention (though the regular army then was smaller than it is at present)? That it was so perfect that even the times of the trains in the railway time-tables had been worked out, as would be seen when two of the army corps were called out suddenly to discover how the system fulfilled his expectations ; that "the labour, the toil, the intelligence devoted to the scheme by those who had worked out its details " were such that "no one could deny that great care and enormous diligence had been exercised in its preparation." Yet now Lord Wolseley tells us that equal care has been exercised during the last few months, and will, after eleven years, the voting of increased numbers, and with an increased expenditure, give us two army corps at home in place of eight.

In two admirable articles on the army and our unreadiness for war which appeared lately in the *Contemporary Review* and the *National Review,* it is pointed out that we could place in the field in Europe a force about equal to that of Servia or Bulgaria; that is, a force by far inferior in numbers to the Roumanian army, and while certainly superior to the Servians in efficiency, not certainly superior to the Rouma-nians. This costs us nominally over eighteen millions a year (from which a deduction for naval guns should be made, however), and by the expenditure in India of from eighteen to twenty-one millions a year we can place in the field a similar force (for the native army cannot be employed against the Russian enemy). The writers (or shall I say the writer, for the articles are pretty evidently by the same hand) tell us that although, looking to the largeness upon paper of our permanent army as compared with the smallness of our reserves, we ought to be able to mobilise quickly, it would take us "almost as many months to mobilise one army corps as the Germans now require days to mobilise nineteen." Even the two army corps of Lord Wolseley's speech will not be believed in by the best informed among his own friends until they see them both completely mobilised at the same time; it is so easy, in our want of system, to rob the Peter of Corps 2 to pay the Paul of Corps 1. Taking the plan, however, as it stands on paper, it certainly seems of little use for Lord Salisbury to frame large schemes for taking over the Egyptian finances with a British guarantee, when not only does he know the House of Commons singularly little for one who sat in it so long, but lets his Army Office sketch a military future for the country which puts it out of the question that we should, under any circumstances, hold Egypt in time of war, and which, indeed, by their own showing, confines us to defence in England and defence in India.

It is a little difficult to make an exact comparison of the expenditure of each Great Power upon its army. Germany spends about eighteen and a half millions upon her army, or about the same as England, and rather less than India on the average of the last three years; on the whole, rather less than half what the British Empire spends, without counting the charges borne by the Australian and Canadian colonies themselves for colonial defence. Some people are

x 2

under the impression that Russia spends as much as we do to keep up her peace army of about 890,000 men, but this is an error, founded upon the belief that the rouble is worth two shillings; as a matter of fact the rouble has so greatly fallen in value that it is idle to take the Russian military expenditure at anything like the thirty-seven millions sterling which we, without counting our self-governed colonies, and without counting the recent expenditure out of "the eleven millions," shall spend in the present year. In my Russian chapter I said that Russia spent rather more than Germany and Austria together—that is, rather more than the thirty and a half millions sterling which those two Great Powers devote to keeping up a peace force of about 750,000 men. Of course, while our military expenditure is greater than that of any other Power, our defence expenditure, combining army and navy, is enormously greater than the defence expenditure elsewhere. Even without apportioning to the present year any part of the extra eleven millions spent a few years ago—which, so far as it was spent on ironclads and ordnance, ought, in part, to be so added—and without allowing for the local expenditure of the Colonies, we are spending about fifty-two millions sterling. Russia and France come next, but they are neither of them spending anything which in the least approaches that enormous sum. In spite of our vast expenditure we have not, however, kept pace with either France or Germany in the introduction of repeating rifles or of the new shells. In the estimates for the present year, although we contemplate the gradual introduction of a repeating rifle, it is not even suggested that preparations should be made for arming the whole of our forces with the new weapon. We have really no security that, in the schemes of the present moment of which Lord Wolseley tells us, we are getting that which we are promised. It is possible that as, according to the present Conservative Secretary of State for War, the grand schemes of 1875, of which so much was made by previous Conservative Secretaries of State, were "academic exercises" which "never had more than a paper existence," so now even our two army corps, to exactly compose which of the right proportions of the various arms the horse artillery has been reduced, have also only a paper existence.

The reduction of the "theatrical" element, which appears to be Lord Wolseley's name for the horse artillery, seems, I repeat, to place that general upon one side, and almost all other soldiers upon the other. Inspired paragraphs have told us that "before proposing the change" our War Office "took pains to ascertain precisely what the proportion was of horse artillery to other arms in European armies." But it is a fact that the Germans are gradually increasing the number of batteries (both horse and ordinary field) which have six guns in time of peace, or in other words, of batteries which are always ready for war. This, and not the proportion of horse to ordinary field batteries, is the real point on which attention should be fixed. The talented writer whom I have already quoted, says that there is no soldier in the country who is not astounded at our reduction of horse artillery. If he believed that we were really increasing our good field artillery he would probably not have used strong language.

Our field batteries are now more mobile than they were, and they are cheaper than horse batteries. We might possibly gain by the exchange if it were a real one without reduction. But the writer from whom I am quoting, shows how every Power in Europe but ourselves is moved by the sense of danger. He is perhaps guilty of some little exaggeration when he says that "we now touch France on the one side and Russia on the other, in Asia," because France in Asia, so long as we hold the command of the seas, is far from dangerous to us; but on the other hand, it is impossible to over-estimate the danger which we incur there from Russia. He lays down the absolute military necessity, if we are successfully to defend ourselves either in Europe or in India, of being ready to assume the offensive. He shows how we could not hope to defend India against Russia unless we were prepared to make counter expeditions, and looking upon our two army corps as intended for that purpose, and not for that mere defence of England to which Lord Wolseley's words appear to confine them, he proves that the two corps require exactly the total force of artillery that we have available. It certainly seems clear, even to those who are not great scientific soldiers, that there is sufficient risk of invasion to make it essential to our position that we should have plenty of cavalry and artillery, plenty of officers, plenty of guns, ammunition, and other stores, always in readiness to supplement the large force of infantry which is provided for us by the militia and volunteers. Non-commissioned officers, who are as important in their way as officers, can in these days of improved education be found largely in the ranks of the army, but the things which we need to keep on hand are the things which cannot be suddenly improvised—cavalry, artillery, transport, officers, and stores. We can, whatever some soldiers may say, make effective infantry of our volunteers in a short space of time. We are beginning to recognise the splendid combination of military aptitude, personal courage, and sense of discipline which characterises our race: but while we can improvise infantry privates to any number, if we have the officers and the guns, we need to support them largely with cavalry and artillery to make them an effective force. Yet it is exactly in officers and artillery that we are trying to economise, and it was in transport and stores that we were economising until a year or two ago. While we are diminishing our artillery Italy is doubling hers ; no increase of infantry is proposed, but an increase in the Italian cavalry, engineers, horse and field artillery, and officers of reserves. The recent fit of economy promoted by Lord Randolph Churchill has taken the form of that decrease of our strength in horse artillery which is not so much important in itself as it is terrible as a sign. Mr. Stanhope's position really is that we are to have a sufficient force of field artillery to accompany two army corps, and that we are to have no field artillery at all, either horse or other, for the great mass of infantry which we are able slowly to put into the field to defend the country. On the other hand, Mr. Stanhope assures us that guns are to be given to the volunteers ; but the guns which are to be given to the volunteers are not field-guns at all, and volunteers as a rule are far more

usefully employed as infantry than in that artillery service
in which they cannot compete with more carefully-trained
men. It is certain that an enormous horde or mob of volunteers, unsupplied with field artillery, would be destroyed
by a much smaller French or German force. As far as it
is possible for a civilian to understand Mr. Stanhope's
figures, the net result of the changes of the horse artillery
and reduction of guns within batteries is a loss of eighteen
guns now; but there is a more serious loss arranged for
the moment when the whole army would be placed on
a war footing. During a campaign each battery carries
ammunition enough for one battle; afterwards its limbers
and waggons have to be filled up again, and its damaged
material replaced from organisations behind the fighting
army, called ammunition columns. These columns are not
fighting units at all, but supply-units, and may be classed
with commissariat trains and services of like nature. The
proper plan is to have a nucleus of these in time of peace,
and arrangements made for filling them up rapidly from
the reserves in time of war. But what the Government
has done is to tell off fourteen field batteries out of our
small existing force to become ammunition columns on mobilisation, which is a reduction of eighty-four guns in the
event of a great war, or a reduction of one hundred and two
guns in all. The guns which are being issued to the volunteers form no compensation, for they are unable to go out
of a walk or across fields. Scientific officers whom I have
consulted, tell me that while horse artillery, and even field
artillery, for a short time, is more mobile than a dog-cart, the

volunteer guns of position are only about as mobile as a laden Pickford's van. The volunteers as a rule cannot possibly give the time for training as field artillery, and to try to get them to do so is to take them from their own work which they do well, and put them to work for which they are unsuited. It must be remembered that the reduction of the artillery in the present year is a further reduction upon a reduction which took place last year, for the field artillery was reduced last year by the number of guns sent to increase the force in India.

Lord Wolseley tells us that all that has been done is to convert "horse artillery into field artillery, which, while more serviceable, requires fewer horses and fewer men," and he is very angry with those who do not approve the change. It is an amazing fact that years after we have been told that we have a small force, a very small force, ready at all times for war, we now discover that there were and are no ammunition columns in existence, even for a single army corps, and that the only way in which this wealthy country can create them is by turning into ammunition columns that artillery which is remarkably good, but at the same time already far short in numbers of what it should be. The deplorable effect which has been produced by the reductions, and by the language used in defence of them, is chiefly caused by the fact that the defence itself has revealed more strikingly than any criticism had done the miserable inefficiency of the machine upon which such enormous sums are spent at the present time. What can be thought of a defence, in the case of an army which costs over eighteen millions sterling a year, when one of the heads of the defence is, " iii. The provision of ammunition columns. Up to the present time no arrangement whatever had been made for this purpose, even in the case of our first army corps." The public will be almost inclined to think that head iii. would justify the hanging of a few ex-Secretaries of State for War. Lord Wolseley misapprehends the point which weighs with the public, if he supposes that anyone not a horse artillery-man much cares whether our force should or should not contain a large proportion of horse artillery as against field artillery. What the public do feel is that the total artillery force is far too weak for our requirements, and, in connection with the defence offered, they find out that many things which ought to have been done years ago, have been left undone up to the present time; moreover, the reduction which is made when an increase was wanted is made in the particular force in the efficiency of which we are most superior to other Powers, and for the creation of which most time is needed. This country in the event of invasion would put some 300,000 militia and volunteer infantry in line, and in order to feel secure with such a force we ought, according to the ordinary rules of war, to have 900 properly worked guns at home: the defence made for the reduction of the horse artillery has revealed the fact that for all practical purposes we may be said to have none. The official War Office view appears to be that after providing garrisons we could put about 130,000 infantry in the field at home to resist invasion, and that to these 130,000 men volunteer field artillery is to be attached until 390 guns are in a position to take the field ; but unfortunately the reduction is a fact, and the creation of the volunteer artillery is a theory or an experiment of the future. Another fact which has been entirely neglected is that it will be impossible to supply the horses needed on mobilisation, and the drain on the horse artillery in the field, from any force which exists at home. It takes a long time to train both the men and the horses for the work, and there will be no force out of which our horse artillery in the field can be replenished. It is ridiculous to compare our system with the German system for peace and war, because the men and horses are told off in Germany for their war positions, and the peace batteries can be swollen out into war batteries in about six days. The volunteers, however useful they may be as garrison artillery, will never be able in large numbers to manage field artillery ; and it is absurd to represent the occasional horsing of old forty-pounder guns for a few hours—say four or six times a year —as the creation of field artillery. Every other Power is increasing its proportion of real artillery just at the moment when we are decreasing ours. Sir Edward Hamley, indeed, has suggested that it is a positive advantage to this country, that while the force which will attack us will by the nature of things be provided only with field artillery, our defending force will be supplied with guns of position, that is with guns of heavier weight; as though a small trained army making a dash on London would be likely to advance directly upon entrenched positions, armed with heavy guns, when it could so easily march into London by twenty other different routes.

If the question involved in the recent changes were only one between horse artillery and other mobile field artillery, I should as a civilian not fitted by my training to take part in the discussion, leave it to military writers in the service papers.   As a matter of fact, field batteries are now very much more mobile than they were on the occasions quoted against them in Parliament.   Each gun can carry on its gun-carriage five gunners, besides the mounted non-commissioned officer who is always with it.   It has therefore a detachment of six men, who are amply sufficient to serve the piece under any circumstances likely to present themselves. With five gunners mounted on the gun-carriage a field battery can trot long distances, and even gallop for a short time.   Its weak point is that the extra weight of the gunners, who in the horse artillery would be mounted upon horses, handicaps it heavily for long marches, and as a part of the gunners are not mounted at all, or only on waggons, a field battery cannot as a complete unit act in the independent manner necessary for guns which have to accompany cavalry. On the other hand, field batteries are a good deal less expensive than horse artillery, and we might have more guns for the same price.

I have said above that I shall never believe in the two army corps until I see them both at once.   In order to send even the diminished number of horse artillery batteries into the field in war a large number of additional horses will be needed; and those horses ought, in order to secure perfect manœuvring power, to be trained horses, for untrained horses notoriously cannot do the work.   I have yet to learn where those horses are to come from suddenly, and I myself firmly believe that those of the first army corps are still likely to be sought for in the second. There is, no doubt, a good deal of unreality about beautiful manœuvres in exact line, and much of the display is open to Lord Wolseley's epithet of "theatrical." But the Germans have raised their number of batteries that have six guns in time of peace to 41 batteries with 246 guns, and this is not the moment to diminish ours. No practical man would even object to the reduction of two guns a battery in time of peace, provided that we had a system by which the commanders of four-gun batteries could lay their hands instantly on the horses, the guns, and the men required to make them up to the full war strength in, say, three or four days. This might perhaps be worked out if once the principle of localisation were loyally adopted and carried to its full consequences. All Continental nations have this power of mobilisation of artillery immediately on the outbreak of war. We have not, but have instead of it the suicidal principle of making up the batteries likely to go on service from other batteries, so that these latter have their efficiency absolutely destroyed, and have to begin at the beginning again, almost as if they were newly created. Therefore, when two guns are taken away from a battery, they are clean gone for all purposes of rapid mobilisation.

There is less to be said in a hostile sense with regard to the present position of the navy than may be said, or must be said, about the army. Clever German officers may write their *Great Naval War of* 1888, and describe the destruction of the British fleet by the French torpedo-boats, but on the whole we are not ill-satisfied with the naval progress that has been made in the last three years. There is plenty of room for doubt as to whether we get full value for our money; but at all events our navy is undoubtedly and by universal admission the first navy in the world, and relatively to the French we appear to show of ships built and building a number proportionate to our expenditure. The discovery of the comparative uselessness of automatic torpedoes is an advantage to this country, and no great change in the opposite direction has recently occurred. M. Gabriel Charmes has pointed out to France the manner to destroy our sea-borne trade, but excellent steps have been taken since his book appeared to meet the danger which he obligingly made clear to us. It remains a puzzle to my civilian mind how Italy can manage to do all that in a naval sense she does for her comparatively small expenditure, and how, spending only from a fourth to a sixth what we spend upon our navy, she can nevertheless produce so noble a muster of great ships. But our naval dangers are, no doubt, dangers chiefly caused rather by military than by naval defects. Our navy is greatly weakened for the discharge of its proper duties by the fact that duties are thrown upon it which no navy can efficiently discharge. As Admiral Hoskins has said, it is the duty of the commander of the British fleet to drive the hostile squadrons from the seas, and to shut up the enemy's ships in his different ports; but on the other hand, he has a right to expect that our own ports and coaling-stations shall be protected by batteries and by land forces. This is exactly what has not yet been

done, although the defence of our coaling-stations by fortresses and by adequate garrisons is essential to the sus-
taining of our maritime supremacy in time of war.

It is only, however, by comparison with our army that I
think our navy in a sound position. In other words, our
military situation is so alarming that it is for a time desirable to concentrate our attention upon that, rather than
upon the less pressing question of the condition of the navy.
I must not be thought, however, to admit, for one single
instant, that our navy should give us no anxiety. As long
as France remains at peace, and spends upon her navy such
enormous sums as she has been spending during the last few
years, she will be sufficiently near to us in naval power to
make our position somewhat doubtful; make it depend, that
is, upon how the different new inventions may turn out in
time of war. Our navy is certainly none too large (even
when the coaling-stations and commercial ports have been
fortified, and made for the first time a source of strength
rather than of weakness to the navy) for the duties which it
has to perform. It would be as idle for us, with our present
naval force, to hope to thoroughly command the Mediterranean and the Red Sea against the French without an
Italian alliance, as to try to hold our own in Turkey or in
Belgium with our present army. Just as the country seems
now to have made up its mind to abandon not only the
defence of Turkey against Russia, but also the defence of the
neutrality of Belgium, so it will have to make up its mind,
unless it is prepared to increase the navy, to resort only to
the Cape route in time of war. Italy being neutral and we

at war with France, we could not at present hope to defend the whole of our colonies and trade against attack, and London against invasion, and yet to so guard the Mediterranean and the Red Sea as to make passage past Toulon and Algiers, Corsica and Biserta, safe. Our force is probably so superior to the French as to enable us to shut up their ironclads; but it would probably be easier to shut in their Mediterranean ironclads by holding the Straits of Gibraltar than to attempt to blockade them in Toulon. I confess that I cannot understand those Jingoes who think that it is enough to shriek for Egypt, without seeing that Egypt cannot be held in time of war or the Suez route made use of with the military and naval forces that we possess at present.

As against a French and Russian combination of course we are weaker still. Englishmen are hardly aware of the strength of Russia in the Pacific, where, if we are to attack at all, we must inevitably fight her, and where, if we are to adopt the hopeless policy of remaining only on the defensive, we shall still have to meet her for the protection of our own possessions. Just as the reduction of the horse artillery, comparatively unimportant in itself, has shown that the idea of the protection of Belgian neutrality has been completely given up, so the abandonment of Port Hamilton, instead of its fortification as a protection for our navy, seems to show that we have lost all hope of being able to hold our own against Russia in the North Pacific. On the 1st of August Russia will have upon her North Pacific station —cruising, that is, between Vladivostock and Yokohama—

three new second-class protected ships: the *Vladimir Monomakh* and the *Dmitri Donsköi* of nearly 6,000 tons apiece, and the *Duke of Edinburgh* of 4,600 tons; one older protected ship, the *Vitiaz*, of 3,000 tons; four fast-sailing cruisers: the *Naïezdnik*, the *Razboïnik*, the *Opritchnik*, and the *Djighite;* and four gunboats, of which two are brand-new this year. While talking about their European fleets, the Russians are paying no real attention to them, and are more and more concentrating their strength in the North Pacific.

I have said that the reduction of the horse artillery means, to all who can read the signs of the times, the end of all idea of intervention in support of the neutrality of Belgium. In January last there was the gravest doubt in my mind as to what would be the response that the questions asked by me with regard to Belgium would produce; I did not know whether or not England meant to fight for Belgium, but I did feel certain that England ought to know her mind upon the point, and I thought it right that marked attention should be directed to a matter so important. A great deal of discussion followed, but that discussion has been all one way, and my questions of last January now read like some of the speculations of ancient history. The principal party organ of the Conservatives of England has declared that our intervention in support of Belgium, which up to last year was assumed as a matter of course by both parties in the State, " would be not only insane, but impossible." It has been suggested by "Diplomaticus" and the *Standard* that we are to allow Belgium to be temporarily

utilised "as a right of way," and the *National Review* has
endorsed the suggestion of "Diplomaticus," and told us that
it might be "possible to obtain a guarantee that the territory
of Belgium, if traversed for military purposes, should not
be permanently violated, and that, at the end of the struggle,
the neutrality and independence of that country should be
religiously respected." It is hardly necessary to argue
seriously upon the religious respect which the neutrality of
Belgium would receive after this non-permanent violation.
My belief remains as strong as it was when I wrote
articles which appeared in January and February last, that
when once the neutrality of Belgium is violated the independence of Belgium is gone. It is the Belgians who, when
Germany and France fall out, if the struggle is a long or
doubtful one, will have to pay the piper. The erection of
Belgian fortresses on the Meuse, and the proposed adoption
of personal service—matters which have been recently discussed in Belgium and elsewhere at enormous length—have
caused a great accumulation of books and papers upon my
table, but I put them aside into their drawer with the feeling
that a question which was worth arguing at length six
months ago has now been solved in England.

The Belgians themselves, very wisely, are beginning to
think of their own defence. We shall not save them, but
if they choose, they still can save themselves. Their fortifications at Namur and Liége, their possible adoption of
personal service, and a large increase of their army and of
their expenditure upon defence, may save them if they have
also courage. All that has become clear is that it is not by

England that they will be saved. The Swiss are able to make their own frontiers safe; both the neutrality and the independence of Switzerland will be respected; and, if the Belgians will give themselves the trouble, what the Swiss do, they can do. They will be safer in their own hands than the outcome of the recent discussion shows them to have been in ours. The *Morning Post* in writing upon this question has used these words: ". . . It is not likely that we should allow treaties to be violated with impunity without a protest. People may remark that protests are a very poor sort of compensation. But it would be far more natural and far more dignified for us to protest against a violation of Belgian territory than to look complacently on while such Powers as France or Germany marched their armies across Belgium, satisfying ourselves with the assurance that at the close of the conflict the territory of Belgium should remain intact as before." "Diplomaticus" and the *Standard*, then, would have us come to an understanding to give the right of way, while the *Morning Post* would have us protest against its use. I do not myself think that the Belgians, who are after all the people most concerned, would see much difference.

The response to my first chapter has been virtually unanimous, and it is clear that my question whether we intend to fight for Belgium according to our treaty obligations, or to throw treaty obligations to the winds under some convenient pretext, is already answered. On the other hand, it is now plain that Belgium desires, although still in a rather tepid way, to preserve her own neutrality, and through it her independence. She is gradually learning the lesson that she will have to preserve it by the power to give hard knocks. Unfortunately we have misled Belgium for many years. The highest modern European strategic opinion upon the existing system of defence of Belgium, written only in 1884, runs as follows : " All has been sacrificed to the intention to afford a landing-place to the army of succour to be furnished by a great naval Power. It is England that is meant, for the neutrality and independence of Belgium have no more firm defender than Great Britain." This was written three years ago, when a Liberal Government was in power ; but it could not be repeated now, although we are under the rule of the party which is supposed to be the more inclined to interfere abroad. Treaties die out no doubt in time. The Treaty of 1839, with regard to Belgium, is after all much older than the Treaty of the 21st November, 1855, with regard to Sweden. France and England would now think it an insane idea that they should attempt to preserve the integrity of Sweden against Russia, and similarly, to all appearance, thinks England with regard to Belgium now.

As we turn aside the head from Belgium and leave her to protect herself, perhaps we shall have the satisfaction at least of seeing a bolder spirit spring up in that country, now left to her own devices. There are signs of an awakening on her part. When first the Belgians began to move in the middle of January last, and confessed that the discussion had stirred them up, they mobilised, with much satisfaction to themselves, one battery of artillery ; but now they talk of an experimental mobilisation of their whole army. The Belgian artillery mobilisation somewhat reminded me of our own: just as we have now become officially aware that if we had sent two corps to Antwerp or to Turkey a few years ago, we might have had a few guns left for the defence of England, but that if we were to do so now, there would not be one organised field-gun left for all the remaining infantry who are to defend us; so in Belgium when one battery of artillery was mobilised, it was only by taking the guns and the men and the horses from three others. So proud were the Belgians of what they had done, that the battery was reviewed in front of the Ministry of War, where the Minister of War, the Minister of Foreign Affairs, and the Minister of Finance, with a great number of officers, were at the windows to appreciate the full result. It came out, however, in connection with this mobilisation, which was described at great length in all the Belgian journals, that even the small existing Belgian army would have in the event of war to suddenly buy 8,000 horses and to find a very large number of officers, for the provision of whom no arrangement has been made. Moreover, even the number of privates who are required to complete the Belgian army on a war footing cannot be found, as was shown a year and a half ago in the excellent notes of the Journal of the Royal United Service Institution. Supposing that they could be found, and that the Belgian system was in reality that which it is on paper, it is a system which, as has been shown by great foreign writers, abandons to the enemy almost the whole kingdom, which would be occupied without resistance and laid under contribution. "Moreover, in face of the rapidity of the mobilisation of the armies of the adjoining countries, it is to be feared that the concentration of the Belgian army would be hindered, and that the Belgian troops would not be all able to bolt into their hole." The " réduit " of course is Antwerp.

After the exposure of January last so much attention was called to Belgian defence that the King himself took part in the discussion, and inspired an article in the *Revue de Belgique* on "The Defence of Belgium from the National and European point of view," which was signed by the Director of the Ministry of Foreign Affairs. If *La Meuse* is right, the King sent also for the Prime Minister and the Minister of War, and spoke to them so seriously that the Belgian clerical Conservatives are about to undertake the whole of those measures which they formerly opposed when they were proposed by the Belgian Liberals. They have begun with the fortification of the Valley of the Meuse, which, conversely, is now opposed by some of those Belgian Liberals by whom it was formerly recommended. This statement is denied, but politicians often draw distinctions where other people cannot see them. Belgium does not need to adopt the Prussian military system. The Swiss system would suffice for her. She need not keep her men in barracks, she may keep them at their homes. She needs that which she is now about to obtain—a series of fortifications on the Meuse, and a very rapid possible mobilisation of a large force to man the walls—a service for which even half-trained infantry would suffice. Neither Germany nor France will violate her neutrality if it can only be done by shooting down myriads of men: neither of the Powers would face the delay; and although military critics may laugh at loss of general or outside sympathy being counted as an element in their calculations, still even that would have some weight.

If the British protection of Belgium has gone, how much more has that of Turkey disappeared into the background? It is a curious reflection that both should have finally vanished while Lord Salisbury is in power. In the autumn of last year the Continental newspapers spoke of the " extraordinary abandonment of the traditional policy of England in Europe, so clearly expressed in Lord Randolph Churchill's Dartford speech," and certainly that abandonment was only looked forward to at that time as resulting from the alliance upon this question of Lord Randolph Churchill with the Liberals. In the few months which have elapsed, the policy of non-intervention in support of Turkey appears to have become a fixed or settled national view, although it is possible that Lord Salisbury and a few others among the older men on the Conservative side still fail to recognise the almost universal change of English opinion. I am not here concerned to defend it, but only to state it as a fact.

It is, indeed, doubtful whether it was ever really intended that the Anglo-Turkish Convention should be acted upon. The Russian engagement towards us, made before the Treaty of Berlin, may, or may not, be still in force, but certainly has little value. The Anglo-Turkish Convention was never properly ratified, for Lord Salisbury insisted upon a ratification pure and simple, which the Sultan would never consent to give him.   There is too much reason to believe that the Anglo-Turkish Convention itself was part of merely theatrical arrangements, which were only intended to secure majorities in Parliament, which indeed they yielded, and in the country, which they failed to secure.   As Sir Samuel Baker wrote at the time, although he was something of a Jingo, " We have assumed the enormous responsibility of the protectorate of Asia Minor under conditions which we must know will never be fulfilled."   In the Parliamentary recess which followed the conclusion of the Treaty of Berlin, Lord Salisbury, at Manchester, ventured to declare that the Treaty would be absolutely fulfilled, and held out hopes to us that not only would Greece and the other smaller Powers be contented, but Turkey restored to her former strength, reformed and made secure for a distant future.   In the famous speech of the 18th July, 1878—the Titus Oates speech—Lord Salisbury had assured us that the "military supremacy " of the Sultan in Eastern Roumelia had been secured.   It was in the same speech that he said that " the presence of English troops, and the accumulation of English material of war at Cyprus would be material elements in assisting to maintain the independence of Asia Minor."   It was pointed out at the time that there was no material of war at Cyprus, except the " Hut Palace " and a large number of warming-pans which had been sent out there by mistake, and no English troops except three hundred men on the top of a high hill ; but what every soldier knew then, namely, that we could not defend Asia Minor against Russia unless we were prepared to make sacrifices, of which there has been as yet no sign, is now known by every civilian in the country.

While it is impossible for us, looking to the inability that we have shown to reorganise our army, to defend Asia Minor for the Turks, even if the people of this country wished to do so, it is certainly necessary for us to defend India, which is not under present circumstances a very much easier task. Little fault has been found with what I have said upon this point, except by Colonel Malleson in an article which appeared in *Blackwood's Magazine* for April last. Under the title of "The Fortnightly Reviewer and Russia," Colonel Malleson, in the politest language, was good enough to say that I had not only dealt "in a masterly manner with the causes which have embittered the relations between Russia and England," but had also submitted "with perfect fairness the conclusions of the military experts of foreign countries" "upon the question of the possibilities of a Russian invasion of India." "These conclusions point to the probability of the success of the invader, and this the Reviewer combats." Colonel Malleson proceeded to argue at length, and with ability, that I took too optimistic a view in contending that it would be very difficult for Russia to bring a large force of Turcoman cavalry into the field, or to supply the train which would be necessary for marching 100,000 men from Herat to Kandahar. My statement upon the point as to the train expressed the opinion of some of the highest authorities whom it would be possible to name, authorities to whom I am certain Colonel Malleson would be the first to yield. At the same time, Colonel Malleson is perhaps right in thinking that I have said less than I might of the possibility of Russian advance through Persia. He probably is justified in thinking that not only is it the manifest interest of Russia to absorb Northern Persia—as Russia alone of European powers can absorb an Eastern country—before she attacks India, but also that the idea has got hold of the minds of the Russian Nationalist party. On the other hand, I think that Colonel Malleson is prepared to allow that he over-estimated the possibility of our striking a real blow against Russia in the Caucasus, and I think that he and I are in agreement as to the necessity, if we are to defend India by counter-attack, of making that counter-attack from the Pacific.

If I have sometimes fallen foul of those whom I look upon as belonging to the Jingo school of 1878, it is because I doubt their wisdom ; of their patriotism I have a profound conviction, and it is only of their methods that I complain, believing as I do that the inflated language of 1878 was a mere insult to our intelligence, and that the occupation of Cyprus was a blunder calculated to divert the country from the penitential consideration of its own real military weakness, and of the true ways in which that weakness should be remedied. Holding, as I do, that the evacuation of Kandahar and the attempt to create a united and friendly Afghanistan were wise, and that those who advocated the retention of Kandahar were mistaken in their policy, nevertheless I hate to contend with them because I feel all the time that upon the essential points we are in real agreement, namely, that we are living in a fools' paradise; that we are not in a military position, in spite of the enormous sums that we have been spending, to defend the Empire against attack. I feel all the time that instead of contending the one with the other, to the advantage of the so-called economists, we ought really to be standing side by side.

It is impossible to prove in this chapter that it is desirable that our rule in India should be maintained. There are assumptions which I am forced to make, and this is one of them, and I shall therefore venture to assume that it is worth keeping India at all hazards, for the sake both of its people and of ourselves, and that leaving India would mean the destruction of the peace of nearly a quarter of the human race. Neither, on the other hand, can there be any doubt for any reasonable man that the progress of Russia over Central Asia has been, on the whole, an advantage to civilisation; the Russian Government, however incompetent to govern liberally Bulgarians or Poles, being infinitely superior to the Governments which held sway at Samarcand or Merv. But now the Russians have reached the frontiers of Afghanistan, and looking to the burning love of their national independence which in all their civil turmoils the Afghans have displayed, I doubt if many can be found to wish that Russian rule should, against the unanimous wishes of the people, be allowed to spread itself over the country. The Russians have lately taken for their arms in Central Asia, "On a field, azure, a Russian imperial eagle, or, between a rising sun and a setting moon." The Russians are trying to inspire the Afghans with the belief that in these arms it is Russia which is the rising sun and England the setting moon. Nevertheless the Afghans however much they may fight among themselves, are still united against foreign attack, and at least as little anxious to see the Russians in Cabul as to see the English there. When, therefore, there are found Englishmen to declare that they think that it would be a good thing that the English and Russian outposts should meet in friendly fashion upon the Helmund, I am always disposed to suspect the reality of their belief in the excellence of this expected future, and to fancy rather that it may be by cowardice that they are inspired. It is as certain as almost anything can be that sooner or later we shall be engaged in war with Russia, and the nearer she is to us upon our Indian frontier the more difficult it will be for us to fight her. But I have tried to show that there is no need for the growth of a hopeless feeling, inasmuch as we can, for many years to come, both hold our own upon our Indian frontier, and, if we properly organise our forces, carry the war into the enemy's camp by an attack upon the Russian possessions on the Pacific. In this, it is now clear, I take the middle view. I am called on the one side a Jingo in sheep's clothing, and on the other side I am attacked by the real Jingoes because I believe that we can still hold our own. Let me make, then, one more appeal to the so-called economists, that they will weigh well the considerations that

I have put forward and ask themselves whether there is not at least cause for anxiety in our military position.

When I declared that we could hold our own upon the Indian frontier, I believed in the possibility of our being able in the event of war, without dangerously reducing our force at home, to pour troops into India, and also to organise an expedition for an attack on Vladivostock. Since I wrote the Russian article to which I allude grave doubts have been thrown by Lord Wolseley's speech upon our ability to do even this. There are many who, knowing that we have in India a large native military police, think that we could put in line against the Russians virtually the whole of the white army and the whole of the native army too. This is a dangerous delusion. There are many scientific officers who have seen the Russian troops, as I have seen them often, and who believe, as I believe, that they are among the best soldiers in the world. Those who do not fully take that view are generally of the opinion that most of the Russian troops are of this quality, and that others of their regiments are very inferior to the average. It is certain, however, that if transport difficulties prevent the possibility of the attempted invasion of India by an overwhelming Russian force, the troops who do advance beyond Herat will be of a first-class quality. Picked men will be sent upon this expedition, and it is simply idle to believe that our native regiments, going into action with about four white fighting officers each, and liable after a few minutes of hot fire to find themselves commanded by a subaltern just out from home, can be counted upon to stand up to picked Russians. No man knows the

Indian army better than Sir Frederick Roberts, and no man is more popular in its ranks, but I feel certain that upon this point Sir Frederick Roberts cannot be quoted upon the optimistic side. We shall be happy if, in the event of a Russian attack upon India, we can count upon our native army to keep watch over the enormous forces unfortunately maintained by native princes, and to hold our communications against possible attack. I repeat what I have said before, that if we can spare the best of the Punjaub cavalry, the Bengal lancers, and the Goorkha, Sikh, or Pathan infantry to send against the Russian force, we must estimate for an equal number of British troops to be left behind. No doubt in the course of time the native Indian army will be reformed, and we may even live to see the day arrive when we may rival the Russians themselves in giving scope to the military energies of the picked men among subject populations; but I have in these articles to deal with facts as I find them, and I speak of the Indian army as it exists at the present moment.

To hold our own, then, upon the north-west frontier, and to carry the war into Russian territory by an attack upon Russia's Pacific shores, is the most that we can expect to be able to do. With a Chinese alliance, which we ought to be able to gain and to retain, our position in Manchuria would be very strong. It is there, and there only, that in the event of war Russia can be bled to death, for of the attack upon the Caucasus and the attack upon Cronstadt, both of which Colonel Malleson originally recommended, I fear that the one and the other are about equally unlikely to succeed.

Major Buxton has pointed out in his admirable book that
armies must be supposed to exist for the purpose of fighting
battles, and " that an army which should be unable to wage
war, would be worthless." Yet according to the tests which
he gives us by which to estimate the existence of a real army,
it must be admitted that while we have an army in India,
we have no army at home in England. The notion that,
although we have not an army at the present time, we should
be able suddenly to collect one in time of war, is a dangerous delusion which ought to be got rid of as soon as
possible. When Sir E. Hamley brought before Parliament
his very doubtful suggestions for the defence of London, in
which however the doubtful point was not the need for
defence or the danger of the present situation, but the character of the suggestions made, a Radical member rose to
protest against " the assumption that we ought always to be
spending money on military and naval armaments." He
went on to say that " periodical panics were much to be
deprecated, as they caused great expenditure from time to
time," and that " we could not afford to lavish our treasures
upon expensive armaments if we were to supply the people
with free schools and technical instruction ; " but it is
doubtful whether the freedom of free schools will in itself
enable us to resist invasion, or whether the gain to our trade
by technical instruction is not neutralized by the increase of
risks against which it seems reasonable to insure. If
periodical panics cause great expenditure, it is perhaps
because our military situation is such that panic from time
to time is certain to occur ; and while one may agree that

336 THE PRESENT POSITION OF EUROPEAN POLITICS.

it is undesirable to spend money by fits and starts, it is
hardly an unjustifiable " assumption " to contend that such
interests and such a trade as ours should be insured.   If
this Radical member had, instead of following Lord Randolph
Churchill, suggested to us considerations which confirm the
notorious fact that we are not at present getting sufficient
value for the money that we spend, his remarks might
possibly have produced a more beneficial result.   Now in
his reply the Secretary of State for War went beyond the
already very terrible statements in his memorandum, and
deliberately informed the House of Commons not only that,
in spite of our immense expenditure, " military stores have
been allowed to fall into a condition absolutely unjustifiable,"
but "that economy has been more than once produced by
an absence of all stores."   On another day he said, " Batteries
would in time of war be absolutely useless without ammunition columns.   We have at present not one of these columns,
or any organisation for furnishing them on the outbreak of
hostilities."   It is against such horrible treachery to the
interests of the country that we have to guard in future, and
it is not the Randolph Churchill policy or the new Radical
policy which will help us to guard against it.   For men who
have not made a special study of military affairs to promise
to save five millions a year upon the Army and Navy
Estimates is somewhat rash ; but economy has always a sufficient surface popularity to make it worth while for us to
combat steadily every suggestion of the kind, and to ask at
least for chapter and verse as to the manner in which the
saving is to take place, and at the expense of what department

of the service. If, on the other hand, we were told that the money which we spend is not well spent at present, and that we do not get value for it, then the economists would be able to work along with the army reformers, who to a man agree with the justice of this view. I am sorry to say that the more inquiry one makes, and the more time one spends upon the Army and the Navy Estimates, the more one comes to the belief, nay, I might almost say the certainty, that while we have a small efficient white army in India, even in India the greater portion of the troops we nominally possess are non-efficient, and in England, with an equal expenditure, our army in a modern sense may be said to be non-existent. In these days armies cannot be forced like mushrooms, and however great the patriotism and the military aptitude of Englishmen—and I for one certainly do not undervalue them—a sudden rush on London by a small well-trained army would find before it nothing but a mob. The opponents of all military expenditure are apt to talk as though fortification were an admitted waste of money, whereas it is a military axiom even with the most economical of Powers, such as Germany, for example, which never spends an unnecessary penny, that "fortification is the most economical way of securing a position from attack," leading as it does to direct economy in war by enabling the defenders to be made less numerous, and in peace in the lesser cost of maintenance as against that of other means of defence. In this country we not only have no army in spite of our expenditure, and no defence of our commercial ports such as in these days they undoubtedly require, no protection of our coasts and of our coaling-stations sufficient to enable our navy to exercise to the full its powers, but by the absence of all these things we expose ourselves to the certainty that sooner or later we shall have suddenly to do our best, probably unavailingly, to make up for our deficiencies by lavish expenditure in the most uneconomical way possible.

There is a difficulty in obtaining consideration for these views when a Conservative Government happens to be in office. The chief organs of the Press are in this case too commonly silent, and the "service members" and the House of Lords are powerless. There is always upon the Liberal side a general desire to associate Liberalism with the principles of economy and of peace, and if a Conservative Government under pressure from Lord Randolph Churchill diminishes expenditure upon one point or resists the necessity for increase upon another, the Liberals are afraid to criticise; on the other hand, when the Conservatives are in Opposition, any such economy is certain to be met with a storm of outcry both from the Conservative party as a whole, and from every member of "the services." Full criticism is insured in the one case and absence of criticism is certain in the other. But, after all, Liberals ought to remember the great Liberals, and even the great Radicals, who have insisted, in the interests of peace itself, on the maintenance of the defensive strength of England; and every Englishman should at least be willing to face the full discussion of the question whether we are in a fit condition to defend ourselves at the present time.

I shall take some future occasion of stating more fully my

views—which, though they are the views of a civilian, I know are in agreement with those of some distinguished officers—upon the system which might give us a better return for our expenditure than does that which we pursue at present. Generally speaking, my remedies would rest in the first place upon a careful consideration of the duties which we wish our army to perform. It has become unlikely that we shall engage in Continental war, but it is still certain that we ought to possess the means of sending out an expeditionary force capable either of aiding directly in the defence of India, or of making a counter-attack. In India itself we must always keep up a large white force. The other colonial garrisons, excluding those which are, or easily may be, supplied by the colonies themselves, do not require a sufficient number of men to make them of much importance in the consideration of the problem. What we have to look to, then, are mainly the defence of India, the defence of England, and the supply of a possible expeditionary force.

For the defence of India, or rather for the garrisoning of India in time of peace, and for a portion of her defence in time of war, we still need, according to an opinion which I expressed at the date of the first introduction of short service, a long-service army. Short service is admirable for European service, and in these days necessary, whether admirable or not; but it is inapplicable to the condition of affairs which the French have to face in Indo-China, and which we have to face in India, the Straits, Ceylon, and Hong-Kong. Sir John Adye, writing in the *Fortnightly*

z 2

Review of April, misapprehends our views when he says that most of us, who are for this change, are of opinion " that only men of mature age—say between thirty and forty —should be called on to serve in the tropics." We do not in the least wish to raise the age of the men sent out. As regards reliefs and cost he also misapprehends the position. We do not wish regiments sent out and brought home, young and old together, but permanent Indian regiments never brought home and continually renewed with men of twenty years of age, joining, practically, for any period they please. Some years ago, when we suddenly changed our military system, we partly did so in imitation of foreign Powers, which, however, have as a rule a wholly different set of facts to meet. The rule of not sending men to India under twenty continues, whatever the care taken, to weaken the regiments at home. The short-service system with its rapid changes involves great expense to India, and is one cause of that continual increase in her military burdens which makes the Indian army as costly as the French or German, and sometimes the most costly in the world, with the exception of that of Russia, with its peace establishment of something like 890,000 men.

The chief argument against the reconstitution of a separate army for India (under which term I include, for military purposes, certain of the tropical colonies) is the danger of white mutiny, or at least of the existence of a trades-union feeling leading to military strikes. I meet this danger by proposing to make the separate army a popular business, which a man could go into or go out of when he chose, guarding only by an extremely short minimum service against the possibility of losing our money by the return of the men immediately after their enlistment. As Major Buxton says, " For home service and European warfare, we are in the same position as any Continental nation ; we need a Reserve, and therefore a short-service army. What difficulties do not hamper us in striving to reconcile short service with foreign service ! Divide the two services, and all becomes simple. The foreign service army . . . requires yearly fewer recruits, becomes acclimatised, and has fewer green young men in its ranks ; it is never relieved home, though it moves about abroad. The question of home and foreign reliefs is closed for ever. Recruits go out, and time-expired men come home ; that is all." On the other hand, for the home army I should rely very largely upon the militia or volunteers, and for the infantry privates of the expeditionary army, upon special volunteers from the militia or volunteers. The feeling of England is so much against the adoption of a conscription that we are never likely to accept that system here ; but there is no difficulty with us of obtaining men for home service in time of peace, and volunteers for special foreign service in time of war, and therefore while encouragement to volunteering is desirable, the adoption of a conscription is unnecessary. The providing of openings in civil life for retiring non-commissioned officers, towards which Lord Wemyss and Sir E. Walter have done so much, will also be of high importance. Speaking as one who has seen, as a civilian, a good deal of war, I am convinced that the time which is required, provided that your officers and non-commissioned officers are well trained, to make an infantry private, is not very great. If this be so, is it not clear that our money should be spent upon fortifications, upon guns, upon torpedoes and coast mines, and upon the scientific branches, or the portions of an army which it is difficult suddenly to create—upon cavalry, upon horse and field artillery, upon engineers, upon officers and non-commissioned officers—and that in times of peace we should keep up the smallest permanent force of infantry privates which is necessary for the purpose of the training of the non-commissioned and the commissioned officers? This would serve as a model, and also as a nucleus for the expeditionary force. If a separate army were once more made for India, the force at home might be highly localised, which would increase the popularity of the service and facilitate the mobilisation of the reserves in time of war. Each regiment would organise and look after its own reserve, and a great saving of money would also be the result. The adventurous men who now flock into the army would go into the Indian force. The expeditionary army would be easily provided in time of war, after mobilisation had taken place, by volunteering from the home force. Its cavalry, artillery, engineers, commissariat and train would all be ready; a full number of highly trained officers and non-commissioned officers would be ready to join the men, who would themselves be already trained in the ordinary duties of an infantry private. Both recent Prussian and recent French experience has shown that under such circumstances it takes but very little time for the men to get to know the officers and the officers the men, and for regimental feeling to be formed. We have in our well-fed and powerful youth of the upper and middle classes a fighting stock which no other country in the world possesses ; and if every opportunity were taken to utilise the advantage we are given by this fact, I am convinced that our new army would be a pattern to the world. Instead of this, we see, at the present time, every opportunity taken to starve the volunteer force, as recently, for example, since the report of the committee on the Capitation grant.

Instead of trying to imitate at one time the Prussians and at another time the French, we ought in my belief to strike out a thoroughly national system for ourselves ; and I am convinced that by an expenditure of far less than the 36 to 38 millions sterling which we spend already upon our army, we could create a force which would make our enemies pause before they ventured to attack us. This is not the time to work out, as I intend soon to do, the possible relations in the new infantry system between what might be called the guards, the militia, and the volunteers. Some of the Australian colonies, in their new military system, have recognised the distinction which should exist, in order to call out the full local military strength, between various classes of what they style volunteers. Some of them have a force in the nature of a volunteer militia, which is paid; some have also a force in the nature of a purely volunteer force, which is only armed and instructed, but not paid ; and it will be interesting at a future time to consider whether the various Australian military systems do not point out to us the way in which we should walk in the future, just as many of their political ideas are likely also to be ultimately adopted in the mother-land. They cannot, however, rob us of the glory of having shown them the way in true volunteering, first in 1803, and again in 1859.

If the theory upon which our existing army system is based had any relation at all to fact, there might be much, indeed, that could be said for it. When, however, we find that after years upon years of reorganisation, and years upon years of fabulous expenditure, we are virtually without an army, and that England and India together, with an expenditure greater than that of Russia, can put into the field a force capable of fighting against European troops only equal to the force of Roumania, surely the time has come when revolutionary measures should be tried. To see our Reserves called out for little wars in Egypt or the Soudan has shown that our present scheme of army organisation is a total failure. I am certain that in the main it is the view which has been put forward by Colonel MacAndrew, Major Buxton, and other thoughtful soldiers which is likely to prevail; but even supposing that our opinion in favour of a return to a separate army for India were to be rejected, it is still possible, without making that largest and in my belief most important change, to do much in the direction which I have indicated, namely, the giving of high efficiency to the elements which cannot be rapidly created in the home army, and the loyal adoption for the infantry of the principle of localisation and of union with the militia and volunteers.

The army must resign itself to certain changes which

will be involved in that adoption of more business-like principles which has become a necessity. Both the War Office and the Horse Guards need considerable change; and whenever the Duke of Cambridge is driven by advancing years to give up his post, the man who is to be the new General commanding the forces, should not be a young prince, but one of the most hard-working officers of the army, Sir Frederick Roberts, Lord Wolseley, or some other man of the same type. The danger with a young prince would be that politeness would incline him always to agree with the last person who talked to him, and that he would be unable to take, what is necessary in these days, a decided line of his own. I am not complaining in this matter of the present Commander-in-Chief, for the Duke of Cambridge is not a young prince at all, and not a prince of this type, and is certainly not open to this objection. In future, however, it will be better that the natural connection between the Crown and the army should be retained in practice only in those matters to which, as a fact, the royal family attach the most importance. There can be no reason why the king for the time being, or why, if it were thought undesirable to place the king in this position, the young military representative of the family—such, for example, as the Duke of Connaught is at the present time—should not be chairman of a small committee, consisting of four or five of the superior officers in great commands, who should meet once or twice a year to settle the infantry promotions, and chairman of similar committees dealing with the cavalry and other branches. All that we ask is that there should be full recognition of the fact that, until a complete change in our army system has taken place, there is a great deal of hard work and of rough work that will have to be done.

Colonel MacAndrew, of whom I spoke above, in the conclusion of one of his articles upon army reform, expressed, just two years ago, the hope that many then living might see the federation of the British Empire for general defence. The two years which have passed since those words were written have already seen the successful accomplishment of a long step in that direction. Whatever blame the impartial observer may have to allot to some of the other steps which the present Government have taken, he can have nothing but praise for their recognition, in their circular of last autumn, of the place of the colonies in the future military organisation of the Empire. It is a strange fact that Mr. Stanhope, the author of that excellent circular, should have been the Minister of War to take the longest step which for some years past has been taken in the wrong direction, by his reduction of the artillery, and still more by the grounds of his defence of that lamentable step. The conference which has been lately held was nominally a general conference with the self-governing colonies, but practically it was an Australian conference, and for the present it would seem that the chief strength that can be gained from our colonial possessions, for general imperial defence, must come from Australia. As regards Canada, the predominant feeling is friendly; but it is useless to disguise the fact that there is a good deal of separatist feeling in Canada, and that there are at times dangerous ups and downs in Canadian sentiment about the

Empire and its advantages. Moreover, Canada has an over-shadowing neighbour of enormous power in the United States, with whom she has from time to time causes of sharp difference. The South African Colonies have a vast preponderance of native population. The Australians alone are in the happy position of being completely masters in their own house, and of having no very near neighbours, and certainly no neighbours of whom they are afraid.

It is, perhaps, rather to the credit of the Government than a reproach to them, that they are somewhat sparing of anything which can fairly be described as "humbug" or "bunkum" in their talk about the colonies. At the same time they perhaps fail on the imaginative side, and are likely to continue to have differences from time to time with the colonists because of this defect in their intelligence. It ought, perhaps, not to be made a charge against the Government, looking to the "cheapness" of the other line, to use a happy term of modern Oxford slang, that in the Queen's speech, at the beginning of the session, they failed to advertise their Colonial Conference. At the same time this modest policy may be pushed too far. The defect of imagination which it displays came out very strongly in the speech of Lord Salisbury to the Colonial delegates about the New Hebrides. Those who were present at its delivery, described the scene as dramatic in the extreme, through the contrast between Lord Salisbury's apologetic humility and diplomatic reserve, and the outspoken youthful British enthusiasm of the Australians. The abridged account of the discussion which appeared in the *Standard* of the 6th

of May was mildly disavowed by Sir Henry Holland and
Lord Onslow on that day, but was, as a fact, within the
mark, and less inaccurate than any " official *verbatim* report "
would be.

Lord Salisbury, who had armed himself with the support
of one prominent New Zealander (immediately denounced as
a traitor by the out-and-out representatives of Colonial
feeling), seemed to think that the colonists would accept
platitudes in the same calm fashion in which they would be
accepted by the House of Lords. He was rudely undeceived:
the moment he sat down, the Australians told him that his
speech was a wet blanket, or, as others put it, " a douche of
cold water; " that they were almost sorry that they had left
Australia, that they were very glad that they were immediately
returning to its healthier atmosphere, and that such speeches
might be suited to an old country, but would be received
with dismay by the Colonial Cabinets. One of the leading
colonists, who is likely soon to be the Prime Minister of one
of the most powerful colonies, declared plainly that he had
heard Lord Salisbury's speech " with confusion and dismay,"
and that Lord Salisbury must understand that if France did
not go out of the New Hebrides of her own accord she would
have to go out of New Caledonia too. Lord Salisbury in
reply admitted that the French were bound to leave, and
were apparently staying in the New Hebrides in virtual
breach of their own word, but added, "You cannot negotiate
great Powers out of islands; " to which the retort was,
" Then France seems to have negotiated us out of the New
Hebrides." Lord Salisbury, in a deprecatory fashion, ex-

plained that there had been so many Governments lately in France that "chaos" had ensued "in the French offices;" whereupon a Victorian (I believe it was) answered : " A little chaos seems an excellent thing, and perhaps we should do better if we had some here," which was not polite towards the host. A portion of the storm afterwards fell, I hear, in private upon Sir F. Dillon Bell, who had been "interviewed" by a French correspondent, and had been imprudent enough to admit that " personally he had been favourable to M. Waddington's proposal " (that the French should keep the New Hebrides but stop transportation), though he now agreed that "the refusal of Australia had made everything impossible except the complete independence of the New Hebrides." " The refusal of Australia!" Shades of Colonial ex-Secretaries of State!

I have fully stated in the chapter on France the case of the colonists against the French with regard to the New Hebrides, and generally with regard to transportation and the Pacific. It looks now as though France were beginning to recognise the strength of the Colonial feeling upon the subject. A short time ago the French newspapers of all shades declared that France intended to stay in the New Hebrides, to get "labour" thence, and to send convicts thither if she chose; but now the subject is seldom mentioned, and the French appear to be prepared to back out. As I tried to point out to them in my article on France, which was much noticed but unfavourably received in Paris, it is the part of a true friend to tell the French that the colonists intend that they shall go, and are strong enough to make them go. The best way in which they can buy safety for New Caledonia, to which their lawful claim is undoubted, is to yield rapidly with regard to the New Hebrides and other points on which they are in the wrong. They are dealing with young countries, who are perhaps more vigorous than altogether respectful of strict rights; and as America drove them out of Mexico, the Australians are likely to drive them out of the South Pacific. Nobody in England cares much one way or the other about this question, except so far as our Australian colonists care, or as we are swayed by our wish for peace; but no English Government would be strong enough to protect the French in the South Pacific against the Australian colonies. It is unnecessary for me to repeat the arguments by which I showed the altogether unlawful nature of the French occupation; but I am bound to say that, looking forward a few years, I do not myself believe that the lawful Dutch and German occupations of portions of New Guinea, or the lawful French occupation of New Caledonia are, because they are lawful, likely therefore to last very long. The young peoples of Australia cannot be dealt with in the same way in which an old Power like England can be dealt with, and France cannot afford to trifle with Australian feeling.

There is a certain fear on the part of nervous people that in the case of the New Hebrides the Colonies will have been found to have tasted blood. It is the fact that at the time when I wrote my second article, that on France, which appeared on the 1st of February last, the question of the New Hebrides had been settled against the Colonies. The

Government, which had decided not to run the risk of offending France upon this point, and which felt its hands fatally weakened by certain similarities presented by the case of Egypt, had decided, while protesting, to allow in practice the French occupation to continue. If this decision has been lately changed, it has been changed entirely through the strength of Colonial language. Even on the day after the Colonial speeches to Lord Salisbury had been made the whole of the French newspapers published a list of " Requests for passages to the Colonies," in which the second and third places in point of numbers were occupied by two countries which the French in many of their books claim as " colonies," although in each case there is an official denial made or an official veil set up—Madagascar with 6,812 requests, and the New Hebrides with 4,917 requests. After what the French had heard privately of the intention of the British Government with regard to the New Hebrides, to snatch the islands from them will indeed be to take the bone out of the mouth of the dog. It is possible that Colonial interference may lead, not only in this case but in others, to increased risk of war with France. At the same time I myself am disposed to doubt this, for I believe that we oftener run into war through saying less than we mean than through telling the exact truth about our feelings.

The partial success of the Australians with regard to the New Hebrides will no doubt encourage the friends of New-foundland to hope that there also the colonial view may ultimately prevail. This is indeed a different case, more

nearly resembling the French position in New Caledonia or
the German position in New Guinea, than the French
unlawful position in the New Hebrides. The full demands
of our colonists in Newfoundland with regard to the "French
Shore" are really demands for a change in a treaty-situa-
tion. The powers which were unfortunately conferred on
France in the last century are incompatible with the growth
of the colony of Newfoundland, and sooner or later I have
no doubt that they will disappear ; but at present the risk
of serious trouble in taking steps to end them is such that,
the Newfoundlanders not being Australians, and the French
rights being better upon paper than in the case of the New
Hebrides, I expect, in spite of the passing of the Bait Bill,
to see the Government continue to be yielding towards
France. Certainly in these days the Empire will have
enough to do if it is successfully to espouse the cause of each
of the Colonies against powerful interlopers. If we are to be
guided only by unanimous colonial feeling we may have to
fight for Canada against the United States upon the Fisheries
question, as well as for Newfoundland against France. The
simplest test, however, that we can take to find the cases in
which we ought to interfere and the cases where our attitude
should be one of reserve, is to examine for ourselves into the
right and wrong. We may depend upon it that in the long
run our wisest course will be steadfastly to maintain our
position and the position of our colonists when, as in the
New Hebrides, we have right upon our side, and to negotiate or try to search out acceptable compromise when, as in
the case of Newfoundland, the matter is very doubtful. If,

however, we are to maintain a high standard of national integrity ourselves, and to expect it in turn from others, we shall have to act very differently, in other parts of the world as well as the South Pacific, from the manner in which we have been acting lately. If, in the interests of the Empire as a whole, we are to allow no breach of the word that has been plighted to us, then we must not consider in each case whether that particular case is, taken by itself, worthy the risk of war, but we must adopt a severer standard and an equal standard. The influence of Lord Randolph Churchill has made itself felt of late in the Departments. Although that noble lord upon some subjects agrees with Mr. Chamberlain, it is notorious that in imperial questions they often hold very different views, and that Mr. Chamberlain has shown in the case of the Cameroons, of the Niger, and in other similar matters on which he had to pronounce an opinion as head of the Board of Trade, that he understands the bearing upon our commerce and upon our future of the habitual assertion of our rights. I doubt whether he would have been the man to permit the murderers of Dabulamanzi to go unpunished. That chief was killed in the Native Reserve—that is, practically, in British territory—by Boers who had an official connection with the new republic upon our borders. For some time past no attempt has been made to bring these ruffians to justice. Yet if we do not take action in such cases we damage the individual rights of Englishmen and of those who are under the protection of this country, as we damage our imperial rights and our imperial future by inaction in such cases as that of the New Hebrides.

A A

The chief outcome of the Colonial Conference has been the establishment of a joint system of naval defence in the Australian seas, and this is, no doubt, an excellent new departure, but it is only a very small point actually gained, when we consider the amount of the contributions, as compared with what remains to be done in taking measures for the future security of the Empire. At the present moment India alone contributes her fair share, with the United Kingdom, towards imperial expenditure. The Colonies obtain great advantages from our diplomacy, from our consuls, and in a thousand other ways, without sufficient return; and it will be necessary to continue in the course upon which we have entered, and to increase and generalise the amount of their contributions, while providing for a more efficient expenditure of the sums raised than has been assured in the past. The present condition of our coaling-stations in the China seas shows the need of which I speak, for improvement in efficiency. The recent elaborate articles in the French military review of foreign countries, which is compiled by the General Staff at the Ministry of War, on the defence of Hong Kong and other British possessions, are not pleasant reading for us. The French scientific writer begins, for example, with regard to Hong Kong by pointing out the enormous importance of the third port of the British Empire, and the probability of the increase of that importance through the opening of the Canadian Pacific Railroad. He shows that the military and strategic importance of Hong Kong is as great as the commercial. He next states what has been the past condition of the fortifications, and points out the improvements which are being made in them. The writer then, several times over, remarks upon the feeble numbers of the garrison, and informs us that it is evidently insufficient for the defence, and that while we have some idea of protecting the port we entirely neglect the southern part of the small island. He adds, by way of conclusion, that want of money, both in the mother country and in the colony, makes it impossible to complete the fortifications of the island, but says that unless we complete them and increase the garrison, our Pacific fleet must be tied to Hong Kong for its defence. The position, therefore, of Hong Kong, according to a foreign scientific writer, appears to be pretty much the same as the position of Port Hamilton while we held it, namely, that however important the station may be, it is impossible to defend it except by the presence of the fleet, or by the spending of large sums of money upon fortifications, and upon the increase of the garrison. The reasons which led to the abandonment of Port Hamilton in spite of what might be called the strategic necessity of holding it, are the same reasons as those which make Hong Kong weak. From the military point of view it was essential to have held Port Hamilton. The ablest of the foreign writers who have discussed the chances of a war between Russia and Great Britain has given high praise to Mr. Gladstone's second Administration for the seizure of Port Hamilton, and has pointed out how essential is the occupation of that post to any chance of successful offensive action on the part of England against Russia. The port itself has, since the publication of that book, been evacuated by our forces, and evacuated only because it was a weakness to our Pacific squadron to be tied to it for its defence. If we are ever to be at war with Russia we shall have to attack her at Vladivostock and on the Amoor ; and, under such circumstances, we shall need as a base a fortified station to the north of Hong Kong.

It would be of some interest to consider whether the commencement of military federation of the Empire which has been made, is a step towards the future adoption of any scheme of general imperial federation, but we have hardly as yet reached a point at which it is useful to spend much time on the details of that inquiry. We are beginning already to see something of practical federation. There was lately a race upon the Thames for a sculling championship, in which an Australian beat a New Brunswicker, no home-staying Englishman competing in the race ; and it would look as though in certain lines of interest England is becoming only a resting-place or a meeting-place for her colonial children. Facts oppose themselves to any attempt to hurry the solution of the problem of federation. It is impossible for the Government so much as to move in it until at least the leading colonies are ready. At the present moment some of our chief colonies are either in doubt of or opposed to all federation schemes. The great merit of what the Government have lately done, is that they have been neither behind nor in advance of public opinion, and have done therefore, at the right moment, exactly that which could be successfully accomplished. It is an excellent thing that irresponsible societies should debate the conditions of the problem of the future, but the matter has not reached the stage at which it can have any bearing upon "the present position of European politics."

If one were in a scoffing humour, one might be disposed to ask whether it was indeed of much use for even mere voluntary societies, or for individuals, to discuss colonial federation, if we are so little disposed to take steps towards the union of the Empire as to allow our Treasury to impose upon the Post Office its present prohibitive price for letters to the outlying portions of the dominions of the Crown. That an English letter to India should cost 5d., while a letter to British India from Calais costs 2½d., and a post-card to British India from Calais a penny, is an anomaly which it is strange that even an overworked Parliament should have permitted to continue for many years. There are some who will begin to believe in earnest in the possibility of a fair consideration of imperial unity when Parliament makes the Treasury allow us to post our letters to India and the Colonies from London at the same price, instead of at double the price, that it costs to post them from Calais to the same addresses.

There can be no doubt, however, that even in the absence not only of strict federation but of general military agreement among the various portions of the Empire, England does nevertheless carry with her into European council much of the weight which comes from the possession of India and the Colonies. She cannot appear in Europe merely as Great Britain or merely as the United Kingdom, but takes with her wherever she goes, both the strength and the weakness

that attach to her world-wide position.   I may, perhaps, be
permitted to speak as one who gave timely attention to this
side of our national position, inasmuch as the class of
considerations to which I alluded in the preface to *Greater
Britain*, written in the spring of 1868, had attracted little
attention before I gave to the expansion both of the Empire
and of the British nationality the name which has since
become familiar of " Greater Britain."   I hardly dare venture now to claim my own when two such personages as
Professor Seeley and Professor Freeman have been contending in volumes about the meaning of my title.   Professor
Freeman, indeed, has given a portion of his *Greater Greece
and Greater Britain* to considering whether I invented the
title of Greater Britain for myself, or took it from that of
Britannia Major, which in the twelfth century was used for
what we now call Great Britain, in contradistinction to
Britannia Minor, or the Brittany of France.   In answer to
his question as to whether the name of Greater Britain grew
from the Major Britannia of the twelfth century used for
Britain, or whether it grew from the Magna Græcia, Great
Greece, applied as the received name to the expansion of
Greece in Italy, I can only reply that the title seemed to me
so obvious that it never occurred to me when I made use of
it for the first time that it was destined to any special
celebrity or remark.   When Professor Freeman suggests
that, in the intention of the original author of the phrase,
"Greater Britain" means the countries inhabited or governed
by the English-speaking people, and includes the United
States, and when Professor Seeley answers, in his chapter,

" What is Greater Britain ? " " By Greater Britain we mean an enlargement of the English state and not simply of the English nationality," I cannot but side with the former rather than with the latter, and refuse Professor Seeley's attempt to narrow the use of the phrase and to exclude the most numerous of the peoples who speak the English tongue and exalt our laws and principles of liberty. I, for one, still have hope that the causes of estrangement between Great Britain and the chief of her daughter-countries, which are mainly to be found in the friction produced by the Irish Question, may even within our lifetime be removed, and the tie of blood, and tongue, and history, and letters, again drawn close.

In *Greater Britain* the doctrine which I attempted to lay down was that both the English-speaking and the English-governed lands should attract a larger share of the attention of the inhabitants of the United Kingdom ; that in all these, whether subject or not subject to the British rule, the English race was essentially the same in its most marked characteristics ; that in the principal English-speaking country not subject to the Queen, the United States, England had imposed her tongue and laws upon the offshoots of Germany, Scandinavia, Spain, and I might now add of Russia ; and that the dominance of our language throughout this powerful and enormous country was in itself a vast assistance to our trade, and must produce in the future political phenomena to which our attention ought more persistently to be called. In the English-speaking countries, or true colonies of England in Professor Freeman's sense, there

is also a vast population which has been born in the United
Kingdom, and the majority of the four and a half to five
millions of people born at home who are now abroad are to
be found within the United States ; a number with which
we should compare the quarter of a million of foreigners
who alone are to be found in the United Kingdom, in order
to form in our minds some conception of our expansive force
In the English-governed lands, or expansion of the English
state, to which Professor Seeley turns his attention, we have
however countries which in the long run may become even
more remarkable than the United States themselves. As
compared with the thirty-five millions of people who live in
the United Kingdom, we have in the whole Empire two
hundred and fifty-five millions directly subject to our rule,
or if we include protected territories, some three hundred
and twenty millions. Of territories directly subject to us
we have in Australia a country virtually of the size of the
United States, which is now known to be (what was not
believed when I wrote *Greater Britain*) habitable throughout
its length and breadth. Canada, which is nominally even
larger than the United States, contains no doubt some unin-
habitable districts, but it is capable also of ultimately sustain-
ing a white population little inferior to that of Australia
or of the United States. The area which is protected or
ruled by us is two and a half times as large as Europe,
and it is possible that the day will come when Australia,
which is considerably more than three times the size of
India, will support a white population which may be counted
by hundreds of millions. It is impossible to leave these

facts, and the dreams which may be founded on them, wholly out of account when writing of the present strength of the United Kingdom, and if on the one hand imperial federation is not feasible at the moment and is not a force to lean on now; on the other hand, we ought to bear in mind the danger that an attitude of weak effacement may make our colonies feel that there is here at home insufficient energy to continue to hold together the Empire as it stands.

There is one special source of national weakness to the United Kingdom and to the Empire, both military and general, which I ought to name, although it is impossible here to deal with it at length: that, namely, which is to be found in the condition of Ireland. At the time of the accession of the Queen, Catholic Ireland was devotedly loyal to the throne and to her person. There can be no doubt as to the loss of power to the whole country which has been caused by the change that has taken place, but it would carry us too far were we to attempt to discuss the reason for the change. It is impossible to suppose that we can rest content to leave the Irish difficulty as it stands, a constant menace to the very existence of the Empire. As long as even one district of Ireland remains distraught, its wrongs will be a grievance to the whole Irish race, furnishing throughout the Empire a pretext for disaffection and a justification for every variety of disorder, furnishing also dangerous causes of estrangement between ourselves and the people of our race who live outside our boundaries We have not only to redress whatever wrongs may still exist, but—and this is a task of even greater difficulty—we have to allay the very sentiment of discontent, to try, if even unhopefully, at least to try, for a settlement which may be permanent. Looking at the position from an Imperial point of view, which takes chiefly into account the necessity for the contentment of local opinion in order to stop the present incessant drain of strength, it is a matter of indifference whether the method employed be Nationalist Home Rule, in any form in which it is likely to be approved by Parliament, or such Unionist Home Rule as Mr. Chamberlain may think better calculated to secure the objects described by him in his speech at Ayr: " Home Rule without danger to the supremacy of the Imperial Parliament; Home Rule without danger to the unity of the Empire." If the Irish question were once settled, not only would England be able to take once more a better place in Europe, but lasting friendship would become possible between Great Britain and her chief daughter-country. The Canadian fisheries troubles would not themselves be found difficult of solution were it not for Irish discontent. Given the existence of this friendship it would be to us a source of pride that the independent branch of our race which is seated in America, rapidly becoming as flourishing and as powerful as the whole of Europe, affords a pleasanter picture than that which Europe itself just now presents.

The writing of this volume will have been to me truly a labour of love if it may help in any degree, by pointing out our dangers, to strengthen the position of England in the defence of our own liberties against attack from

without, and also for the purpose of enabling us better to
perform our duty in the world. In the last considerations
at which we have looked, we have found causes for hope, or
for congratulation, which the condition of Continental
Europe does not afford. The reign of force under which
the Continent has fallen, and which to some extent affects
our own position, has but little bearing upon the proud
growth of Canada, Australia, or the United States. While
all with them is bright, the picture which we in Europe
present is sad indeed. If we look to the position of the
majority of the human race there seems no special ground
for dejection; but if we turn to that part of it which lives in
Europe, the simplest principles of human progress seem to
be forgotten or denied. Dealing as I have done with facts
rather than with tendencies or with wishes, I find a relief,
after surveying the increasing power of discord and hatred
in European international affairs, in letting in the flood of
light which comes to us from across the greater seas. On
the Continent we see taxation daily increasing for the support of armies and fleets which necessarily must grow, and
underneath the organised fabric of society a consequent
mining of anarchic principle. When we look towards
America and the lands in the southern seas we find, on the
contrary, some ground for hoping that all which we have
been taught to believe of human progress is not a lie;
that, whatever may be the momentary power of self-interest
and oppression in one portion of the globe, in larger parts
of it, occupied by the picked men of our own race, the same
principles of liberty seem to bear the same good fruit in

364 THE PRESENT POSITION OF EUROPEAN POLITICS.

the life of nations which we have been taught to expect that
they must bear in the lives of individuals. While in Europe
all seems dark, elsewhere, as young and pushing portions
of our race gain for themselves at length the leisure which
is necessary for cultivation, there is reason to believe that
mankind will recognise the spirit of self-sacrifice and the
desire to do good to others which seem gone from the old
world. Reverence may once more be paid to duty instead
of to might, and the principle of human brotherhood receive
new recognition through the action of men of our own
race.

VII.

CONCLUSION.

———•———

In publishing in collected form these six essays upon the Present Position of European Politics, I may be permitted to repeat that my object has been to state facts rather than wishes, and to concern myself with the existing position of affairs rather than with the history of the events which have brought it about.

I have to thank the public for the manner in which the articles have been received. While a good deal of notice seems to have been attracted to them, on only two points have I met with much hostile English criticism. Those points are my comparison of the military strength of Austria with that of Russia in the articles on Russia and on Austria-Hungary, and my incidental statement that the conduct of Austria lured France to destruction in 1870, which has been denied in the name of Count Beust in the English introduction to the translation of that Saxon statesman's memoirs. If I may first dispose of the latter point, which is one of history and outside the scope of my work, I may be permitted to refer to the preface to a book lately published by General Lebrun. In it the General promises that we shall one day see his copies of the diplomatic, as well as of the military, engagements taken by Austria in 1870 ; if, indeed, we are not allowed to see the originals, which are still, I believe, in the French Ministry of War. It has been lately pointed out that there are many who have seen the Austrian engagements which were communicated to the French Cabinet of January —July, 1870, members of which are still alive and have no reasons for not freely discussing the subject with their friends.

Count Beust admits in his memoirs that "the great rapidity of events and the consequent excitement of the writers of some of the letters sent from Vienna to Paris, caused some expressions to be employed that had not been sufficiently weighed. . . . In this category may be placed the often quoted words, 'fidèles à nos engagements.'" Count Beust has also admitted that he expected that the French would have beaten Germany, and that he was in doubt for some time whether or not to ask for money from the French and to begin a war on their behalf. As to Beust's duplicity there can hardly be a doubt, for even Rothan, who is friendly to him, quotes his terrible words, "make a grand fuss over the value of our engagements and over our fidelity and respect for them." We shall some day have the details of the missions of the Archduke Albert and of Count Vitzthum to Paris, and of General Lebrun to Vienna; but in the meantime we have the revelations of the Duc de Gramont. There is no real difference between the Duc de Gramont and Count Beust, except as to the actual signature of a Treaty at the end of July which provided for the military steps to be taken by Austria. The

Duke has proved that the despatch of Count Beust to the
Austrian Ambassador, dated the 11th of July, was never
made known to the French Government; that it was written
only to be afterwards made public for use with Prussia; that
all traces of the coldness caused by the sudden declaration of
war disappeared during Count Vitzthum's subsequent visit
to Paris; and that it was after Count Vitzthum's return to
Vienna that Beust wrote, on the 20th July, "faithful to our
engagements as laid down in the letters exchanged last year
between our Emperors, we consider the cause of France our
own and will as far as possible contribute to the success of
her arms." It was on the 24th July that the Austrian
Ambassador was instructed to tell the French that Austria
could not actually take the field before September; and it
was after that that Count Vitzthum returned to Paris, and,
the Duc de Gramont says, drew up a treaty as to the means
and the form of Austrian co-operation against Prussia, the
details being suggested by Austria. It is this last point
alone which Beust has in fact denied. What was Count
Beust's language at this time may be judged from the despatch of the Prince de Latour d'Auvergne, dated the 26th
July, from Vienna, in which he says that Count Beust fully
intends to "hurry his military preparations so as to be able
to give us his armed support as soon as possible." Some day
we shall have interesting memoirs of M. Emile Ollivier,
which will probably contain documents which will make this
matter completely clear. There can be no doubt that the
declarations of Prince Metternich at Paris were absolute and
free from any doubt or hesitation. He informed the

Emperor, over and over again, that Austria would give France her military support. So much for this matter of history which has been only incidentally introduced by me.

The other point upon which fault has been found in England with my statements is, as I have said, that which concerns my comparison between the military forces of Russia and of Austria-Hungary. I do not see my way to modify my views. An anonymous writer in the *St. James's Gazette* found fault with all my figures, but as against him I must maintain the accuracy of those figures. He has been replied to by an able military writer, and I know from the letters which I have received that I have the support for my facts and figures of some of the best informed of military critics. I must repeat that the "Budget-peace-effective" of Russia, excluding constabulary and customs guards, is at least from 850,000 to 890,000 men, while that of Germany, adding one year volunteers, is about 460,000 and that of Austria about 290,000, so that the two latter are together seriously inferior to that of Russia. I have also to repeat that Colonel Rau has clearly established that Russia has a number of instructed men closely approaching to four millions in the portions of her Empire which are subject to the European conscription system, a number which has to be supplemented by a large force of Cossacks and other irregular troops which can be drawn from the remainder of the Empire. This force exceeds, therefore, the combined number of instructed men possessed by Germany and Austria. But while these facts, and also those which I stated with regard to the Russian cavalry, are facts indeed,

my critics in the *St. James's Gazette* and the *Spectator*
made me appear to have drawn from them deductions which
I carefully abstained from drawing. I do not for one
moment pretend to believe that Russia is equal in fighting
strength upon her frontier to Germany and Austria combined. I never said so, and I do not think so. If a
struggle were to take place in which France would not
move, for example, for the possession of Poland between
Russia on the one hand, and Germany and Austria on the
other, I am as certain that Russia would be defeated as
can be my critics. But in the statements which I made I
see no inaccuracy either of fact or of deduction. As regards
the chances of a single-handed contest between Austria and
Russia, the able critic of the *Spectator*, who evidently knows
the Austrian cavalry well, has formed a very different
opinion from my own. There is no means unfortunately
but war of testing who is right. I may add that one of
those of my Hungarian correspondents who was the most
displeased with portions of my article on Austria-Hungary,
and who is a gentleman who holds a position which enables
him to speak with much weight in the name of Hungary,
begins by saying, "I agree with you in your judgment as
to the inferiority in strength of Austria-Hungary as compared with Russia. I have no fault to find with what you
say of the military strength, or rather weakness, of our
monarchy." I cannot in justice to this gentleman give his
name on account of the position which he worthily fills.

While on these two points only, which I have named,
have my conclusions been seriously attacked in England, I

have to confess that my essays have not been over-popular
abroad. Serious fault was found in France with the second
of them,—the one upon that country; my third was pro-
hibited in Russia; and the French Review which translated
the first, second, and fourth, was afraid to give the third
for fear of hurting Russian feeling, and the fifth because I
declared the continuance of the alliance between Italy and
Germany to be certain. On the other hand, my fourth
article was grievously attacked in Austria. This no
doubt is natural enough; and I fear the sixth essay,
that on England, has not been over-popular in this country.
I have tried all through to state as accurately as I
could the exact position: but as many Powers, and notably
Austria, are to some extent living upon a prestige founded
upon their past, to dissect the present position is to do
that which is most painful to the parties concerned. My
comparison, therefore, between Austria and Russia has been
still more unpopular in Austria than it was in certain
quarters in this country. I have been assured that while I
know something of France and Germany, and while in consequence my articles on those countries may be of some
value, I have no knowledge of Russia and Austria, and that
my pictures of the strength of Russia are partly based on
worthless Russian government statistics, and partly on a
vague impression that Russia must necessarily be as strong
as she is big and populous. I do not know how it is possible
to try harder to get to know countries than I have tried to
acquaint myself with the position of Russia and Austria;
certainly if repeated visits and very lengthy journeys can

do anything in that direction, those means of acquiring information have not been omitted; and when I am accused of basing my impressions of the strength of Russia on a mere glance at maps, I can only repeat that I have visited for myself the Asiatic possessions of that country more than once. Be it remembered, moreover, that I am writing against my wishes, and therefore that presumably I should not be likely to exaggerate in the direction in which it is suggested that I have erred. In the event of that war between Russia and Austria which I dread, it is the success of Austria for which I should hope, though it is the success of Russia which I should expect. I can only say therefore to my Austrian critics that I am almost as anxious as they are that I should prove to have been wrong, and that no one will rejoice more than I shall if that should be the result of the inevitable war when the day for it shall have arrived. The best article which was written upon my unfavourable estimate of the future of the Austrian empire, if I may be allowed to discriminate among my critics, was one which appeared in the *Levant Herald*, in which I could not but fancy that I detected on the one hand the desire to maintain the prestige of Austria as against that of Russia before the Turks, and on the other hand, in an undertone, the feeling that after all I unfortunately might be right. The ablest of the critics of my views maintain that Russia cannot find more than 2,700,000 men to place in the field at all points, Central Asia, the Amoor, the Armenian frontier, and Europe; that the corrupt combinations between officers and contractors are such as to enfeeble Russia to a remark-

able extent; that the quality of a large proportion of the
Russian troops is not equal to that of the Austro-Hungarian
army; that Germany in the last resort would save Austria,
and is strong enough to save her even if France should
move ; that the Turkish mobilisation of last year shows that
the Turkish army might still be of formidable service in a
general war against the Russians; that there is still hope
for a Balkan Confederation under Turkish leadership, and
an alliance between this federation and the Central Powers.
A good deal in this view is merely in the nature of a
pleasant dream ; but the one point upon which I think
a serious impression has been made upon my argument
is where I have indicated an opinion that Germany
does not share the view that the capture of Constantinople by Russia would be any danger to the world. I
think it is probably true that Germany is rather anxious
to say this, than that she really means it. Russia at Constantinople would mean the destruction of Austria and the
Russification of a large portion of her Slavs. When Austria
had disappeared or had been transformed out of all knowledge, Germany, placed between France and Russia, would
be still weaker in her military position than she is at present.
It is no doubt impossible that Germany can really contemplate that contingency with complacent satisfaction. And if
she cannot get other people to help Austria to keep Russia
away from Constantinople, it is probable that she would be
forced to interfere to help to do so, however stoutly her rulers
may make the opposite declaration. One of my most valued
correspondents, whose criticisms have been of the highest

use to me, admits that to place Turkey at the head of a Balkan Confederation would be "adding a badger to your three unfriendly cats and altogether hostile dog;" but, nevertheless, he thinks that such a combination would be possible on account of the overwhelming dread of the danger of absorption by Russia; and I think it right to state his view, although I am unable to modify that which I have said as to the difficulties which the dispute for Macedonia causes.

Some very serious criticism of my French article appeared in France, especially an article in the *Revue Politique et Litteraire* (*Revue Bleu*), and an article in the *Nouvelle Revue* by Madame Adam. I have to thank both writers for their personal politeness, and cannot but agree with them in deploring that inability to understand one another's positions which appears to characterize the English and the French. Madame Adam charged me with "ferocious selfishness" and combated the view that we had any ground for complaint that the French should seize countries belonging to other people and then put on differential duties against our goods. She seemed to think that my desire was that England should herself be able, in her own favour, to accomplish a similar commercial stroke. What, of course, I asked for, as will be clear to any one who reads the first chapter of this book, was not exclusive advantages for English trade but simply a fair field and no favour. Madame Adam also thought I did not blame the spoliation of Turkey by England but only the spoliation by France. I used, however, precisely the same language with regard to the taking of Cyprus which I used with regard to the taking of Bosnia, and the taking of Tunis by France. I could, however, have drawn a sharp distinction had I chosen so to do. Tunis is a Mahommedan country; Cyprus, and the two provinces occupied by Austria, both have a Christian majority, although there is a large Mahommedan minority in each. This perhaps affects the situation. That which certainly affects it is that Tunis has been taken away from the Ottoman Empire without the slightest regard for the Sultan's authority, whereas Cyprus is rented from the Sultan and the rent religiously paid.

My French critics have altogether misunderstood the meaning of my remarks in my first two articles with regard to Belgium. I need perhaps only say that I abhor the doctrine of "Diplomaticus," in the *Standard*, which they charge me with having started. My views on the subject of Belgium I should have thought had been clearly enough expressed, but at all events they have been entirely confirmed by one of the most representative of Belgians, General Brialmont, in his authorized "interview" with a representative of the *Pall Mall Gazette*, which appeared on the 15th of April last, and the expression of them has, I am happy to think, had some effect in stirring up, as is now admitted on both sides in Belgium, the recent patriotic movement in that country.

I cannot but think that the impression of the existence in me of Gallophobia, which was created in France by my second article, is to be traced to the consideration that the readers of each article are apt to give undue attention to the points upon which they differ from me, even though these may be comparatively few as contrasted with the more

numerous points on which we are in agreement. Because I
attacked the French breach of solemnly plighted national
word in the case of the New Hebrides; because I showed
how much England feels the one-sided violence of a portion
of the Parisian press, I am accused of hostility to France,
just as I am accused by others of hostility to Austria. The
main point, however, which concerned the European position
of France at the moment at which I wrote was one upon
which I found myself upon the French side. Not only the
German press, but a portion of the press of England, was at
that moment writing of France as a dangerous and aggressive
power, whereas in what I said in the first and second articles
I showed pretty clearly that, as regards that which after all
was the principal French external question of the day, my
sympathies were on the French side. I fear that the anger
which portions of my articles created in France was largely
due to the fact that my French readers had an uneasy
impression that my statements, as, for example, those about
the New Hebrides, were true, and that it was not altogether
easy to make an answer to them.

I have received some communications from scientific
officers with regard to my remarks upon military questions.
It is pointed out that the argument by Lord Wolseley's
friends in favour of the reduction of the horse artillery,
which I have quoted, does not take into consideration the
fact that we have at home a very large force of militia and
volunteer garrison artillery which would be useful behind
fortifications, but no auxiliary field artillery, and that the
latter could not be rapidly created in the event of war. In

the South-eastern district, for example, there are, counting militia and volunteers as well as regulars, nearly 6,000 garrison gunners, of whom one-half would probably suffice for our needs, but there are in the same district only 12 field guns, that is three field batteries of four guns each. This is a specimen of the state of things which exists all over England.

I am also told on all sides that black as is the military portion of my article on the United Kingdom it is far from being black enough. For example, I have assumed that the recent failure of the automatic torpedo for sea-going use is an advantage to us, but it is pointed out to me that, while this is so, as regards the safety of all our iron-clads, the position is reversed as regards the possibility of invasion. Invasion of course implies a large convoy of transports crammed full of troops, and as these are of necessity widely scattered and at a distance from the protecting ironclads, the havoc which might be effected among the transports in a short time by a few sea-going torpedo-boats of high speed, commanded by energetic officers, is very great; and the fact that automatic torpedoes soon get out of order when being carried at sea on board ships going at a high rate of speed, is somewhat against us on this point. Again I am told that I have set too high the power of the British forces in India to resist attack, because it is assumed that Russia would be able to cause local outbreaks of disaffected natives in India as a diversion, and that we should have to face the fact that the British force in India is only just sufficient to garrison the country.

Some of the criticisms which have reached me from India upon my Russian article show that there has been a certain growth of pessimism among our best Indian officers of late. It is pointed out that in their belief the ability of Russia to attack India depends mainly on her relations and our relations with the Afghans and the tribes on our immediate border, and that the side which these join will have the game in its own hands. The danger we have to meet is more political than military, and is enhanced by the effect which the danger itself will have upon our native troops. Were the whole of our Indian army composed of troops which could take the field against an European foe our position would be unassailable, but much as our Indian officers believe in the loyalty and the fighting qualities of some of our native soldiers, they cannot hide from themselves that under certain circumstances we might not be able to depend upon them. So long as our supremacy is undisputed the native army will remain faithful to us, but it is thought that their belief in us would be shaken if another Power were permitted to approach near enough to India to dispute our hold over the country. At the present time the northern part of Afghanistan is, practically speaking, in Russia's hands; as soon as her military communications are a little more complete, her appearance in force on the banks of the Oxus would ensure her the possession of Herat and the whole of Afghan-Turkestan, probably without the striking of a single blow. The garrisons of Herat, Balkh, and Maimena, would be disposed of by the Russians as easily as the garrisons of Cabul and Kandahar were disposed of by us in 1878-9. I myself fear that there is reason to believe that the people of Afghan-Turkestan would welcome the Russians as deliverers from the Afghan yoke which they detest. The presence of a Russian army south of the Oxus would cause wide-spread consternation in Afghanistan. It is impossible to foretell what the effect of this would be on the tribes south of the Hindu Kush. A common danger might result in even the Ameer and the Ghilzais making friends; but this is doubtful, as there is no real homogeneity in the Afghan nation. Under any circumstances it would be impossible for the Afghans unaided to stem the advance of the Russians, who, once masters of Afghan-Turkestan, would speedily find their way to Cabul, where their power and the promise of the loot of India would attract to them the whole of the Afghan peoples as well as the tribes on our immediate frontier. In order to prevent the arrival of this state of things, and to win over the tribes, we must push on roads, railways, and irrigation schemes, and in this way open out the country and increase the value of their land. As money flows into their pockets they will come to appreciate the value of peace and order. A marked change has come over the tribes of late, especially those living in the Khyber and in Beluchistan, owing to their having seen more of us, and our popularity among them has greatly risen. There are some signs that this feeling is spreading to the Afghans, but it would be more likely to gain ground rapidly if they felt that we were able to perform our promise to defend their country. We are solemnly pledged to defend against Russia the integrity of Afghanistan, and if there is hesitation or timidity in doing so the tribes will certainly attribute delay to fear. Should they take to thinking that we are afraid of Russia all hope of their casting in their lot with ours will be at an end. The highest authorities in India are now convinced that unless we are able thoroughly to attract the Afghans and other frontiermen to our side, Russian invasion of India is merely a matter of time, and not of long time.

I have only to add that I have made a few changes in other portions of my articles by which I intend to bring up to date the information which they contained, but I have been unable to keep pace with the rapid changes in French politics.

INDEX TO NAMES.

Tunis, the Bey of, 70, and *see* Tunis
Turcoman Cavalry, 329
Turcomans, the, 122, 166, 172
Turin, 255
Turkestan, 173
Turkestan, Afghan-, 377, 378
Turkey (and the Turks), *passim*
Turkey, the Sultan of, *passim*
Tyrol, 120, 184, 193, 195, 222, 232, 240-2

Ugrian (Asiatic Finn), 196,
Ulster, a German, 190
United Kingdom, *passim*
United Service Institution, 304
United States, 56, 107, 123, 126, 134, 135, 264, 275, 283, 287, 347, 352, 358-60, 363
Union Générale, the, 211
Uralian Cossacks, 122

Valangin, 137
Valbert (Pseudonym). *See* Cherbuliez
Vambéry, Professor, 170
Vannutelli, the Brothers, 260
Vassiltchikoff, Prince, 132, 141
Vassiltchikoff, Prince A., 141
Vatican, 103, 226, 244, 254, 255, &c., and *see* Pope, the
Vatiki, the, 122
Vaudois, 137
Venice, 3, 241
Venice, Republic of, 233
Verne, Jules, 289
Viale, General Bertolè, 253
Victoria, 108-10, 349
Victor Bonaparte, Prince, 62
Vienna, Chap. i. 6, 15, Chap. ii. 70, 145, 152-4, Chap. iv. 181, 184, 189, 192, 193, &c., Chap. v. 234, 259, 260, Chap. vii. 366, 367
Vincent, Mr. Howard, 289
Vistula, 15, 135

Vitzthum, Count, 366, 367
Vizier, the Grand, 27
Vladikavkas, 156
Vladivostock, 18, 155, 174, 175, 320, 333, 356
Vlangaly, General, 119
Volga, the, 122, 142

Waddington, M., 92, 349
Wales, H.R.H. the Prince of, 30
Walter, Sir E., 341
Warsaw, 153, 209
Washburn, Dr., 142
Waterloo, 14, 21, 47
Weiner Neustadt, 204
Weiss, M., 76, 77
Wellington, the Duke of, 179
Wemyss, Lord, 341
Wends, the, 198, 200, 201
West Australia, 108
West Indies, 289, and *see* Jamaica
White, Sir William, 25, 208
Whitehall, 258
White Russia. *See* Russia, White
White Sea, the, 18, 167
Whitworth, Lord, 164
William, Prince, of Prussia, 9
Wilna, 153
Windhorst, Herr, 269
Wolff, Sir H. D., 25
Wolseley, Lord, Chap. vi. 299, 300, 301, 303-6, &c., Chap. vii. 375
Woolwich, 292

Yate, Captain, 156
Yokohama, 320

Zanardelli, Signor, 229, 231, 253
Zanzibar, 54, 88, 95, 106, 237, 278
Zemstvoes, the, 150
Zinovieff, 137
Zulfikar, 178
Zululand, 95, 278

THE END.

PRINTED BY J. S. VIRTUE AND CO., LIMITED, CITY ROAD LONDON.